STEPHEN FOX

COLOURS

ENGLISCH FÜR INTENSIV- UND KOMPAKTKURSE

LEHR- UND ARBEITSBUCH

MAX HUEBER VERLAG

The author would like to thank
Sally Cleesattel, Gail Heidenhain and Heinrich Schrand
in particular for their input during the development of this course,
family and friends for their continued support
and the staff and students of the Volkshochschulen Grafing
and Pfaffenhofen/Ilm for their cooperation in conjunction
with the many pilot courses in which this material was tested.

Das Werk und seine Teile sind urheberrechtlich geschützt.
Jede Verwertung in anderen als den gesetzlich zugelassenen Fällen bedarf
deshalb der vorherigen schriftlichen Einwilligung des Verlages.

4. 3.	Die letzten Ziffern bezeichnen Zahl
2002 2001 2000	und Jahr des Druckes.

Alle Drucke dieser Auflage können, da unverändert, nebeneinander
benutzt werden.
1. Auflage
© 1995 Max Hueber Verlag, D-85737 Ismaning
Verlagsredaktion: Context, Bad Münstereifel; Stephen Fox, München
Zeichnungen: ofczarek! Brühl/Köln
Herstellung/Layout/Umschlag: Alois Sigl, München
Lithographie: ROYAL MEDIA Publishing, Ottobrunn
Druck und Bindung: Ludwig Auer, Donauwörth
Printed in Germany
ISBN 3–19–002430–8

Vorwort

Colours ist ein einbändiges Lehr- und Arbeitsbuch, das sich an KursteilnehmerInnen mit geringen bzw. vor langer Zeit erworbenen Englischkenntnissen wendet. Ziel dieses Lehrwerks ist es, bereits vorhandene Kenntnisse zu festigen und zu erweitern. Besonders für Kurse, die zum schnellen Erlernen von praktischen Fähigkeiten führen sollen, ist *Colours* sehr gut geeignet.

Ein Intensivkurs mit *Colours* zeichnet sich durch folgende Merkmale aus:

- Erwerb von grundlegenden Fertigkeiten im Hörverständnis, Sprechen, Lesen und Schreiben,
- Systematisierung und Festigung von Grammatikkenntnissen, die für die Verständigung in wichtigen Situationen des Alltags, im Beruf und auf Reisen benötigt werden,
- Angebot an Übungen und Aktivitäten, die Einzel-, Partner- und Gruppenarbeit ermöglichen,
- Darbietung unterschiedlicher Texte, die der Alltagssprache entnommen sind,
- praxisnahe Themen, die den Interessen und Bedürfnissen erwachsener Lerner in besonderer Weise entsprechen.

Jede der insgesamt 12 Lektionen

besteht aus fünf Lernabschnitten:

First words: Einstieg in den Wortschatz der Unit,
Focus: Ausgangstexte mit Übungen zur schrittweisen Ausbildung von praktischen Fertigkeiten,
Follow-up: Übungen zur Festigung des Lernstoffs,
Special focus: weiteres Material zum zentralen Thema der Unit,
Summary: systematischer Überblick über die grammatischen Strukturen und Redeabsichten der Unit.

Self-Study Section

Ein in das Lehrbuch integrierter Arbeitsbuchteil, die *Self-Study Section*, bietet zusätzliches Übungsmaterial zur Ausspracheschulung, zur Entwicklung des Hörverständnisses und zur schriftlichen Festigung des Lernstoffs. Außerdem befinden sich in der *Self-Study Section* anschauliche Erklärungen zur Grammatik der Unit *(Sprachtip)*.
Die *Self-Study Section* dient vor allem der Eigenarbeit. Die Einführung *Lernen zu Hause* (S. 98–99) enthält Anregungen, wie das Lernen angenehm und effektiv gestaltet werden kann.

Im Anhang des Lehrbuchs

finden sich

- eine Kurzgrammatik,
- die Lösungen zu den Übungen der *Self-Study Section* zur Eigenkontrolle,
- ein nach Units geordneter Wortschatz mit deutscher Entsprechung,
- ein alphabetisches Wörterverzeichnis.

Außerdem bietet das Lehrwerk zwei Cassetten bzw. CDs an. Cassette/CD 1 enthält die mit dem Symbol gekennzeichneten Texte des Lehrbuchteils. Cassette/CD 2 enthält die Aussprache- und Hörverständnisübungen der *Self-Study Section*.

Wir wünschen Ihnen viel Spaß und Erfolg beim Lernen!

Autor und Redaktion

Inhalt

Seite 8 – 13

REDEABSICHTEN
Begrüßungen, sich und andere vorstellen, um Auskunft bitten
GRAMMATIK
I/my, you/your; das Verb *be*; Fragewörter; *this/that*
THEMEN
Auskunft über Personen, das Alphabet, die Zahlen 1–20

Seite 14 – 19

REDEABSICHTEN
jemand beschreiben
GRAMMATIK
he/his, she/her, it, we, you, they; das Verb *be* (Aussagen, Verneinung, Fragen und Kurzantworten); *the, a/an*
THEMEN
Herkunft, Eigenschaften, Familie und Freunde

Seite 20 – 27

REDEABSICHTEN
über Mengen sprechen, Besitz und Zugehörigkeit ausdrücken, nach der Zeit fragen und antworten
GRAMMATIK
die Mehrzahl von Hauptwörtern; *have got*; *there is/are*; *how many*
THEMEN
die Familie, die Uhrzeit, die Zahlen ab 20

Seite 28 – 33

REDEABSICHTEN
über seine Arbeit /den Tagesablauf sprechen, einen Standort beschreiben
GRAMMATIK
die einfache Gegenwart (Aussagen); *can*; *always, usually, often, etc.*
THEMEN
Berufe, der Alltag, das Frühstück

Seite 34 – 39

REDEABSICHTEN
nach Freizeitbeschäftigungen/Vorlieben fragen und darauf antworten, über die Dauer einer Reise sprechen
GRAMMATIK
like + ing-Form; Fragen und Kurzantworten, Verneinung mit *don't/doesn't*
THEMEN
Freizeitbeschäftigungen, Geschäfte/öffentliche Einrichtungen usw.

Inhalt

Seite 40 – 47

REDEABSICHTEN
nach dem Weg fragen und darauf antworten, einen Standort beschreiben, laufende Handlungen beschreiben

GRAMMATIK
Verhältniswörter; die Verlaufsform der Gegenwart

THEMEN
unterwegs in der Stadt, Fortbewegungsmittel, Farben

Seite 48 – 55

REDEABSICHTEN
über Pläne sprechen, um etwas bitten, sich entschuldigen

GRAMMATIK
die Verlaufsform der Gegenwart zum Ausdruck der Zukunft

THEMEN
Wohnen, das Datum

Seite 56 – 63

REDEABSICHTEN
im Restaurant etwas bestellen, spontane Entscheidungen äußern, Vorhersagen machen, Vorschläge machen

GRAMMATIK
die Zukunft mit *will*; *some/any*; *mine*, *yours*

THEMEN
Essen (im Restaurant), Reisen

Seite 64 – 71

REDEABSICHTEN
über die Vergangenheit sprechen

GRAMMATIK
die Vergangenheit: Aussagen, Verneinung, Fragen und Kurzantworten; regelmäßige und unregelmäßige Verben

THEMEN
der Tagesablauf, Urlaub, über seine Vergangenheit sprechen

Seite 72 – 77

REDEABSICHTEN
über seine Kindheit sprechen, nach Vorlieben fragen, nach dem Wetter fragen und antworten

GRAMMATIK
die Vergangenheit von *be*

THEMEN
Möbel, das Wetter

Inhalt

Seite 78 – 85

REDEABSICHTEN
eine Meinung äußern, Vergleiche anstellen, jemand/etwas loben
GRAMMATIK
die Steigerung von Eigenschaftswörtern
THEMEN
Kleidung, Einkaufen, Werbung, der Körper

Seite 86 – 91

REDEABSICHTEN
nach Vergangenem fragen und darauf antworten
GRAMMATIK
present prefect: Aussagen, Verneinung, Fragen und Kurzantworten
THEMEN
Englisch lernen außerhalb des Kurses, Urlaub, Ländernamen

Seite 94 – 96   **EXTRAS**

Seite 97 – 135   **SELF-STUDY-TEIL**

Seite 136 – 147   **GRAMMATIK IM ÜBERBLICK**

Seite 148 – 153   **SCHLÜSSEL ZUM SELF-STUDY-TEIL**

Seite 154   **WÖRTERVERZEICHNIS NACH UNITS**
Seite 176   **ALPHABETISCHES WÖRTERVERZEICHNIS**

Nice to meet you

First words: Greetings

1 Match the greetings to the pictures.

Good morning. ◆ Good afternoon. ◆ Good evening. ◆ Good night.

1

2

3

4

5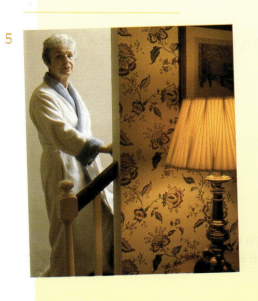

6

Focus: Saying hello

Dialogue: *Hello.*

○ Hello, my name's Julia.
● Hello. My name's Gabi.
○ Gabi. That sounds German. Are you from Germany?
● Yes, I am.
○ Where in Germany?
● Well, I'm from a place near Hanover, but I live in Berlin. Where are you from?

2 And you?

Germany ◆ Austria ◆ Switzerland
a place / a town near …

▶ Hello, my name's _____
– Hello. My name's _____
Where are you from?
– I'm from _____ And you?

Dialogue: *How are you?*

□ Hello, Mike. How are you?
■ Fine, thanks. And you?
□ Not bad, not bad!
■ Anne, this is my wife, Kim.
   Kim, this is Anne Mundy.
□ Hello, Kim.
△ Hello, Anne. Nice to meet you.

4 And you?

Mr (Schmidt) ◆ Mrs (Schmidt) ◆ Ms (Schmidt)
my wife ◆ my husband ◆ my friend
my colleague

▶ Hello, _____, how are you?
– Fine, thanks, and you?
_____
– _____, this is _____.
_____, this is _____.
Hello, _____, nice to meet you.
– Nice to meet you, too!

Dialogue: *Goodbye!*

☆ See you next week.
★ Bye!
☆ Goodbye!

nine

Follow-up

1 Match.

hello — your
this — goodbye
my — night
morning — no
yes — that

2 Listen and repeat.

My name's Schmidt.
Are you from Germany? – Yes, I am.
I'm from a place near Hanover.
This is Kim.
Nice to meet you.
How are you? – I'm fine, thanks.

3 Listening

a)

Are they friends?	Yes, they are.	No, they aren't.
Sue and William		
Tim and Mr Hewitt		
Mrs Dunn and Mrs Court		
Meg and David		

b) Listen again and circle the items you hear.

How are you?   Are you from ...?   I'm fine, and you?   Not bad.   Goodbye.
My name's ...   This is ...   Nice to meet you.   See you next week.

4 Fill in.

Where are you from?
Good night!
Susan, this is John.
How are you?

Follow-up

5 Numbers

0	"oh" / zero						
1	one	6	six	11	eleven	16	sixteen
2	two	7	seven	12	twelve	17	seventeen
3	three	8	eight	13	thirteen	18	eighteen
4	four	9	nine	14	fourteen	19	nineteen
5	five	10	ten	15	fifteen	20	twenty

6 Listening

Fill in the gate numbers.

Departures

Flight		to	gate	time
BA	70	Sydney		10.05
LH	205	Frankfurt		10.10
DL	36	Atlanta		10.15
AF	534	Paris		10.20
TWA	112	Chicago		10.25
SR	33	Geneva		10.30
SAA	44	Cape Town		10.35

7 Make a list.

Make a list of people in your class with their telephone numbers.

▶ *Can I phone you?*
– *Yes, of course. / Sorry, I haven't got a phone.*
What's your name?
– *Andrea.*

And what's your telephone number?
– *My number at work is ... / My number at home is ...*
Thank you.
– *You're welcome.*

Name	Telephone number (at home / at work)

Special focus: The alphabet

1

a	b	c	d	e	f	g	h	i	j	k	l	m
[eɪ]	[biː]	[siː]	[diː]	[iː]	[ef]	[dʒiː]	[eɪtʃ]	[aɪ]	[dʒeɪ]	[keɪ]	[el]	[em]

n	o	p	q	r	s	t	u	v	w	x	y	z
[en]	[əʊ]	[piː]	[kjuː]	[aː]	[es]	[tiː]	[juː]	[viː]	[dʌbljuː]	[eks]	[waɪ]	[zed]

2 Listen and repeat.

a – k – j
b – c – d – e – g – p – t – v
f – l – m – n – s – x – z
i – y
q – u

3 Can you say these English abbreviations?

VW ◆ PC ◆ DJ ◆ IQ ◆ VCR ◆ TV ◆ UFO ◆ CD ◆ BMW
EU ◆ UK ◆ USA ◆ TWA ◆ UN

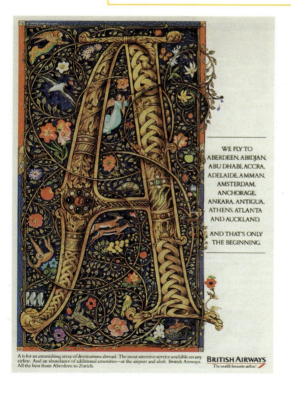

4 Can you spell that, please?

▶ What's your name?
– It's _____
Can you spell the surname, please?
– Yes, it's _____

What's your address?
– It's _____
Can you spell the name of the street, please?
– Yes, it's _____

Summary

Grammar

I'm (am) from Germany.
You're (are) welcome.
My name's (is) Gabi.
This is Anne Mundy.

Are you from Germany?   Yes, I am.
Are they friends?   Yes, they are. / No, they aren't.

My name's David.
Your number is 6457.

this ↓   that

What's your surname?
Where are you from?
How are you?

in   near

Phrases

Hello.
Good morning/afternoon/evening.
Goodbye.

My name's Julia.
This is my wife, Maria.
Nice to meet you.

Where are you from?
I'm from Hanover.

How are you? – Fine, thanks, and you?

Can I phone you? – Yes, of course.

Thank you. – You're welcome.

"Hey, how's it going?"

What's she like?

First words: People

1 Listen and repeat.

untidy
shy
athletic
romantic
pessimistic
funny

Now match the words to the pictures 1–6.

2 What are they like?

he

she

▶ I think he/she's ... /
He/She isn't very ...

Focus: Describing people

1 Do this personality test.

Are you...?

- tidy
- outgoing
- funny
- athletic
- optimistic
- realistic
- untidy
- shy, reserved
- serious
- not very athletic
- pessimistic
- romantic ?

2 And you?

▶ Are you an outgoing person?
 – Yes, I am.
   Yes, I'm rather/very outgoing.
   No, I'm not.
   No, I'm not very outgoing.

3 Report to the class.

▶ Heinz and I are/aren't (very) tidy.
 We're/We aren't ...
 He's/He isn't ...
 She's/She isn't ...

4 Dialogue: Two friends at the office

KATE: Who was that?
MARY: Who?
KATE: The tall girl with long blond hair.
MARY: That's my new colleague.
KATE: A new colleague? What's her name?
MARY: Chris Wilson.
KATE: Where's she from?
MARY: From Devon. She's from a place near Exeter.
KATE: What's she like? Is she nice?
MARY: Yes, she is. But she's a bit reserved.
KATE: People are when they're new.
MARY: Right!

UNIT 2

5 Quick check

1 Who's the tall girl?   ▶ Mary's new colleague.
2 What's her name?
3 Where's she from?
4 What's she like?

Follow-up

1 Who's your best friend? Ask a partner.

your boyfriend/girlfriend ◆ a school friend/an old school friend
a colleague/a former colleague
a neighbour/a former neighbour ◆ a member of your family:
your husband/wife, mother/father, sister/brother, son/daughter

▶ Who's your best friend?
– My best friend is my ... / is a/an ...
What's his/her name?
– His/Her name's .... .

2 Listening

Fill in the information.

	best friend's name	What's he/she like?
Person 1 (Simon)		
Person 2 (Anne)		
Person 3 (Jill)		

3 Now ask people in your class.

Student's name	Best friend	What's he/she like?

▶ Who's your best friend?
What's his/her name?
What's he/she like?

4 Report to the class.

▶ Helga's best friend is her sister, Monika.
She's outgoing and funny.
– Is she athletic?
No, she isn't very athletic.

Follow-up

5 **Find out from a partner.**

Student A   Look at this page.   Student B   Look at page 92.

Student A   These people are all new colleagues at TV International. Ask your partner questions and complete the table. You can only ask questions with *Is ...?*

First name	MARK	BEN	SCOTT	BARBARA	JILL	NICOLE
Surname	BRAUN	SMITH			BRETT	
From	AUSTRIA		ENGLAND		ENGLAND	
What like?		ATHLETIC		SHY		RESERVED
	ROMANTIC		REALISTIC		OUTGOING	

Ask about:

Surnames: BAGLEY   BRETT   BRAUN   MILLER   SCHMIDT   SMITH

From: AUSTRIA   ENGLAND   GERMANY   SWITZERLAND

What like: athletic ◆ not very athletic ◆ outgoing ◆ realistic
reserved ◆ romantic ◆ shy ◆ tidy ◆ untidy

▶ Is Scott's surname Bagley?
– Yes, it is. / No, it isn't.
Is Barbara from Switzerland?
– Yes, she is. / No, she isn't.
Is Mark athletic?
– Yes, he is. / No, he isn't.

6 **Answer with a partner.**

▶ *Are Mark and Barbara both from England?*
– *Yes, they are. / No, they aren't.*

1   Are Ben and Jill both from England?
2   Are Mark and Nicole from Germany?
3   Are Scott and Ms Brett both from England?
4   Are Ben and Scott both athletic?
5   Are Ben and Jill both outgoing?
6   Are Barbara and Nicole both outgoing?
7   Are Barbara and Jill both tidy?
8   Are Ben and Scott both romantic?

And now complete this:

▶ ... and ... are both from England, but they aren't both romantic.
Make two more sentences like this.

7 **Who or where?**

1   _____ is that? – That's Miriam, my sister.
2   _____ are you? – My name's Ed Madison.
3   _____ are you? – I'm at the hotel in Pisa.
4   _____ is she? – Her name is Laura Sands.
5   _____ is Toronto? – It's in Canada.
6   _____ is on the telephone? – It's Alan's brother.
7   _____ are your mother and father?
– They're at home.

seventeen   **17**

Special focus: Describing appearance

1 Who's who?

1 "My husband, Larry, isn't tall but he isn't short. He's bald now. He has brown eyes, and he has a beard."
2 "My sisters? Well, they're tall and thin. They have blue eyes and short blond hair. Oh, yes – Emma wears glasses. They're very pretty."
3 "Well, I'm rather tall and heavy. I have blue eyes and brown hair. My hair is very short. Oh, yes – I have a moustache."

2 And you?

Describe the other two people in exercise 1.

And now describe a good friend or a member of your family.

Summary

Grammar

She's **the** girl with short blond hair.
She's **a** colleague.
She's **an** old school friend.

I'm		I'm not	
You're		You aren't	
He/She/It's	from Germany.	He/She/It isn't	from England.
We're		We aren't	
You're		You aren't	
They're		They aren't	

Am I		Yes, I am.	No, I'm not.
Are you		Yes, you are.	No, you aren't.
Is he/she/it	romantic?	Yes, he/she/it is.	No, he/she/it isn't.
Are we		Yes, we are.	No, we aren't.
Are you		Yes, you are.	No, you aren't.
Are they		Yes, they are.	No, they aren't.

I have	
You have	
He/She has	
We have	brown hair.
You have	
They have	

I'm Alan. This is **my** wife.
You're here, but where is **your** brother?
He's from Germany, but **his** wife is from England.
She's new. **Her** name is Betty.

Who is that? – David Bagley.
Where is he from? – From a place near Exeter.

Phrases

What's she like?
Is she nice?
She's quite nice, but a bit reserved.
He's outgoing, but not very tidy.

My best friend is my sister.

She's tall with long blond hair.
He's got blue eyes and a beard.
She wears glasses.

"I love your hair!"

Keeping Count

First words: Numbers

2,134,567

Numbers

21 twenty-one	30 thirty	100	a/one hundred
22 twenty-two	40 forty	200	two hundred
23 twenty-three	50 fifty	350	three hundred and fifty
24 twenty-four	60 sixty	1,000	a/one thousand
25 twenty-five	70 seventy	1,000,000	a/one million
26 twenty-six	80 eighty	2,550,000	two million five hundred and fifty thousand
27 twenty-seven	90 ninety		

2 Circle the numbers you hear.

13 27 40 500 70 30 61 80 72 17 14 30 90
28 71 19 55 16 12 15 91 11 21 1500 60 50

3 Quiz

Countries

How many states are there in the United States?	49	50	53
How many people are there in the USA?	230 million	275 million	300 million
How many people are there in the United Kingdom?	57 million	60 million	65 million
How many islands are there around the United Kingdom?	1200	1800	4000

Now tell a partner:

▶ I think there are ... states in the United States.
What about you?
– I think there are ...

Focus: Talking about quantities

1 True or false?

1. There are three books in the picture.
2. There is one flight attendant in the picture.
3. There is one newspaper in the picture.
4. There are two handbags in the picture.

Now say how many people/men/women/children there are in the picture.

▶ *There is one ... / There are ... in the picture.*

2 Dialogue: *Are you American?*

- 23 E, 23 D, 23 C – here it is! Excuse me, I think this is my seat.
- Is it? Oh. Yes, you're right. I've got 23 B. I'm sorry.
- That's OK. No problem.

- Are you American?
- Yes, I am. Where are you from?
- I'm German, but I live in Philadelphia.
- Oh, really? I've got a sister in Philadelphia and a brother near Philadelphia.
- It's a small world! Where are you from?
- I'm from Washington.

- How many children have you got?
- I've got a son and a daughter. And you?
- I haven't got any children – just my dog, Sam.

twenty-one   **21**

Focus: Talking about quantities

 3   **And you?**

How many brothers and sisters have you got?
Have you got children?
Have you got a dog or a cat?

▶ *I've got ...*

 4   **Find someone who ...**

Find someone who ...	student's name
has got relatives in the USA.	
has got an English-speaking friend.	
has got 15 cousins.	
has got a younger brother or sister.	
has got two boys or two girls.	

▶ *Have you got ...?*
– Yes, I have. / No, I haven't.

Follow-up

1. Listen and circle the word you hear.

friend	friends		name	names
town	towns		number	numbers
computer	computers		address	addresses
eye	eyes		colleague	colleagues
man	men		woman	women
boy	boys		girl	girls
baby	babies		child	children

Now read the list to a partner. Read one word in each pair. Your partner ticks the words you say.

2. How many blocks are there in this pile?

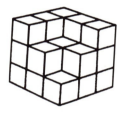

▶ There are ...

3. Ask your partner.

Ask your partner about a member of his/her family.
Use *has he/she got*? Find out as much as you can.

▶ You can ask me about my cousin Ellen.
– OK. Has she got long hair?
Yes, she has. / No, she hasn't.

Here are some ideas.

short/blond/... hair?
blue/brown/... eyes?
a moustache/a beard/glasses?
a big/small family?
children?
a pretty wife/girlfriend / a handsome husband/boyfriend?
English-speaking friends/relatives?
nice neighbours?
a dog/cat with a funny name?
cousins in the USA/England?

4. Now report to the class.

▶ Anja's cousin Ellen has got ...
She hasn't got ...

Follow-up

 Find out from a partner.

Student A   Look at this page.   Student B   Look at page 92.

Student A   This is a photo of the Bartlett family. Your partner has got a different photo of the family. Ask your partner questions and find out who is not in his/her photo.

Ask questions like this:

▶ *Is there a man with a beard in your photo?*
  – Yes, there is. / No, there isn't.

  Are there four children in your photo?
  – Yes, there are. / No, there aren't.

  Have you got a young woman with glasses in your photo?
  – Yes, I have. / No, I haven't.

 What are they like?

Write eight sentences with a partner about the people in the photo.

1 _____ have got _____
2 _____ has got _____
3 _____ haven't got _____
4 _____ hasn't got _____
5 There is _____
6 There isn't _____
7 There are _____
8 There aren't _____

Special focus: The time

1 minute = ____ seconds	1 hour = ____ minutes	1 day = ____ hours
1 week = ____ days	1 month = ____ weeks	1 year = ____ months

What time is it?
It's three o'clock.

What time is it?
It's a quarter past three.

What time is it?
It's half past three.

It's a quarter to four.

It's five to four.

It's almost four o'clock.

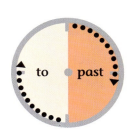

8.00 am

8.00 pm

13 Monday **14** Tuesday **15** Wednesday **16** Thursday **17** Friday **18** Saturday **19** Sunday

on Monday/Tuesday/...   at the weekend

from 8 o'clock till 5 o'clock ◆ from Monday to Friday

twenty-five **25**

Special focus: The time

1 Match the dialogues to the clocks.

Excuse me, what time is it?
– It's almost seven o'clock.
Thanks.

When's the next train to London?
– In twenty minutes, at twenty-five past eleven.

What time is the film tonight, Ed?
– At eight o'clock; we've got only ten minutes!

2 What time is it?

▶ It's ...

 3 **Listening.** Is the information in the table correct?

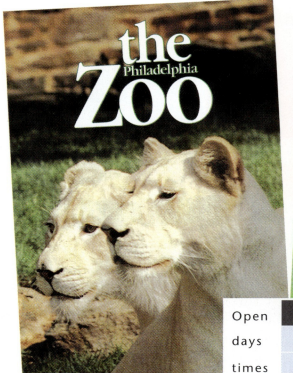 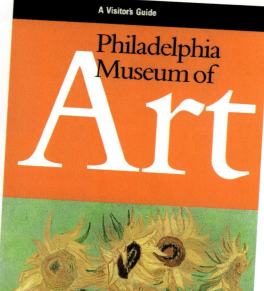

Open	Zoo	Museum
days	Monday – Sunday	Monday – Sunday
times	9.30 – 5.30	10.00 – 5.00

26 twenty-six

Summary

Grammar

book	books	+s [s]
name	names	+s [z]
address	addresses	+es [ɪz]
baby	babies	-y+ies [ɪz]

There is/isn't one newspaper in the picture.
There are/aren't three books in the picture.

Is there a man in the picture? Yes, there is. / No, there isn't.
Are there children in the picture? Yes, there are. / No, there aren't.

I've got
You've got
He/She's got
We've got   a brother.
You've got
They've got

I haven't got
You haven't got
He/She hasn't got
We haven't got   a sister.
You haven't got
They haven't got

Have I got
Have you got
Has he/she got   your book?
Have we got
Have you got
Have they got

Yes, I have. / No, I haven't.
Yes, you have. / No, you haven't.
Yes, he/she has. / No, he/she hasn't.
Yes, we have. / No, we haven't.
Yes, you have. / No, you haven't.
Yes, they have. / No, they haven't.

When's the next train to London?
How many people are there in the picture?

Phrases

How many blocks are there?
There are...

What time is it?
It's a quarter to four.
What time is the film?
It's at six o'clock.
When's the next train to London?

twenty-seven 27

What do you do?

First words: Jobs

1 Can you find these people?

- a doctor
- a policewoman
- a gardener
- a workman
- a teacher
- a reporter
- a secretary
- a shop assistant

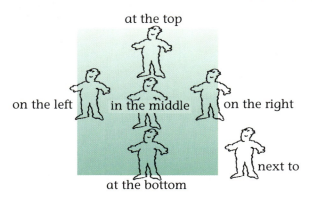

2 Where are they?

▶ Where's the doctor?
– He's at the top (of the picture) on the left./
He's next to the reporter./
I can't find him!

Focus: Talking about jobs and routines

Dialogue: At a party

NIGEL: Alice and Diana, this is Patrick and Sharon Kane. They're old friends from Ireland.
ALICE & DIANA: Hello, nice to meet you.
PATRICK & SHARON: Hello.
NIGEL: Patrick works at IBF.
DIANA: Oh, really. What do you do there?
PATRICK: I'm a gardener. I work outside.
ALICE: And you, Sharon? What do you do?
SHARON: Well, I was a secretary, but now I'm a housewife. We've got two children.
DIANA: That's a full-time job!
SHARON: You can say that again!

2 True or false?

1 Diana is Patrick's husband.
2 Diana and Alice are from Ireland.
3 Sharon was a secretary, but now she's a gardener.
4 Sharon and her husband have got two children.
5 Sharon works at home.

3 Where do they work?

Where do the people in exercise 1 on page 28 work?

in an office ◆ in a school ◆ in a hospital ◆ outside
in a factory ◆ in a shop ◆ in a restaurant ◆ at home

▶ A doctor works...
A policewoman works...

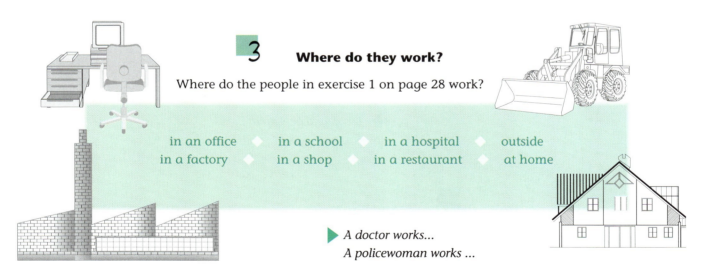

4 And you?

▶ *What do you do?*
 – I'm a ... / I work at ...

Where do you work?
– I work in/at ...

And now report to the class.
▶ Anja is a housewife. She works at home.

Focus: Talking about jobs and routines

5 **Put these activities in order.**

start work ☐   finish work ☐   go to bed ☐   get up ☐   have a shower ☐   have breakfast ☐

▶ First I..., then I ... . After that I ...

SIGRID

6 **A typical working day in Germany**

"Well, first I get up at 6.15 and have a shower. I never have breakfast, just a cup of coffee.
I go to work at 7.30 – I usually start work at 8.00.
I always have a coffee break at 9 o'clock, and I have lunch at 12 o'clock.
Usually I finish work at 4.30, but sometimes I finish at four. I often go shopping then."

7 **True or false?**

Make three true or false sentences about Sigrid and give them to a partner.
Can he/she correct the false sentences?

▶ 1 Sigrid gets up at ...
2 She always ...
3 ...

8 **And you?**

get up ◆ have breakfast ◆ go to work ◆ start work ◆ have a coffee break
have lunch ◆ finish work ◆ go to bed
never ◆ sometimes ◆ often ◆ usually ◆ always
first ◆ then ◆ after that ◆ at ... o'clock

▶ I usually get up at ...

30 thirty

Follow-up

1 Who does what?

talks to people ◆ helps people ◆ phones people ◆ writes letters ◆ reads ◆ cooks
cleans ◆ makes things ◆ repairs things ◆ goes shopping

a housewife   a reporter   a workman   a policeman   a secretary

2 And you?

Talk to a partner and tell him/her what you do at work.
▶ *I talk to people and phone people and write letters and ...*

Now report to the class. Tell the class what your partner does.
▶ *Anna cooks and cleans and helps her children.*

3 Listening

When does Barbara Travers usually do these things?

get up	6.45	read the newspaper	
have breakfast		go to dance class	
have a shower		make dinner	
start the housework		go to bed	

Now say what she does.
▶ *She usually gets up at a quarter to seven.*

Special focus: Breakfast

milk ◆ muesli ◆ toast ◆ ham ◆ cornflakes ◆ butter ◆ coffee ◆ yoghurt ◆ jam
egg ◆ tea ◆ honey ◆ rolls ◆ cheese ◆ bread ◆ fruit ◆ sausages ◆ juice

 Listening

Fill in what Jeff and Penny have for breakfast.

weekdays

at the weekend

Jeff's breakfast table

Penny's breakfast table

▶ Jeff usually has …
At the weekend he has …

 And you?

▶ What do you have for breakfast?
– I always/usually/often/sometimes/never have …

▶ And at the weekend?
– At the weekend I …

Now report to the class.
▶ Anna usually has …

32 thirty-two

Summary

Grammar

I'm **a** secretary.
She's **a** doctor.

I	work	
You	work	
He/She/It	works	in an office.
We	work	
You	work	
They	work	

+ s
work – works
make – makes
repair – repairs

+ es
go – goes
do – does
finish – finishes

	always	
	usually	
I	often	get up at 6 o'clock.
	sometimes	
	never	

I			I		I	
You			you		you	
He/She/It	can read, but	he/she/it	can't cook. Can	he/she/it	make coffee?
We			we		we	
You			you		you	
They			they		they	

on the left/right   at the top/bottom   in the middle   next to

Phrases

What do you do?
Where do you work?
I'm a housewife.
I work in a shop.
I work at IBF.

I write letters and phone people.
A workman makes and repairs things.

I get up at 7 o'clock.
Then I have a shower.
After that I have breakfast.
I usually go to bed at 11 o'clock.

Do you like flying?

First words: Activities

1 Match the words to the pictures.

> travelling ◆ watching TV ◆ cycling ◆ swimming ◆ going to the cinema
> gardening ◆ playing tennis ◆ relaxing ◆ going shopping
> going to the theatre/concerts ◆ reading ◆ hiking

2 Write three things you like and three things you don't like.

> ▶ I like swimming.
> I don't like gardening.

Focus: Asking questions

1 Ask a partner.

Find three things your partner likes.
▶ *Do you like reading?*
  – Yes, I do. / No, I don't.

2 Find someone who ...

Find someone who likes ...	student's name	doesn't like it	student's name
watching TV			
gardening			
swimming			
going shopping			
cycling			
playing football			
playing squash			
hiking			
going to the theatre			
going to concerts			
eating in restaurants			
travelling by train			
just relaxing.			

▶ *Do you like swimming?*
  – Yes, I do. Swimming is my hobby.
    No, I don't. I hate swimming.
    It's OK. I don't do it often.

3 Report to the class.

Write two sentences like this and then tell the class.
▶ *Thomas likes playing football, but Jens doesn't like it.*
  Traudi likes watching TV, but she doesn't like hiking.

4 Listening

A reporter is interviewing people. He wants to know:
Do you like flying? Listen and tick the correct answer.

Person	1	2	3	4	5	6	7	8
Yes, I do.								
No, I don't.								
I don't know.								

And you? *Do you like flying?*
Does your neighbour?

▶ *Yes, I do.*
  I don't mind.
  No, I don't.
  I hate flying!

Focus: Asking questions

 6 True or false?

1. Nick likes flying.
2. Ellen likes flying.
3. The flight doesn't take long.
4. Ellen wants to go by train.
5. Nick doesn't want to go by train.

 5 Dialogue: A trip

NICK: Well, what do you say?
ELLEN: I don't want to go.
NICK: Why not?
ELLEN: You know I don't like flying.
NICK: But the flight only takes an hour.
ELLEN: Only an hour? That's an hour of panic for me!
NICK: I'm there with you.
ELLEN: Sorry, but that doesn't help.
NICK: The train takes all day.
ELLEN: Yes, but you can sleep and read and talk and listen to music and ... You can't do that on the plane.
NICK: You can.
ELLEN: Not when the flight only takes an hour.

 7 Listening

What do these people like to do on a plane?

> sleep ◆ smoke ◆ read ◆ watch the film
> talk ◆ work ◆ listen to music
> eat ◆ have a drink

Person 1   EATS AND WORKS.
Person 2 _____
Person 3 _____
Person 4 _____
Person 5 _____
Person 6 _____
Person 7 _____
Person 8 _____

 8 And you? What do you do on a plane/train? What *don't* you do?

> ▶ *I usually read and eat.*
> *Sometimes I listen to music.*
> *I don't work.*

36 thirty-six

Follow-up

 How well do you know your teacher?

a) Read these questions and discuss with a partner how your teacher will answer.

▶ What do you think? Does he/she smoke?
 – Yes, he/she does. I think he/she smokes.
   No, he/she doesn't. I don't think he/she smokes.

What do you think? Can he/she sing?
 – Yes he/she can. I think he/she can sing.
   No, he/she can't. I don't think he/she can sing.

b) Now interview your teacher and write down his/her answers.
(In exercise 2 you can ask your partner the questions.)

		Teacher's answers	Partner's answers
Do you	smoke?		
	sometimes drive too fast?		
	eat a lot of sweets?		
	see your family often?		
	exercise?		
	take public transport?		
	like children/cats?		
	go to parties often?		
	watch a lot of TV?		
	get angry often?		
Can you	sing?		
	keep a secret?		
	repair things?		
	cook well?		
	play an instrument?		

2 **And you?**

Now ask your partner the questions in exercise 1 and write down his/her answers.

3 **Report to the class.**

Tell the class four things about your partner, one thing he/she does, one thing he/she can do, one thing he/she doesn't do, and one thing he/she can't do.

 ▶ Anja likes cats, and she can keep a secret.
She doesn't see her family often, and she can't cook well.

Special focus: **Shops etc.**

Southland Bank

Chestnut Hill Station

RITZ CINEMA
NOW PLAYING:
LASSIE COMES BACK (AGAIN)

Stilton Hotel ★ ★ ★
Mayfield Street

Super Fresh Supermarket

CRANKS Restaurant

Toilets
← Ladies   Gents →

Booths Chemists

MONTGOMERY HOSPITAL

Merion Post Office

Holiday Travel Agency
"We've got the cheapest air fares"

Très Chique Boutique
Walton High Street

 What is the name of the place?

1. You take a letter here.
2. You can go here when you want to eat.
3. You can change money here.
4. You go here when you want to go by train.
5. A place where you buy food.
6. You can buy medicine here.
7. You go here when you want to see a film.
8. A place where you can stay overnight.
9. The place where you buy T-shirts, jeans etc.
10. A place where you can go and see a doctor.

Summary

Grammar

Swimming is my hobby.
I like gardening.

read, go	→	reading, going
swim, shop	→	swimming, shopping
cycle, hike	→	cycling, hiking

Do | I / you / we / they | like flying?
Does | he / she | like flying?

Yes, I / you / we / they do.
Yes, he / she does.

No, I / you / we / they don't.
No, he / she doesn't.

I / You / We / They don't like flying.
He / She doesn't like flying.

Phrases

I like flying.
I hate flying.
Do you like flying?
– Yes, I do.
– No, I don't.
– I don't mind.

What do you say?

The train takes all day.
The flight only takes an hour.

thirty-nine 39

Excuse me, I'm looking for...

First words: Places

UNDER THE TABLE
IN THE HOUSE
AT THE DOOR
ON THE TABLE
BETWEEN TWO BIG PEOPLE

The toilets are behind the bank.
The taxi is in front of the hotel.
The boutique is next to the bank.
The post office is near the hospital.
The cinema is opposite the supermarket.

First words: Places

1 What is he saying?

over there ◆ on the left ◆ on the right ◆ on the corner ◆ straight on
between ◆ behind ◆ opposite

2 Where is it?

Your teacher is thinking of an object in the classroom.
Ask questions and find out where it is.

▶ *Is it under the book?*
  – Yes, it is. / No, it isn't.
  Is it near the door?
  Is it behind the table?

forty-one **41**

Focus: Asking the way

Dialogue: A tourist in New York

TOURIST: Excuse me, where's the Tourist Information Center?
PASSER-BY: Sorry, I'm not from here.
TOURIST: Excuse me, I'm looking for the Tourist Information Center.
PASSER-BY 2: It's on 42nd Street, near Times Square. Have you got a map?
TOURIST: Yes, here it is.
PASSER-BY 2: OK, we're standing here in Pearl Street. You go down Pearl Street and turn right. That's Grand Street. The subway station is on the left.
TOURIST: Which line do I take?
PASSER-BY 2: You take the B, D or Q train going uptown – the orange line. Change at Washington Square and take the A, C or E train – the blue line. You get off at 42nd Street. The Tourist Information Center is one block east of the station.
TOURIST: Thanks.
PASSER-BY 2: You're welcome.

Focus: Asking the way

2 True or false?

1. The tourist doesn't know where the Tourist Information Center is.
2. The tourist goes to the Information Center on foot.
3. The orange line takes you directly to the Information Center.
4. The Information Center is near Washington Square.

3 Where does the tourist go?

Look at the map. Mark the route from the Grand Street subway stop to the Tourist Information Center.

4 Please match.

right	over
go	up
get off	stop
down	left
under	get on

5 And you?

1. Is there a tourist information center (near) where you live?
2. Are there interesting things to see near you?
3. How can you get there best – on foot, by car, by bus, by subway?
4. How do you get to work – on foot, by bicycle, by car, by bus, by subway, by train?

forty-three

Focus: Asking the way

6 Giving directions

Excuse me, where's the (nearest) ... ?

It's over there.
   on the left/right.
   on the corner.
   next to the hotel.
   opposite the bank.
   in Oxford Street.
   one block east/west.

Go straight on.
   down this street.
   up Oxford Street.

You pass the supermarket/bus stop.

Turn left/right.
   into Oxford Street.
   at the bank.

7 Find out from a partner.

Student A   Look at this page.
Student B   Look at page 93.

Student A   You are at the station looking for these places:
1 a toilet, 2 the Midland Bank, 3 the nearest chemist.
Student B knows where they are. Ask him/her questions and find out.

▶ Excuse me, where's the ...?
   I'm looking for ...
   – It's in ...
   Go ... Turn ... You pass ...

8 Listening

A tourist is asking for directions at the tourist information office.
Look at the map, listen to the directions and write the numbers 1, 2 and 3 on the map.
Where's the   1 bookshop?   2 nearest car park?   3 nearest supermarket?

Follow-up

1 Listening

a) First read these sentences.

> Someone is eating.
> Someone is laughing.
> Some people are speaking French.
> A man is talking about his day.
> Someone is working at a computer.
> A woman is asking the way.
> The telephone is ringing.
> Someone is asking the time.

b) Now listen and write what you hear.

In situation 1 _____   In situation 5 _____

In situation 2 _____   In situation 6 _____

In situation 3 _____   In situation 7 _____

In situation 4 _____   In situation 8 _____

2 What are these people doing?

▶ She's cycling.

3 What am I doing?

▶ Are you hiking?
– Yes, I am. / No, I'm not.
Is he/she swimming?
– Yes, he/she is. / No, he/she isn't.

Now mime an action with a partner.

▶ Are you playing tennis?
– Yes, we are. / No, we aren't.
Are they playing squash?
– Yes, they are. / No, they aren't.

Special focus: Colours

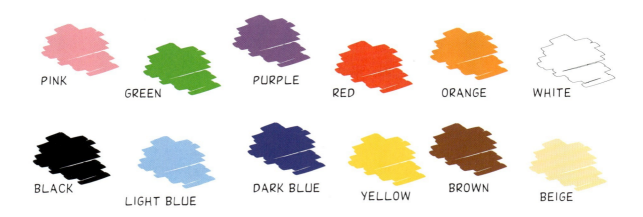

 Which car?

Which car is parked:

1. in the garage?
2. at the corner?
3. behind the bus?
4. in front of the chemist?
5. next to the bus stop?
6. under the tree?
7. near the post office?
8. on the pavement?
9. opposite the supermarket?
10. between the black car and the white car?

▶ 1 The red car is parked in the garage.

 And you?

Ask a partner about colours. Find out as much as you can.

▶ What's your favourite colour?
What's the colour of your car/house/room/neighbour's door/best friend's hair/ ...?

Summary

Grammar

I'm You're He/She's We're You're They're	looking for a bank.	I'm not You aren't He/She isn't We aren't You aren't They aren't	looking for a hotel.	

 behind

 at

Are you playing? — Yes, I am. / No, I'm not.
Is she reading? — Yes, she is. / No, she isn't.
Are they talking? — Yes, they are. / No, they aren't.

in front of

on

between

Which line do I take?

opposite

over

Phrases

under

The red car is in the garage.

Excuse me, I'm looking for the Tourist Information Center.
Excuse me, where's the ...?
 – It's on 42nd Street.
   It's over there.
   It's in Oxford Street.
   It's next to the bank.
   It's on the left/right.
   It's one block east/west.
   Go up/down here.
   Go straight on and turn left/right.
   Take the orange line.
   Get on at Grand Street.
   Change at Washington Square.
   Get off at 42nd Street.

"Excuse me, sir. Which way to Lexington Avenue?"

on foot   by bicycle   by car   by bus   by subway   by train

UNIT 6

forty-seven **47**

We're moving

First words: Homes

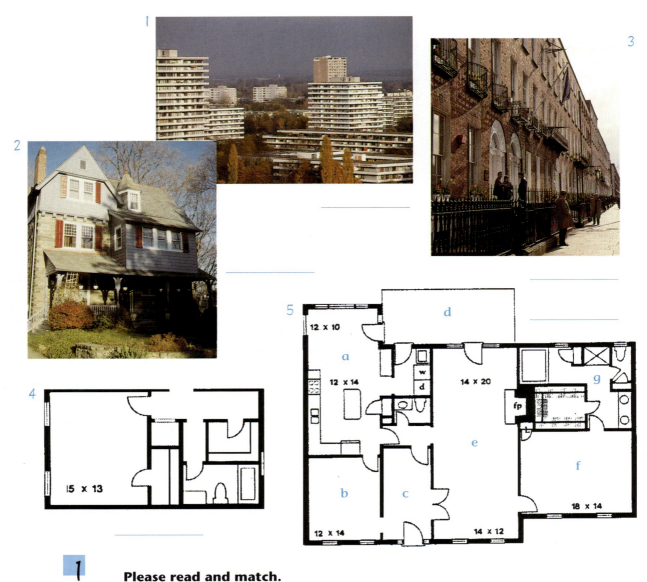

1 Please read and match.

a) Match these words to the pictures above.

house	a building where people live, usually one family
bed-sitter	a room where you live and sleep (AmEng studio)
terraced house	a house which is attached to others (AmEng row house)
flat	a group of rooms including kitchen and bathroom (AmEng apartment)
block of flats	a large building with many flats (AmEng high rise)

48 forty-eight

First words: Homes

b) Now match the names of these rooms to the flat on page 48.

kitchen ◆ bedroom ◆ dining room ◆ entrance ◆ living room ◆ bathroom ◆ balcony

TO LET - 1 BEDROOM FLAT
large living room, modern kit.
5 min. to Woodford tube station
£350 + security 01-274 8954

 2 Listening

Ellen and Nick are looking at a new flat. What's it like?

	new	old	modern	big	small	bright	dark	quiet	noisy	nice	not very nice
living room											
bedroom											
bathroom											
kitchen											

Is there a balcony
           garage
           lift?

▶ *The living room is big, bright and a bit noisy.*

3 And you?

new – old ◆ modern ◆ cheap – expensive ◆ big – small ◆ bright – dark
quiet – noisy ◆ nice – not very nice

What about your flat/house? What is it like?
How many rooms has it got? What are they like?
And your partner's flat/house?

Focus: Invitations and Plans

 1 **Dialogue:** *An invitation*

ELLEN: 372-8094. Hello.
LIZ: Ellen, hello. It's Liz. How are you?
ELLEN: Busy!
LIZ: Why? What are you doing?
ELLEN: I'm packing.
LIZ: Packing? Where are you going?
ELLEN: Well, tomorrow we're flying to Amsterdam, and in three weeks we're moving.
LIZ: You're moving to Amsterdam?
ELLEN: No, we're going to Amsterdam for a long weekend. We're moving upstairs to a bigger flat.
LIZ: Super! Listen, Ellen, I'm phoning because we're having some friends over for dinner tonight. Are you doing anything?
ELLEN: I'm afraid we are, Liz. Nick's friend Simon is coming over. He's helping us paint. But thanks for the invitation.
LIZ: Next time. Now tell me about the flat.

2 **Match and put in order.**

now ◆ tonight
this weekend
in three weeks

☐ Liz is having a party _____ .
☐ Ellen is packing _____ .
☐ Ellen is moving to a bigger flat _____ .
☐ Ellen is going to Amsterdam _____ .

 3 **True or false?**

Make true and false statements. Your partner or the others in the class must say if they are true or false.

▶ *Ellen is moving to Amsterdam.*
   – That's not true.

 4 **And you?**

What are you doing after class? This weekend? And your neighbour?

▶ *I'm …*

Focus: Invitations and Plans

5 Dialogue: Making plans

NICK: So, who can give us a hand when we move?
ELLEN: Well, let's see, there's Tom and Stephen ...
NICK: Tom's working in Oxford at the moment and Stephen's got a bad back.
ELLEN: Michael?
NICK: He usually goes to France at this time of year.
ELLEN: What about Rob?
NICK: Right, we can ask him.
ELLEN: And David? He always asks you for help with his jobs.
NICK: Yes, of course.
ELLEN: Then there's Norman.
NICK: Good idea! And perhaps he can bring Cliff – his friend who's visiting from Harwich.
ELLEN: Nick!
NICK: And then, of course, there's Hank.
ELLEN: Yes, but Kathleen's sister is getting married soon – perhaps the wedding's on that Saturday.

Sorry, I'm ...

6 What is correct?

1 Tom works/is working in Oxford.
2 Michael goes/is going to France at this time of year.
3 David phones/is phoning Nick for help with his jobs.
4 Cliff visits/is visiting Norman.
5 Kathleen's sister gets/is getting married soon.

7 Listening

Nick is phoning friends to ask if they can help. Can they?

Can he help?	Yes, he can.	No, he can't.
Rob		
David		
Norman		
Hank		

Now complete this:

▶ *... can't help because ...*

8 Who can give the best excuse?

Your teacher asks for help. Say why you can't help him/her.

Can you give me a hand?

Sorry, I'm ...

Follow-up

1 Who's coming to the party?
Who isn't?

We're having a party

Who: NICK & ELLEN
Why: HOUSEWARMING
When: SATURDAY 10TH MARCH
Where: 37 ALDEN PLACE
(SAME BUILDING, BUT ONE FLOOR NEARER HEAVEN)

Hope you can come.
RSVP

TOM	OK
STEPHEN	HIKING IN SWITZERLAND
HILLARY	VISITING HER MOTHER
ROB	HELPING A FRIEND MOVE!
NICOLE	OK - IS BRINGING A FRIEND
NORMAN	WORKING AT THE HOSPITAL
KATHLEEN	OK
HANK	FLYING TO SPAIN ON BUSINESS

▶ Tom's coming.
Stephen isn't coming. He's hiking in Switzerland.

2 Please complete.

1 Hillary usually goes by car when she visits her mother, but this time she's ...
2 Hank and Kathleen often just relax at the weekend, but this weekend they're ...
3 Nicole usually goes on holiday in May, but this year she's ...
4 Rob almost always watches TV in the evening, but tonight he ...
5 Norman usually stays at home at the weekend, but this weekend he ...

Follow-up

3 And you?

Make a list. Write some things you usually do at the weekend. Then write three things you're *not* doing this weekend.

▶ At the weekend I usually ...
  This weekend I'm not ...ing ...

4 Find someone who ...

a) First write down the questions with a partner.

▶ Do you eat out often?
  Are you having spaghetti for dinner tonight?

b) Now ask the other students.

Find someone who ...	student's name
eats out often.	
is having spaghetti for dinner tonight.	
likes game shows on TV.	
is going to the cinema this week.	
goes jogging regularly.	
is going hiking next weekend.	
goes to parties often.	
is having a party soon.	
...	
...	

Special focus: The date

March 17, 1999
May 26, 2005
July 17, 1997

November 3, 2001

1st	first	6th	sixth	11th	eleventh
2nd	second	7th	seventh	12th	twelfth
3rd	third	8th	eighth	13th	thirteenth
4th	fourth	9th	ninth	20th	twentieth
5th	fifth	10th	tenth	21st	twenty-first

3. 11. 2001 = the third of November two thousand (and) one / November (the) third two thousand (and) one
17. 7. 1997 = the seventeenth of July nineteen ninety-seven / July (the) seventeenth nineteen ninety-seven

January   February   March   April   May   June   July   August   September   October   November   December

 When is your birthday?

Make a line, with January 1st at one end and December 31st at the other.

MY BIRTHDAY'S ON 2ND JANUARY.

MY BIRTHDAY'S ON 30TH DECEMBER.

▶ When's your birthday?
– In July.
   On the sixth of July.

3 When is it?

1 Easter this year
2 the beginning/end of the school holidays
3 your wedding anniversary
4 the teacher's birthday
5 the fair in ...
6 your holiday

Summary

Grammar

I'm		tonight.
You're		this/next week.
He/She's		this/next weekend.
We're	moving	next Tuesday.
You're		on Saturday.
They're		tomorrow.
		in three weeks.

Phrases

You're moving to Amsterdam?
– No, we're going to Amsterdam for a long weekend.
What are you doing this weekend? – I'm going hiking.
Are you doing anything this weekend?
– No, I'm not. / Yes, (I'm afraid) I'm ...

Can you give me a hand?
– Of course. / Sorry, I'm ...

(I'm) Sorry!
I'm afraid ...

When's your birthday?
– On the fifth of April.

"It's for you."

I'll have the moussaka

First words: Food

 1   **What is there in the picture?**

> beef ◆ bread ◆ cake ◆ carrots ◆ cheese ◆ coffee ◆ cornflakes ◆ chicken
> egg ◆ fruit ◆ honey ◆ ice cream ◆ jam ◆ milk ◆ peas ◆ pie ◆ potatoes
> prawn cocktail ◆ salad ◆ soup ◆ tea ◆ vegetables ◆ wine

▶ There is some meat.   There isn't any honey.
    There are some carrots.   There aren't any cornflakes.

 2   **Starter, main course or dessert?**

Starter	Main course	Dessert
SOUP	BEEF	ICE CREAM

Focus: Decisions and predictions

 1   Dialogue: At a restaurant

NICK: What are you having?
ELLEN: I think I'll have the grilled salmon with fresh vegetables.
NICK: That sounds good.
ELLEN: And what are you having?
NICK: I think I'll have the moussaka.
ELLEN: But you had that last time.
NICK: So?
ELLEN: Don't you want to try anything new?
NICK: I'll have some of your salmon.
ELLEN: No, you won't!
NICK: OK, then I'll have the salmon, too. What would you like to drink?
ELLEN: I'll have a glass of white wine.
NICK: Me, too.

2   What are the questions?

1 _____? – She's having salmon.
2 _____? – He's having the grilled salmon, too.
3 _____? – They're having white wine.

 3   And you?

Judy's High Street Restaurant

Starters

Tomato soup	£2.95
Fresh melon with Parma ham	£4.95
Prawn cocktail with brown bread and butter	£6.25

Main courses

Roast beef	£8.95
Moussaka	£7.25
Chicken Kiev	£6.75
Grilled salmon	£8.75
Grilled Dover sole	£9.75

(all served with fresh vegetables of the day)

Salads

Salad platter	£5.25
Side salad	£1.65

Desserts

Italian ice cream	£2.25
Apple pie	£3.45
Coffee cake	£3.25
Fresh fruit salad	£2.75

▶ What are you having?
– I'll have the ...

Focus: Decisions and predictions

4 **Dialogue: At a Chinese restaurant**

NICK: What does your fortune cookie say?
ELLEN: It says: "You will live a long life and your wife will, too".
NICK: I think we've got a problem.
ELLEN: What does yours say?
NICK: Mine says: "You will meet a tall, dark, handsome man".
ELLEN: Let's swap.
NICK: OK.
 ...
ELLEN: Shall we go?
NICK: Waiter, can we have the bill, please?

5 **Put in the correct order.**

- a) Nick reads his fortune cookie.
- b) It says: "You will live a long life ..."
- c) His fortune cookie says: "You will meet a tall, dark, handsome man".
- d) Nick asks the waiter for the bill.
- e) Ellen reads her fortune cookie.
- f) Nick and Ellen exchange fortune cookies.

6 **Make predictions about your teacher's future.**

meet ◆ fly to ◆ travel to ◆ find ◆ win ◆ have lots of ◆ learn ◆ see
get ◆ be ◆ make ◆ write ◆ buy ◆ move to ◆ help someone to ◆ visit

You won't learn Chinese.   *You will meet lots of interesting people in your English classes.*

Follow-up

 Find out from a partner.

Student A   Look at this page.   Student B   Look at page 93.

Student A   Look at your picture for one minute. Student B has a picture like yours, but it isn't quite the same. Ask questions and find the differences.

▶ *There are some ... in my picture. Are there any ... in your picture?*
 – *Yes, there are. / No, there aren't.*

 Chain game

Teacher: *Let's make dinner! I'll go to the supermarket and buy some chicken.*
▶ Student 1: *He'll/she'll go to the supermarket and buy some chicken. I'll buy some cheese.*
Student 2: *He'll/she'll go to the supermarket and buy some chicken. He'll/she'll go to the supermarket and buy some cheese. I'll buy some cake.*
Student 3: ...

Follow-up

3 Please match.

1. We haven't got any bread.
2. I'll have some of your sole.
3. Someone's at the door.
4. There's one room with a shower.
5. Where are we?
6. All our friends are coming.
7. It's hot in here.

a) I don't know; I'll ask.
b) I'll open a window.
c) No, you won't.
d) I'll take it.
e) I'll see who's there.
f) I'm going shopping; I'll get some.
g) OK, OK, I'll come, too.

4 Listening

a) Match these words with the people you hear.

tired person
cold person
hungry person 1
bored person
dirty person
hot person
thirsty person

b) Listen again. Then choose the correct reaction.

☐ I think I'll go to the cinema.
1 I think I'll get a hamburger.
☐ I think I'll take a shower.
☐ I think I'll get a pullover.
☐ I think I'll get something to drink.
☐ I think I'll go swimming.
☐ I think I'll go to bed.

OH WELL, I'LL CATCH THE 11·25...
THE 11·55...
THE 12·25...

LEICESTER TO LONDON EVERY 30* MINUTES.
*Weekday Service
INTERCITY

Follow-up

5 What will you need?

bicycle ◆ computer ◆ football ◆ glasses ◆ games ◆ guide ◆ hotel reservation
jeans ◆ juice ◆ map ◆ medicine ◆ money ◆ newspaper ◆ plane ticket
restaurant guide ◆ secretary ◆ spaghetti ◆ subway map ◆ sweets

a) You're going to New York on business for five days. What will/won't you need?

▶ I'll need ..., but I won't need ...
Will you need ...? - Yes, I will. / No, I won't.

b) You're going to a holiday flat in the Alps for two weeks with children. What will/won't you need?

6 Making suggestions

open a window
play a game
get something to drink
phone for a pizza
go to the cinema
find a bar
order a bottle of mineral water
make a sandwich
phone Ian and ask what he's doing
get something to eat
sit outside
go swimming

You and a friend are   a) hungry
                       b) thirsty
                       c) hot
                       d) bored.

Make three (or more) suggestions for each situation.

▶ a) I'm hungry. Let's ...
   b) I'm thirsty. Let's ...
   c) I'm hot. Let's ...
   d) I'm bored. Let's ...

Special focus: Eating in a restaurant

1 Who says what?

C = customer
W = waiter / waitress

(I think) I'll have ... ☐

Yes, please. / No, thank you. ☐

Are you ready to order? ☐

For dessert I'll have ... ☐

That sounds good. ☐

I'd like ... ☐

There's ... W

Would you like ...? ☐

Can I have the menu/bill, please. ☐

Could I have some ...? ☐

Here you are. ☐

2 Listening

You will hear some people in a restaurant. What are they having?

	Starter	Main course	Dessert	Drink
Trevor				
Marjorie				
Sue				

3 Roleplay

Work in groups of three or four. You are in a restaurant. Order a meal. One of you is the waiter. Use the menu on page 57.

62 sixty-two

Summary

Grammar

Statements (.):	some	I'll have **some** salmon/carrots.
Negative statements (not):	any	I **don't** want **any** meat/peas.
Questions (?):	any	Have you got **any** bread/potatoes?

I
You
He/She   **'ll (will) have** water.
We
You
They

I
You
He/She   **won't have** wine.
We
You
They

Will I/you/he/... **need** a computer?
– Yes, I/you/he/... **will**. / No, I/you/he/... **won't**.

This is **my** ice cream. It's all **mine**.
There's **your** dessert. That's **yours**.

Phrases

I'll have the salmon.
Would you like some wine?
What would you like to drink?

It's too hot? I'll open the window.
You're thirsty? I'll get you some water.

You will have a long life and your wife will, too.
You'll need your glasses. You won't need a computer.

Could I have some water, please?

Let's swap.

Shall we go?

"First, you will meet Mr. Hot. Next, you will meet Mr. Cool. Then you will meet Mr. Right."

What did you do yesterday?

First words: The past

1 Match the verbs.

I always	work	Yesterday I	made
	have to		took
	make		went
	do		had to
	go		worked
	take		did

2 Match the captions to the cartoons.

a)   My son took my bowler to his playgroup.
b)   What a day! The computers broke down and we had to WRITE!
c)   Where did you work before you worked for us, Mum?
d)   I made a new friend today.
e)   He went to bed at 7.30, 8.15, 10.30 and midnight.

Focus: Talking about the past

1. I looked at the clock
 And saw it was late.
 I got out of bed
 Which is something I hate!

2. I stretched and yawned
 And scratched my head,
 While a little voice told me
 To go back to bed.

3. I took a shower,
 But the water was cold,
 Got dressed, made breakfast,
 But the bread had mould.

4. I flew out of the door,
 Jumped over the gate,
 Waved to the bus driver,
 But he didn't wait.

5. I thought to myself:
 "Now keep a cool head,"
 So I sat down and opened
 My paper and read.

6. The bus never came,
 But what could I do?
 My car's at the garage,
 My bicycle, too.

7. Along came Harry
 And gave me a ride,
 But I had to push
 When his motor died.

8. Things got worse
 As the day went by.
 How many times
 Did I ask myself: Why?

9. I had a feeling
 As I said,
 So why did I ever
 Get out of bed?

(The next time I get that feeling I think I'll roll over and play sick!)

2 Match each verse to a picture.

Focus: Talking about the past

3 **What does the poem say?**

1. The poem says:
    a) Never get out of bed.
    b) Listen to your feelings.
    c) Never take a ride with a friend.
2. Where do you think he's going?
3. How many words in the poem rhyme with red?

4 **Find the verbs in the past.**

a) Can you find the past of these verbs in the poem?

see _____	tell _____	give _____
think _____	have to _____	take _____
say _____	fly _____	get _____
go (by) _____	read _____	do _____
make _____	come _____	be _____
sit (down) _____	can _____	have _____

b) What eight other verbs in the poem are in the past? Write them here.

c) What's the difference between these two groups of verbs?

Follow-up

 1 Listening

What did Annie forget?

Monday   May 26, 1998

09.00	MAKE BREAD
10.00	TELL MR THOMPSON ABOUT PROBLEMS
11.00	WITH THE HOT WATER
12.00	HAVE LUNCH WITH DAD
13.00	
14.00	TAKE BICYCLE TO GARAGE
15.00	GO TO DANCE CLASS
16.00	
17.00	HAVE DRINK WITH PETER
18.00	MAKE SALAD FOR DINNER
19.00	TAPE TV PROGRAMME ABOUT GREENPEACE
20.00	MEG'S FOR DINNER

Now say what Annie did.

▶ At nine o'clock she made bread.
At ten o'clock she ...

2 And you?

Make a list of the things you did yesterday. Then ask your partner about his/her day.

Yesterday

▶ What did you do yesterday?
– Well, I ...

09.00	
10.00	
11.00	
12.00	
13.00	
14.00	
15.00	
16.00	
17.00	
18.00	
19.00	
20.00	

Follow-up

3 Ask a partner.

		me	my partner
Did you	get up on time		
	have a cold shower		
	have breakfast — today?		
	take the bus to work/school		
Did you	read the paper		
	work		
	do anything you don't like — yesterday?		
	watch television		
Did you	see family or friends		
	go shopping		
	go to the cinema — last weekend?		
	go to the theatre or a concert		

▶ Did you get up on time today?
– Yes, I did. I …
  No, I didn't. But I …

4 Listening

-(e)d is the ending for the past of regular verbs. There are three ways to pronounce it: [t], [d] or [ɪd]. Listen to these verbs and put them in the correct column.

[t]	[d]	[ɪd]
WORKED	LISTENED	PAINTED

Follow-up

 Who can tell the best lie about last night?

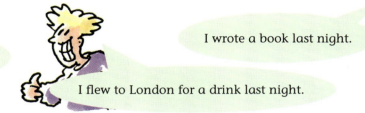

I had dinner with Franz Beckenbauer last night.

I wrote a book last night.

I flew to London for a drink last night.

 What didn't you do on holiday?

Last year people who went to New York State on holiday did these things. What did you do? What *didn't* you do?

They went	swimming, sightseeing, fishing, camping, shopping, sailing, riding and hiking.
They went	to a concert, to the theatre and to the cinema.
They played	golf, baseball and tennis.
Or they just	relaxed!

▶ I went swimming but I didn't play golf.
I didn't go swimming but I played golf.
I played golf but I didn't go hiking or riding or play baseball.

Special focus: Talking about your life

I was born in 1954.

I went to school in 1960.

I left school in 1974.

I met my husband and trained as a newspaper reporter in 1975.

I got married in 1976.

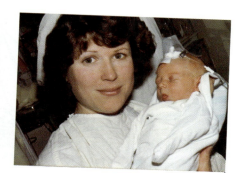
I had a baby in 1980.

We moved to the suburbs in 1987.

I got divorced in 1993.

Last year I found a job with a local paper.

 And you?

Tell a partner about your life. Then ask questions about his/her life.

Summary

Grammar

She **went** shopping and **got** some wine.
I **stretched** and **yawned** and **scratched** my head.

[t]	[d]	[ɪd]
work → work**ed**	live → liv**ed**	paint → paint**ed**
look → look**ed**	listen → listen**ed**	want → want**ed**

break	broke	make	made
can	could	read	read
come	came	say	said
do	did	see	saw
fly	flew	sit	sat
get	got	take	took
give	gave	think	thought
go	went	write	wrote
have	had	be	was/were

Did	I / you / he/she / we / you / they	watch the film?	Yes, I did. / No, I didn't. Yes, you did. / No, you didn't. Yes, he/she did. / No, he/she didn't. Yes, we did. / No, we didn't. Yes, you did. / No, you didn't. Yes, they did. / No, they didn't.	I / You / He/She / We / You / They	didn't read a book.

Phrases

I was born in 1967.
I left school in 1984.
I got married and had a baby.

We lived in a flat

First words: Furniture

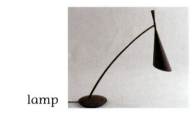
lamp

desk

chest of drawers

sofa

bookshelves

wardrobe

chair

armchair

1 **Label the drawing.**

BED

Focus: Talking about childhood

1 Reading

Which text describes the house on the opposite page, text 1 or text 2?

We lived in a quiet street. Our house was like the other houses except that it was red. I loved to sit in the living room and listen to music; my father was a musician and he had shelves full of records. My mother spent a lot of time in the kitchen; there was a lot of work because we didn't have things like a dishwasher or a fridge then. The kitchen was a very nice room with lots of light – I think it was yellow.

My brother and I each had our own room, and my parents had the big bedroom. Sometimes in the summer the whole family used to sit outside on the porch – the summers were long and hot then.

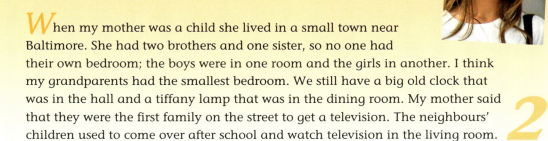

When my mother was a child she lived in a small town near Baltimore. She had two brothers and one sister, so no one had their own bedroom; the boys were in one room and the girls in another. I think my grandparents had the smallest bedroom. We still have a big old clock that was in the hall and a tiffany lamp that was in the dining room. My mother said that they were the first family on the street to get a television. The neighbours' children used to come over after school and watch television in the living room.

2 What do the texts say?

1. How many bedrooms were there in the house that the woman describes?
2. What was nice about the kitchen and the living room?
3. Whose house is the person in text 2 describing?
4. Why was this person's mother popular with her friends?

seventy-three 73

Focus: Talking about childhood

3 And you?

	me	my partner

1. Where did you live when you were a child:
   a) in a city?
   b) in the suburbs?
   c) in a small town/village?
   d) in the country?
2. Did you live in a house or a flat?
3. How many people were there in your family?
4. How many rooms were there?
5. Did you have your own room?
6. What colour was your room?
7. Was it a big room or a small room?
8. What furniture was there in your room?
   Was there: a table?
   a desk?
   a chair?
   a lamp?
   a chest of drawers?
   a wardrobe?
   Were there pictures?
   windows?
   bookshelves?
   plants?
9. What did you do there?
   a) I slept.
   b) I played.
   c) I read.
   d) I did my homework.
   e) I listened to music.
10. Did you like your room?
    Why?

▶ *Did you live in a city?*
– *Yes, I did. / No, I didn't.*
Was there a table?
– *Yes, there was. / No, there wasn't.*

Follow-up

1 Listening

IRIS

TOM

a) Listen to the two interviews on the cassette, one with Iris, one with Tom.

b) Make two groups.
Group A: listen to the first interview, with Iris.
Group B: listen to the second interview, with Tom.

In your groups read the questions below about your person (Iris or Tom). Then listen again and write down your answers.

Iris:
1. Did Iris live in a big city?
2. Did she live in a house?
3. Was her family a big family?
4. Was there a room for each of her brothers?
5. Was Iris's room very big?
6. Did she like playing with her brothers?

Tom:
1. Was Tom born in London?
2. Did he live in a big city?
3. Did he have a room of his own?
4. Was there a picture in his room?
5. Did Tom do his homework in the bedroom?
6. Did he listen to music in the bedroom?

c) Work with a partner from the other group. Ask him/her the questions about his/her person. Answer his/her questions about your person.

▶ *Did Iris live in a big city?*
   – Yes she did. / No, she didn't.
   Was Tom born in London?
   – Yes, he was. / No, he wasn't.

d) With your partner answer these three questions together:
   Were Iris and Tom both born in London?
   Were there bookshelves in both their rooms?
   Were there pictures in both their rooms?

2 And you?

What was different for you? Write five sentences.
▶ *Iris had three brothers, but I didn't have any brothers.*

3 Ask a partner.

▶ *Did you have a favourite ... when you were a child?*

drink ◆ game/sport ◆ animal ◆ story ◆ place in your house
place where you used to go after school ◆ place where you used to go on holiday ◆ time of year
day in the year ◆ friend ◆ teacher ◆ relative

▶ *What / Where / When / Who was it?*

Special focus: The weather

1 What was the weather like?

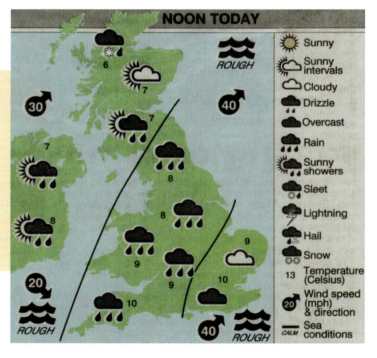

It was	sunny.	The sun shone.
	rainy.	It rained.
	(partly) cloudy.	–
	windy.	The wind blew.
	foggy.	–
		It snowed.

It was hot/cold.
warm/cool.

It was 10° (= ten degrees).

▶ What was the weather like in London?
– It was rainy. / It rained.

2 And you?

What was the weather like where you live…

1 this morning?
2 yesterday?
3 last weekend?
4 last Christmas?
5 last summer?
6 when you were a child?

3 Spring, summer, autumn or winter?

April   November
September   August
May   March
December   June
July   October
January   February

What is your favourite season/month? Why?

Summary

Grammar

I was/wasn't
You were/weren't
He/She was/wasn't
We were/weren't   in the kitchen.
You were/weren't
They were/weren't

Was I		Yes, I was. / No, I wasn't.
Were you		Yes, you were. / No, you weren't.
Was he/she	outside?	Yes, he/she was. / No, he/she wasn't.
Were we		Yes, we were. / No, we weren't.
Were you		Yes, you were. / No, you weren't.
Were they		Yes, they were. / No, they weren't.

There was a bed. **There wasn't** a table.
There were plants. **There weren't** any pictures.

Was there one?	Yes, there was. / No, there wasn't.
Were there two?	Yes, there were. / No, there weren't.

Phrases

Our house was like the other houses.
The whole family used to sit outside.

What was the weather like?
– It was sunny.

Can I help you?

First words: Clothing

1 Match the words to the clothing.

tie ◆ jacket ◆ dress ◆ gloves ◆ coat ◆ trousers ◆ shirt ◆ hat ◆ shoes

Styling by Gillian Annesley
Photography by Tim Platt
Gloves by Cornelia James £ 25
Hat by Hat Shop £35
Ring by Kathryn Post £145
Earrings by Eric Beamon £ 35
Dress by Genny Boutique £ 370
Letter by Royal Mail 26p
By Air, By Land, By Hand
Royal Mail

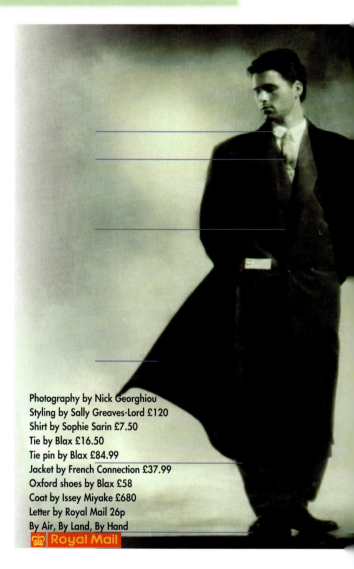

Photography by Nick Georghiou
Styling by Sally Greaves-Lord £120
Shirt by Sophie Sarin £7.50
Tie by Blax £16.50
Tie pin by Blax £84.99
Jacket by French Connection £37.99
Oxford shoes by Blax £58
Coat by Issey Miyake £680
Letter by Royal Mail 26p
By Air, By Land, By Hand
Royal Mail

2 Make a list.

1 What do you wear:
   a) at home/outside?   b) in the winter/in the summer/all year?

2 What clothing do you like buying?
   What clothing don't you like buying?

Focus: Shopping

Dialogue: *The sleeves are too short*

ELLEN: Here, try this one on.
  ...
NICK: I don't think it suits me.
ELLEN: What's the matter?
NICK: The colour's not right and the sleeves are too short.
ELLEN: The sleeves aren't too short; your arms are too long.
NICK: My arms are just right.
ELLEN: This is the last time I go shopping with you.
NICK: I think the last jacket looked better. And the sleeves were longer.
ELLEN: Put it on again.
  ...
  Yes, it is better. It's the cheapest, too.
NICK (to the shop assistant): I think we'll take this one.

2 Who says it? Customer or shop assistant?

		Customer	Shop assistant
1	Can I try this on?		
2	No, thank you; I'm just looking.		
3	I think I'll take this one.		
4	How would you like to pay?		
5	Have you got this in a larger size?		
6	Can I help you?		
7	I'm looking for		
8	What size are you?		
9	I think it's too small.		
10	The changing room is over there.		
11	How much is it?		
12	Do you take Eurocard?		
13	Those pullovers are nice.		

seventy-nine

Focus: Shopping

3 **What are they saying?**

I think it's too small.
Can I help you? (2x)
What size are you?
Yes, I'm looking for a...
No, thank you. I'm just looking.
I'll take this one.
What size are you?

4 **And you?**

You're shopping in England. With a partner decide first what you want to buy, then write a dialogue with the phrases above.
When you're finished, practise the dialogue and roleplay it for the class.

Focus: Comparing things

5 London – A City of Superlatives!

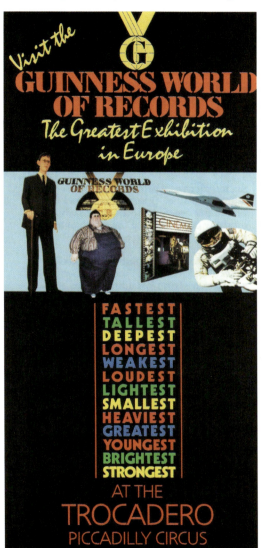

When people talk about London you often hear words like *the biggest, the best, the most famous*, etc. A hundred years ago London was perhaps the most important capital in the world. Even today it is still one of the most important financial centres in the world. In the Houses of Parliament we find one of the oldest parliaments, in the London Stock Exchange one of the busiest stock markets. London has the largest public transport system in the world. (It carries over 5 million people every working day!) London has more parkland than all other world capitals (11% of Greater London). Harrods, the largest department store in Europe, is world-famous, as is Liberty's of London, best known for its fabrics. The British Museum, the National Gallery and the Tate Gallery have some of the finest collections in the world, and Madame Tussaud's the most interesting collection of wax figures. And the list goes on and on.

6 Superlatives

1. How many superlatives can you find in the text? Circle them.
2. What are the oldest/most beautiful/most modern buildings in your city/town?
3. What are the biggest/best/cheapest /most expensive department stores/shops?
4. What are the most interesting things to see and do?

eighty-one **81**

Follow-up

1 The Woods family

Look at this family and write five sentences about the people in it.

tall ◆ short ◆ thin ◆ funny ◆ old ◆ short

▶ Patricia is thinner than Gordon.
Janet is as tall as Patricia.

2 And you?

Now compare yourself with a partner/a friend/a member of your family.

▶ Martina is more outgoing than me.
I'm heavier than Petra.

Follow-up

3 Match the texts to the headlines.

California's Most Elegant ☐

THE FUNNIEST, WARMEST, MOST LOVEABLE COMEDY OF THE YEAR! ☐

Travellers Magazine's Ten Best Cities ☐

The greatest shoe sale of the season! ☐

The quietest, smartest, safest car you can buy! ☐

THE SADDEST WORDS YOU'LL EVER HEAR! ☐

A This is an automobile like no other you have ever seen – or ever driven. We have combined 75 years of technology with the dreams of tomorrow, and the result is the 1995 Tempo II. Come in and test drive it today. You'll be glad you did!

B "Sorry, we're not taking any more reservations." Next time, call a little earlier – you're not the only one who loves our delicious steaks, fish and vegetarian dishes!
The Rittenhouse Square Restaurant

C
1 San Francisco
2 Florence
3 London
4 Vienna
5 Rome
6 Paris
7 Sydney
8 New York
9 Bangkok
10 Berlin

D DON'T MISS THIS ONE: IT WILL MAKE YOU LAUGH TILL YOU CRY. DEFINITELY ONE OF THE YEAR'S BEST!

E Come in and save on the best footwear money can buy. But don't wait – a sale this good won't last long!

F Come and spend a romantic weekend at one of the West Coast's oldest and most beautiful resort hotels. You'll love the difference!
The Catalina Inn

4 Simply the best!

Make up an advert for your English class / your teacher / one of your classmates / your town etc.

Special focus: Parts of the body

Other parts of the body:

1 Match the words to the parts of the body.

hair ◆ eye ◆ nose ◆ mouth ◆ ear ◆ chin ◆ neck
head ◆ chest ◆ back ◆ arm ◆ hand ◆ fingers ◆ waist ◆ leg ◆ foot ◆ toes

2 What parts of the body do you move when you …

watch TV
write a letter
say goodbye
learn English
… ?

Summary

Grammar

new – newer – newest
big – bigger – biggest
noisy – noisier – noisiest

modern – **more** modern – **most** modern
famous – **more** famous – **most** famous

good – better – best
bad – worse – worst

George is thinner **than** Margaret.
Peter is **as** tall **as** his sister, Susan.
Martina is **more** outgoing **than** me.

Phrases

Harrods is the largest department store in Europe.

I'm looking for …
How much is it?
I think it's too big/small. – Do you?

Have you ever ...?

First words: Activities

1 Match the phrases to the pictures.

read a magazine ◆ watch a TV programme ◆ work as an au-pair ◆ visit friends or relatives
go to see a film ◆ listen to the news on the radio ◆ keep a diary ◆ buy a newspaper

2 Have you ever ...?

Have you ever ...	Yes, I have.	No, I haven't.
listened to the news in English regularly?		
kept a diary in English?		
watched a TV programme in English?		
been to see a film in English?		
worked as an au-pair in an English-speaking country?		
bought an English-language newspaper?		
read an English-language magazine?		
visited friends or relatives in an English-speaking country?		

Now ask a partner. ▶ *Have you ever listened to the news in English regularly?*
– *Yes, I have. / No, I haven't.*

Focus: Talking about the past (2)

1   Dialogue: *I've been to Canada*

JACK: Have you ever been to the United States?
JENNIFER: No, but I've been to Canada.
JACK: Really? When?
JENNIFER: In 1989, the year before I got married. I went to Toronto.
JACK: How long did you stay?
JENNIFER: I was there for six months. I worked as an au-pair.
JACK: Have you been back since then?
JENNIFER: No, I haven't, unfortunately.

2   Answer the questions.

		Yes, she has.	No, she hasn't.
1	Has Jennifer ever been to the United States?		
2	Has Jennifer ever worked as an au-pair?		
3	Has Jennifer ever been back to Canada?		

		Yes, she did.	No, she didn't.
4	Did she stay for more than a year?		
5	Did she go to Canada on holiday?		
6	Did she go before she got married?		

3   And you?

Austria	Denmark	Greece	Italy	Spain
Canada	England	Holland	Japan	Sweden
China	France	Hungary	Russia	Switzerland
the Czech Republic	Germany	Ireland	Scotland	the United States

▶ What foreign countries have you visited?
– I've been to (Austria, France, Spain and Italy).
When did you visit (France)?
– I went there (in 1987).

Which places did you go to?
– I visited (Paris).

Follow-up

1 Please complete.

had ◆ been
spoken ◆ flown
driven ◆ asked
eaten ◆ found
heard

1 HAVE you ever BEEN to Greece?
   – Yes, I 'VE FLOWN there three times and I _____ _____ there once.
2 _____ you _____ time to call her?
   – Yes, I _____ _____ to her, but I _____ not _____ her to come.
3 I _____ not _____ anything about it. What happened?
4 _____ you ever _____ Indonesian food?
   – Yes, I _____ _____ it many times – my wife is Dutch.

2 Chain game

a) You are going on holiday to Canada. With a partner make three lists.

Things I'll need in Canada

Clothing

Sports equipment

Other things

b) You have now packed your bags. Play the chain game.

Teacher: I'm going on holiday to Canada, and I've packed my passport.
▶ Student 1: I'm going on holiday to Canada, and I've packed my passport and my tennis racket.
Student 2: I'm going on holiday to Canada, and I've packed my passport, my tennis racket and my address book.
Student 3: ...

3 Listening

Pete and Mary are going on holiday. Listen and decide what is right.

		Yes, he/she has.	No, he/she hasn't.
Has Pete	found his passport?		
	packed the medicine?		
	bought films?		
	called a taxi?		
Has Mary	asked the neighbour to water the plants?		
	packed the guide book?		
	phoned her mother?		

Follow-up

 4 Complete the questions, then ask a partner.

		Yes, I have.	No, I haven't.
1	Have you ever been to _____ ?		
2	Have you ever seen _____ ?		
3	Have you ever read _____ ?		
4	Have you ever found _____ ?		
5	Have you ever met _____ ?		

5 Find someone who ...

Now ask other people in your class.
If they answer "yes", ask questions like this:

> ▶ When were you / did you ...?
> Where did you ...?
> What did you ...?
> Why did you ...?
> How did you ...?

 6 What has just happened?

1   2   3

▶ I think the man/woman in picture ... has just heard/seen/...

 7 What have you learned in this course?

a) Say what you have learned to do in the course.

▶ We've learned to ...

b) Can you remember in which unit it was?

▶ I think we learned to ... in Unit ...

Special focus: Learning English

1 Looking back. Ask a partner.

1 Are you happy with the progress you've made in your English class?
2 Have you learned the things you need?
3 Did you hear enough English? Speak enough? Read enough? Write enough?
4 What things have been most important for you? What did you like best about the course?
5 Is there anything you didn't like? What?
6 What was the funniest thing in the course?

2 Looking ahead

With a partner decide what you will do after your course.

do another course ◆ go to a language school ◆ read some easy readers
buy an English magazine or newspaper regularly
go to an English-speaking country for my next holiday ◆ listen to radio programmes in English
watch English TV programmes ◆ keep a diary in English

▶ In the future I would like to ...
I've decided that I'll definitely ...
I think I'll ...

Summary

Grammar

Have you ever **seen** the film? – Yes, I **saw** it **last month**.
He **has been** to London. He **went** there **in 1993**.

I	have asked		I	haven't asked		have I?	
You	have asked		you	haven't asked		have you?	
He/She	has asked	him, but	he/she	hasn't asked	her. Or	has he/she?	
We	have asked		we	haven't asked		have we?	
You	have asked		you	haven't asked		have you?	
They	have asked		they	haven't asked		have they?	

Yes, I have. / No, I haven't.
Yes, you have. / No, you haven't.
Yes, he/she has. / No, he/she hasn't.
Yes, we have. / No, we haven't.
Yes, you have. / No, you haven't.
Yes, they have. / No, they haven't.

be	have been		hear	have heard
buy	have bought		keep	have kept
drive	have driven		meet	have met
eat	have eaten		read	have read
find	have found		see	have seen
fly	have flown		speak	have spoken
go	have gone/been		write	have written
have	have had			

Phrases

Have you ever been to Greece?   Yes, I have. / No, I haven't.
Have you been back?
I've learned to order food in a restaurant.

Information gap activities

Unit 2, page 17 **Find out from a partner.**

Student B — These people are all new colleagues at TV International. Ask your partner questions and complete the table. You can only ask questions with *Is ...?*

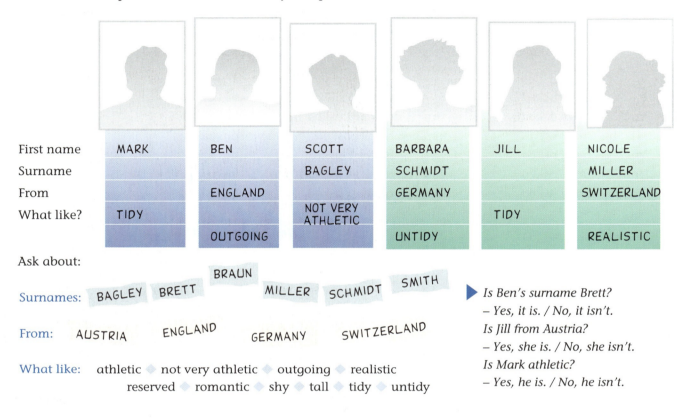

First name	MARK	BEN	SCOTT	BARBARA	JILL	NICOLE
Surname			BAGLEY	SCHMIDT		MILLER
From		ENGLAND		GERMANY		SWITZERLAND
What like?	TIDY		NOT VERY ATHLETIC		TIDY	
		OUTGOING		UNTIDY		REALISTIC

Ask about:

Surnames: BAGLEY   BRETT   BRAUN   MILLER   SCHMIDT   SMITH

From: AUSTRIA   ENGLAND   GERMANY   SWITZERLAND

What like: athletic ◆ not very athletic ◆ outgoing ◆ realistic
reserved ◆ romantic ◆ shy ◆ tall ◆ tidy ◆ untidy

▶ Is Ben's surname Brett?
– Yes, it is. / No, it isn't.
Is Jill from Austria?
– Yes, she is. / No, she isn't.
Is Mark athletic?
– Yes, he is. / No, he isn't.

Unit 3, page 24 **Find out from a partner.**

Student B — This is a photo of the Bartlett family. Your partner has got a different photo of the family. Ask your partner questions and find out who is not in his/her photo.

Ask questions like this:

▶ Is there a man with a beard in your photo?
– Yes, there is. / No, there isn't.

Are there four children in your photo?
– Yes, there are. / No, there aren't.

Have you got a young woman with glasses in your photo?
– Yes, I have. / No, I haven't.

Information gap activities

 Find out from a partner. Unit 6, page 44

Student B   You are at the station looking for these places:
1 the tourist information office,
2 the Parkview Hotel, 3 the post office.
Student A knows where they are.
Ask him/her questions and find out.

▶ Excuse me, where's the ...?
I'm looking for ...
– It's in ...
Go ... Turn ... You pass ...

 Find out from a partner. Unit 8, page 59

Student B   Look at your picture for one minute. Student A has a picture like yours,
but it isn't quite the same. Ask questions and find the differences.

▶ There are some ... in my picture. Are there any ... in your picture?
– Yes, there are. / No, there aren't.

ninety-three   93

A poem

What have you got in your bag?

What have you got in your bag? I asked.
She said, let's have a look:

A pen,
A book –
Whose pen is that?
A hat.
Not mine,
The pen –
I think it's Ben's,
Or Ken's,
Or is it Len's?
Now I know,
It belongs to Joe.
What's this I feel,
A banana peel?
What's this I see?
Of course, my key.
Or is it yours,
Or his or hers?
I think I know,
It's Mrs Sherr's.
A letter I forgot to post,
A sandwich –
Ham and cheese on toast.
Money,
Kleenex,
Photos, too,
Most of them
Aren't new.
Oh, look, here's Beth
When she was two,
Or Barbara or Sally,
Or is it Sue?
What's in my bag?
Excuse me, please –
I think I'll eat
My ham and cheese.

Emily Patrick – artist

I was born in 1959 on a farm in Kent. My parents always said I should have a "sensible" career, so I studied architecture at Cambridge. In my spare time, however, I painted. These paintings sold well in London, and this gave me the confidence to say: "I am a painter!"

I learned to look carefully from John Ward, the artist, and I studied the old masters. I got commissions to paint portraits and when there were no portrait commissions I painted "still lives". In 1987 I was commissioned to paint a portrait of the Princess of Wales.

I got married in 1986 and had my first child in 1987. I managed to continue painting, but then I had a second child and found it almost impossible. It was the first time I found it hard to be a woman and have a career. Now my second child is four years old and I am painting well again. I have had two exhibitions, one in London and one in Japan.

Emily Patrick

Daily routine

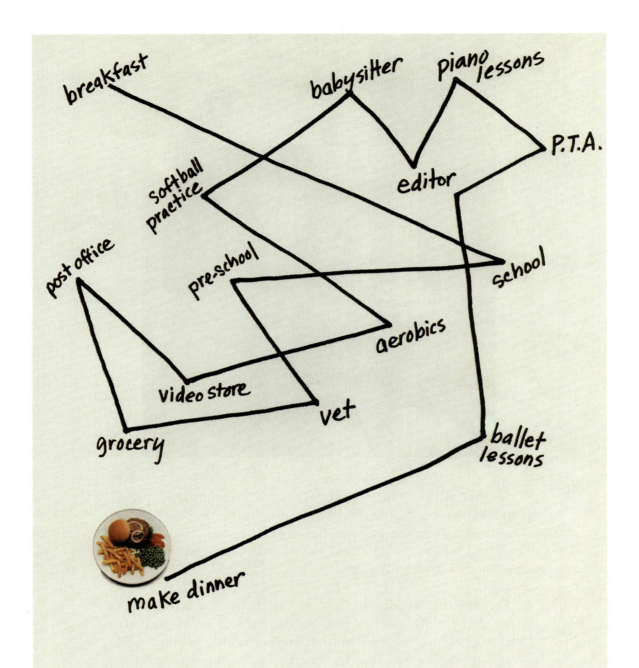

No wonder mothers love Ore-Ida as much as kids do.

Sometimes being a mom is like being a human pinball.

But even after you've bounced around all day, you still want to come up with a nutritious dinner that shows you care.

Which is why there's nothing moms love more than Ore-Ida Golden Fries.

They're delicious and easy to cook.

What's more, when you serve them with a big hamburger, your kids will make a beeline straight for the table.

Ore-Ida Golden Fries. After a day of zigging and zagging, it's nice to know there's still a direct route to a kid's heart.

Ore-Ida
It's All-Rightal

SELF-STUDY SECTION

Lernen zu Hause

Bevor Sie mit den Übungen in diesem Teil Ihres Lehrwerks beginnen, möchten wir Ihnen einige Vorschläge mit auf den Weg geben, wie Sie das Lernen zu Hause erfolgreicher und angenehmer gestalten können. Zuerst einige allgemeine Tips:

- Lieber häufiger kurz als einmal lang! Fünfzehn Minuten jeden Tag oder jeden zweiten Tag ist besser als nur einmal pro Woche eine Stunde oder länger.
- Versuchen Sie, immer zu einer bestimmten Zeit zu lernen; man schiebt oft hinaus, was nicht fest eingeplant ist, und schon ist die nächste Unterrichtsstunde da, ohne daß man was dafür getan hat.
- Versuchen Sie, zu Hause zusammenzufassen, was Sie im Unterricht gelernt haben. Ihnen wird dadurch klar, was Sie verstanden haben und was nur so halb. Dann können Sie mit Hilfe Ihres Buches Klarheit schaffen oder, wenn Ihnen das nicht gelingt, Ihrem Kursleiter/Ihrer Kursleiterin bei der nächsten Gelegenheit Fragen stellen.
- Fragen Sie die anderen Kursteilnehmer, wie sie lernen. Vielleicht hat der eine oder andere einen guten Tip. Vergessen Sie dabei aber nicht, daß jeder Lerner seinen eigenen Stil entwickeln muß.
- Investieren Sie ein paar Minuten, um herauszufinden, wie Ihr Wörterbuch funktioniert. Es lohnt sich!

Hinweise zu den einzelnen Bereichen

Wortschatz

Die erste Regel beim Vokabellernen lautet: Wörter immer im Zusammenhang zu lernen. Es gibt viele Methoden, sich neue Vokabeln einzuprägen, aber die unwirksamste aller Methoden ist, sie in einer alphabetischen Liste zu lernen, völlig ohne Zusammenhang. Hier einige Vorschläge, wie Sie Ihre Wortschatzarbeit effektiver gestalten können:

- Es gibt Wörterbücher für Kinder (*picture dictionaries*), die Vokabeln in Wortgruppen bildlich darstellen. Diese sind meist farbig und eignen sich gut, sich einen gewissen Grundwortschatz anzueignen.
- Man kann Gegenstände, die sich im Haus befinden, mit dem Namen des Objektes (auf einem Zettel) versehen, damit man jedesmal, wenn man den Gegenstand sieht, an dessen englische Bezeichnung erinnert wird. Wenn sich diese Begriffe eingeprägt haben, kann man ein passendes Verb dazuschreiben (*lamp – turn on/off*).
- Wenn man sich etwas merken will, ist es nützlich, es zusammen mit einem anderen Reiz im Gehirn zu verankern. Das kann ein Bild, ein Gefühl, eine Bewegung oder eine andere Sinneswahrnehmung sein. Durch die Melodie schaffen es Kleinkinder z.B., längere Texte in Form von Liedern auswendig zu lernen.

Versuchen Sie mal, Verben mit einer körperlichen Bewegung zu verbinden, so daß Sie an das englische Wort denken müssen, wenn Sie die Bewegung machen. Oder denken Sie an ein Geräusch, mit dem Sie eine Tätigkeit und deren englische Entsprechung verbinden.

- Eine weitere Möglichkeit, sich Vokabeln zu merken, besteht darin, sich dafür ständig neue Zusammenhänge auszudenken, indem Sie sie sinnvoll ordnen, klassifizieren, assoziieren usw. Sie haben zum Beispiel das Wortfeld *animals* (Tiere) im Unterricht gelernt und möchten zu Hause diese Wörter wiederholen. Versuchen Sie es mit Hilfe einer sogenannten „Wortspinne".

Hier einige Möglichkeiten:

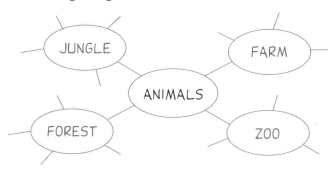

Denkbar wäre auch folgende Gruppierung:

ANIMALS THAT LIVE ON LAND / ANIMALS THAT LIVE IN WATER / ANIMALS THAT FLY

Lernen zu Hause

Eine gefühlvollere Unterteilung wäre z.B. folgende Rangordnung:

MY TEN FAVOURITE ANIMALS

Lassen Sie Ihrer Fantasie freien Lauf: Je ausgefallener die Gruppierung, desto besser wird man sich die Wörter merken.

Grammatik

Sie werden schon gemerkt haben, daß Grammatik in *Colours* nicht die Rolle spielt wie vielleicht früher in der Schule. Sie ist kein Lernziel an sich, sondern dient nun lediglich zur Systematisierung und Kontrolle des Gelernten.
Viel wichtiger als Grammatikregeln ist es, sich die Sprache anzueignen, die Sie brauchen, um Ihre Bedürfnisse und Meinungen mitzuteilen und die von anderen verstehen zu können.

Hörverstehen

Sie sollen wissen, daß Sie nicht jedes Wort einer Hörverständnisübung verstehen werden, ja verstehen müssen. Vielmehr geht es bei diesen Übungen darum, die gestellte Aufgabe zu lösen. Wenn Sie in einem englischsprachigen Land um eine Information bitten, werden Sie wahrscheinlich auch nicht jedes Wort Ihres Gesprächspartners verstehen und können dennoch folgen. Genau diese Fertigkeit soll trainiert werden.
Sollten Sie trotz mehrmaligen Hörens einen Hörtext nicht vertehen, können Sie den genauen Wortlaut im Schlüssel lesen. Tun Sie dies aber nur, nachdem Sie versucht haben, die gestellte Aufgabe zu lösen!

- Machen Sie es sich zur Gewohnheit, täglich die Nachrichten auf englisch zu hören. Die wichtigsten Ereignisse, Namen, Orte und einiges mehr werden Sie aus der Tagespresse schon kennen. Das erleichtert das Verstehen, und Sie werden bald merken, daß Sie genug mitbekommen, um einzelne unbekannte Wörter nachschlagen zu können.

Lesen

Machen Sie nicht den Fehler, jedes Wort eines Textes auf Anhieb verstehen zu wollen. Versuchen Sie vielmehr, die globale Bedeutung zu erfassen. Entscheiden Sie dann, welche Wörter für ein genaueres Verstehen von Bedeutung sind und schlagen Sie diese nach. Zur Kontrolle können Sie dann versuchen, den Text schriftlich zusammenfassen.

- Abonnieren Sie eine wöchentlich oder monatlich erscheinende Zeitung oder Zeitschrift in englischer Sprache, eine, die Ihnen zusagt, damit Sie sie gern lesen.

Sprechen

Richtiges Sprechen können Sie nur mit jemandem üben, der die Sprache beherrscht. Es gibt allerdings einiges, das man tun kann, um mündliches Kommunizieren vorzubereiten:

- Üben Sie die Aussprache und Satzmelodie. Das können Sie anhand der Übungen in der *Self-Study-Section*. Nachdem Sie die Aufgabe gelöst haben, können Sie die Wörter/Sätze nachsprechen. Vergleichen Sie Ihre Aussprache mit der, die Sie auf der Cassette/CD hören.
- Wiederholen Sie die Dialoge mit Hilfe der Cassetten/CDs, aber belassen Sie es nicht dabei. Versuchen Sie auch, die Dialoge mit eigenen Worten zusammenzufassen. Oder schreiben Sie verschiedene Varianten des Dialogs, z.B. mit anderen Figuren oder an einem anderen Ort.

Schreiben

Wenn Sie die Übungen in der *Self-Study-Section* gemacht haben, vergleichen Sie Ihre Lösungen mit denen im Schlüssel. Schreiben Sie mit Bleistift, damit Sie zu einem späteren Zeitpunkt Ihre Antworten ausradieren und nochmal schreiben können.

- Versuchen Sie, eine Zeitlang Tagebuch auf englisch zu führen. Beschreiben Sie darin Ihren Tagesablauf, oder auch den vom Vortag, wenn Sie nicht täglich genügend Zeit zum Schreiben finden.

Aussprache: Wortbetonung

Die richtige Wortbetonung ist der erste Schritt zur richtigen Aussprache. Hören Sie die folgenden zweisilbigen Wörter aus Unit 1. Kreuzen Sie an, ob das Wort auf der ersten Silbe (= O o) oder auf der zweiten Silbe (= o O) betont wird.

	O o	o O
morning	☐	☐
twenty	☐	☐
goodbye	☐	☐
address	☐	☐
English	☐	☐
people	☐	☐
hello	☐	☐
welcome	☐	☐
evening	☐	☐
repeat	☐	☐
listen	☐	☐

 Aussprache: Wort- und Satzbetonung

Hören Sie zu und sprechen Sie nach. Übertreiben Sie ruhig die Betonung!

Good morning.
Good afternoon.
Good evening.
Good night.
Hello.
Bye.
Goodbye.
Nice to meet you.

 3 Begrüßungen

Schreiben Sie den passenden Gruß.

Good afternoon.
Goodbye.
Good evening.
Good morning.
Nice to meet you.

1 _____   2 _____

3 _____   4 _____   5 _____

4 Das Verb *be*

Setzen Sie die richtige Form des Verbs *be* ein.

1. My name _____ Lea. What _____ your name?
2. _____ you from Paris? – Yes, I _____ .
3. Henry, this _____ my husband, Bob.
4. I' _____ from Dublin. – Where _____ you from?
5. This _____ my telephone number at home.
6. What' _____ his name? – I think it' _____ Robert.
7. How _____ you? – Fine, and you?

SPRACHTIP

Zusammengezogene Formen (*I'm, you're* usw.)

In der gesprochenen Sprache (und in ihrer schriftlichen Wiedergabe) kürzt man das Verb *be* in der Regel ab, z.B. *am* zu *'m*, oder *is* zu *'s*. Beispiele haben Sie in der Unit vorne im Buch kennengelernt. Aber: am Satzende muß man die Vollform benutzen, weil hier die Betonung liegt. Vergleichen Sie:

Are you English? – No, I'm not.   (zusammengezogene, unbetonte Form)
Are you German? – Yes, I am.   (Vollform, weil hier die Betonung auf *am* fällt)

5 Verhältniswörter

Setzen Sie das richtige Verhältniswort ein.

at ◆ from ◆ in ◆ near ◆ of

1. I live _____ Berlin, but I'm _____ a town _____ Hanover.
2. What's the name _____ your town?
3. What's your telephone number _____ work?
4. Susanne's _____ Switzerland.
5. Are they _____ home?

6 Fragen

Wie lautet die Frage?

1. _____ My name's Linda.
2. _____ My number at home is 6741938.
3. _____ It's Klenzestraße 24, 33160 Paderborn.
4. _____ I'm from Manchester.
5. _____ Yes, I am. I'm from London, but my husband is from Germany.
6. _____ Fine, thanks.

7 Hörverstehen

Hören Sie zu und füllen Sie das Formular aus.

Surname _____
First name _____
Address _____
_____
Telephone _____

8 Übersetzung

Übertragen Sie folgende Sätze ins Englische.

1 Ich heiße Schmitz. _____
2 Ich komme aus Deutschland. _____
3 Woher kommen Sie? _____
4 Das ist Nina. _____
5 Nett, dich kennenzulernen. _____
6 Wie geht's? _____
7 Gut, danke. Und dir? _____
8 Danke! _____
9 Nichts zu danken! _____
10 Bis nächste Woche! _____

9 And you?

Beantworten Sie folgende Fragen zu Ihrer Person.

1 What's your name? _____
2 Are you German? _____
3 Where are you from? _____
4 How are you? _____

1 Aussprache: Wortbetonung

a) Hören Sie folgende drei- und viersilbige Wörter. Ein Wort in jeder Spalte gehört nicht dorthin; kreisen Sie es ein.

o O o	O o o	o o O o
appearance	dialogue	pessimistic
untidy	serious	romantic
family	beautiful	realistic
athletic	optimistic	information
_____	_____	_____

b) Tragen Sie nun die drei eingekreisten Wörter in die richtigen Spalten ein.

c) Hören Sie noch einmal und sprechen Sie nach.

2 Aussprache: *th* im Englischen

th kann stimmhaft [ð] (*this*) oder stimmlos [θ] (*three*) ausgesprochen werden. Im Deutschen kann z.B. der s-Laut stimmhaft [z] (*super*) oder stimmlos [s] (*Gruß*) sein.
Hören Sie folgende Wortpaare aus den Units 1 und 2. Sind die *th*-Laute in den zwei Wörtern jeweils gleich oder verschieden?

			gleich	verschieden
1	thanks	these	☐	☐
2	their	thin	☐	☐
3	this	that	☐	☐
4	thanks	athletic	☐	☐
5	think	the	☐	☐
6	brother	thirteen	☐	☐
7	these	father	☐	☐
8	they	mother	☐	☐

Aufgepaßt! Die *th*-Laute können nur richtig ausgesprochen werden, wenn die Spitze der Zunge die oberen vorderen Zähne berührt. Sonst entsteht ein [z]- oder [s]- Laut ("zis" statt *this*, zum Beispiel).

3 Wortschatz

Schreiben Sie einen Satz mit einem Eigenschaftswort, das mit demselben Buchstaben anfängt wie der Name.

1 Andrew IS ATHLETIC.
2 Barbara and Brenda ARE BEAUTIFUL.
3 Fran _____
4 Greg and George _____
5 Harry _____
6 Nick _____
7 Owen _____
8 Paula and Pamela _____
9 Ruth _____
10 Sam _____
11 Tina and Tanja _____
12 Ursula _____

4 Hörverstehen

a) Larry erzählt von seiner Familie. Hören Sie zu und schreiben Sie die Namen der Familienmitglieder zu den richtigen Bildern.

b) Was stimmt hier nicht?

1 Sam's daughter's name is Wendy.
   SAM'S DAUGHTER'S NAME ISN'T WENDY. HER NAME IS JENNIFER.

2 Larry is Sam and Wendy's son.
   Larry isn't _____. He's _____

3 Rita is Jennifer's mother.
   Rita isn't _____. She's _____

4 Frank is Rita's wife.
   Frank _____

5 Jennifer is Frank's daughter.
   Jennifer _____

SPRACH TIP
Die Kurzantwort

Fragt man im Englischen, z.B. *Are you outgoing/German/Kevin?*, lautet die Antwort *Yes, I am* oder *No, I'm not*. Mit dieser Kurzantwort vermeidet man die Wiederholung von Bekanntem. *Yes* oder *No* allein wird dagegen als barsch empfunden.

5 Kurzantworten

Antworten Sie mit *Yes, he/she/it is* oder *No, he/she/it isn't*; mit *Yes, they are* oder *No, they aren't*.

1 Is her name Hilary? (She's Julia.)   NO, IT ISN'T.
2 Is this English? (Il mio nome è Carlo.) _____
3 Is this right? (Two and nine are eleven.) _____
4 Are your friends English? (They're Kurt and Anna from Villach.) _____
5 Is she in New York? (She's in London.) _____
6 Is Jill's boyfriend outgoing? (He's reserved.) _____
7 Are your neighbours nice? (They're your best friends.) _____
8 Is Jack at home? (He's at his office.) _____

6 Personen beschreiben

Was können Sie über folgende Personen sagen?

1 SHE'S TALL AND THIN.
2 THEY AREN'T VERY TALL.
3 _____
4 _____
5 _____
6 _____
7 _____

7 Wie sagt man es auf englisch?

1 Wie fragt man, wie eine Person ist? WHAT'S HE/SHE LIKE?
2 Wie sagt man, daß eine Person nicht sehr romantisch ist? _____
3 Wie fragen Sie jemand, ob er/sie aus Kanada kommt? _____
4 Wie antwortet man höflich „nein" auf Frage 3? _____
5 Wie stellen Sie jemandem Ihren Mann/Ihre Frau vor? _____
6 Wie fragt man, wer am Telefon ist? _____
7 Wie sagt man, daß zwei Personen aus der Nähe von Berlin sind? _____
8 Wie fragen Sie jemanden, ob Sie ihn anrufen dürfen? _____
9 Wie sagen Sie, daß zwei Personen Ihre besten Freunde sind? _____

8 And you?

Schreiben Sie einige Sätze über sich.

1 I'm _____ and rather _____.
2 I've got _____ hair and _____ eyes.
3 I think I'm a(n) _____, _____ and _____ person.
4 My best friend is _____.

1 Aussprache von Zahlen

a) Hören Sie zu und sprechen Sie folgende Zahlen nach.

☐ thirteen	☐ thirty
☐ fourteen	☐ forty
☐ fifteen	☐ fifty
☐ sixteen	☐ sixty
☐ seventeen	☐ seventy
☐ eighteen	☐ eighty
☐ nineteen	☐ ninety

b) Hören Sie zu und kreuzen Sie die Zahlen an, die Sie hören.

 2 Aussprache von Mehrzahlformen

a) [s], [z], oder [ɪz]? Tragen Sie folgende Mehrzahlformen in die richtige Spalte ein.

> wives ◆ weeks ◆ girls ◆ streets ◆ offices ◆ friends ◆ addresses ◆ eyes
> classes ◆ states ◆ glasses ◆ tests

[s]	[z]	[ɪz]
_____	_____	_____
_____	_____	_____
_____	_____	_____
_____	_____	_____

b) Hören Sie nun die Wörter und kontrollieren Sie Ihre Lösungen.

SPRACH TIP
Wortarten

Diese Wortarten haben Sie in den ersten drei Units kennengelernt. Sie finden hier die deutschen Begriffe (einschließlich der aus dem Lateinischen) und die englischen Begriffe.

Deutsch		Englisch	Beispiel
Hauptwort, Namenwort	Substantiv, Nomen	noun	sister, telephone
Fürwort	Pronomen	pronoun	she, it; my, your
Geschlechtswort	Artikel	article	a/an, the
Eigenschaftswort	Adjektiv	adjective	outgoing, tall
Zeitwort, Tätigkeitswort	Verb	verb	is, make
Hilfszeitwort	Hilfsverb	auxiliary verb	can
Umstandswort	Adverb	adverb	now, here
Verhältniswort	Präposition	preposition	in, at

Können Sie die Wortarten im folgenden Satz benennen?
You can phone the new museum on Monday.

3 there is/there are

Was liegt auf dem Bett?

book	1	THERE ARE THREE BOOKS.
alarm clock	2	
photo	3	
handbag	4	
film	5	
laptop computer	6	
portable phone	7	
newspaper	8	
cat	9	

4 Fragewörter

Setzen Sie das richtige Fragewort ein: *who, what, where, when, how*.

1 _____ are you from? – Zurich.
2 _____'s your surname? – Thompson.
3 _____ many children have you got? – Three.
4 _____ are you? – Fine, thanks, and you?
5 _____'s got a cat? – I have. I've got a dog, too.
6 _____ have you got here? – A new computer.
7 _____'s my English book? – Here, with the newspapers.
8 _____ is there tonight? – A new film with Anthony Hopkins.
9 _____ is there a train to London? – At 6 o'clock.

5 Hörverstehen

Hören Sie die Uhrzeiten. Bringen Sie die Uhren in die richtige Reihenfolge, indem Sie die Ziffern 1–10 in die richtigen Kästchen schreiben. (Benutzen Sie Ihre Pausetaste, wenn nötig!)

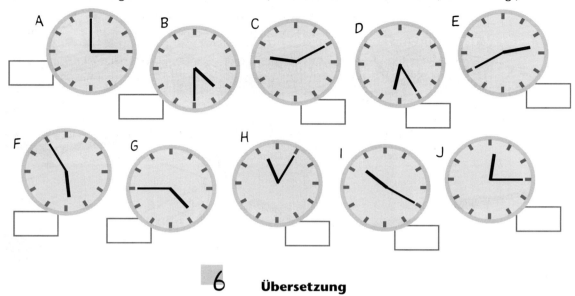

6 Übersetzung

Übertragen Sie folgende Sätze ins Englische.

1. Entschuldigen Sie. _____
2. Wie spät ist es? _____
3. Es ist Viertel nach acht. _____
4. Wann fährt ("ist") der nächste Zug nach Paris? _____
5. Es gibt zwei Züge. _____
6. Haben Sie jetzt Zeit? _____
7. Ich habe keine ("nicht") Kinder. _____
8. Sie hat eine Katze. _____
9. Es gibt 50 Staaten in den USA. _____
10. Wie viele Menschen gibt es in deiner Klasse? _____

7 And you?

Schreiben Sie einige Sätze über die Familienmitglieder/Verwandten/Freunde/Haustiere, die Sie haben bzw. nicht haben. Was haben Sie und was haben Sie nicht? Wie viele haben Sie? Wo sind diese Menschen zu Hause? Wie heißen Sie?

1. I'VE GOT _____
2. _____
3. _____
4. _____
5. _____
6. _____

Aussprache: Betonung

Nicht alle Wörter eines Satzes sind gleich wichtig. Manche liefern neue Informationen, andere nicht. Im Englischen gilt allgemein die Regel: Wichtige Wörter werden betont, weniger wichtige Wörter werden weniger deutlich ausgesprochen und in der Betonung abgeschwächt (daher der Begriff *weak forms*). Zu solchen Wörtern zählen vor allem Verbindungswörter (z.B. *and, but*) und Hilfsverben (z.B. *can*).

Hören Sie den Betonungsunterschied zwischen den folgenden beiden Beispielen:

bread and butter   (*and* wird nicht betont und wie *'n* ausgesprochen)
bread and butter   (*and* wird betont)

Ist *and* betont oder unbetont (= wie *'n*) ? Kreisen Sie die Aussprache ein, die Sie hören.

1	cornflakes 'n milk	cornflakes and milk
2	tea 'n coffee	tea and coffee
3	toast 'n jam	toast and jam
4	ham 'n egg	ham and egg
5	milk 'n honey	milk and honey
6	milk 'n cheese	milk and cheese

Aussprache: die -s-Endung in der dritten Person

Die Endung des Verbs in der 3. Person Einzahl -(e)s wird auf unterschiedliche Weise ausgesprochen, je nachdem welcher Laut vorausgeht. Hören Sie dazu folgende drei Beispiele.

[s]   work*s*
[z]   repair*s*
[ɪz] finish*es*

Hören Sie den folgenden Text und tragen Sie die <u>unterstrichenen</u> Verbformen in die richtige Spalte der Tabelle ein.

" Susan <u>works</u> at home. She's a writer. She has an office at home where she <u>writes</u>, but on Mondays and Thursdays she <u>goes</u> with her husband, Tom, to his office where she <u>phones</u> people and <u>helps</u> with problems. At the weekend Susan <u>cooks</u> and Tom <u>cleans</u>. She <u>finishes</u> her work, and then she <u>reads</u>. Tom <u>does</u> sports. "

[s]	[z]	[ɪz]
___	___	___
___	___	___
___	___	___
___	___	___
___	___	___

SPRACH TIP
Die einfache Gegenwart (The simple present tense)

Form: Die einfache Gegenwart ist identisch mit der Grundform des Verbs; nur in der dritten Person Einzahl (*he, she, it*) wird *s*, bzw. *es* angehängt.

Funktion: Diese Zeitform verwenden wir, wenn wir von Zuständen (*She's a doctor, He lives in Barcelona*) und von wiederholten Handlungen (*I get up at 6.00, She goes to dance class on Monday*) sprechen. Umstandswörter (*Adverbs*) wie *usually, often* usw., die die Frage „Wie oft?" beantworten, zeigen oft, daß eine wiederholte Handlung vorliegt.

3 Verbformen

Ergänzen Sie den folgenden Text mit der richtigen Form des angegebenen Verbs.

„My day? Well, my wife (get up) _____ at seven o'clock, and I (get up) _____ about fifteen minutes after her. Hillary (go) _____ to work at a quarter to eight, so I (make) _____ breakfast. We (eat) _____ cornflakes or muesli. Hillary sometimes (have) _____ toast and jam.

When Hillary (be) _____ at work, I (do) _____ the housework, then I (start) _____ my other work. I'm a designer. I (have) _____ a partner. We (work) _____ in an office in her house. She usually (cook) _____ lunch, but sometimes I (do) _____ it. My partner and I usually (finish) _____ work at 5 o'clock. My wife (finish) _____ at 6."

4 Die einfache Gegenwart mit Umstandswörtern der Häufigkeit

Formulieren Sie Sätze nach dem vorgegebenen Muster.

1 I get up at 6.30. (usually) SARAH USUALLY GETS UP AT 6.30.

2 I have toast and jam for breakfast. (often) SARAH OFTEN

3 I start work after 8.30. (never) SARAH NEVER

4 In my job I talk to people with problems. (sometimes) IN HER JOB SARAH

5 I have lunch in a restaurant. (usually)

6 After lunch I read and write reports. (often)

7 I go shopping after work. (sometimes)

8 On Monday evening I go to a dance class. (usually)

110 one hundred and ten

5 Hörverstehen

Hören Sie, wie zwei Leute von ihrem Arbeitstag erzählen.

a) Was machen die Leute beruflich?
1 Ruth Cohen is a   a) teacher   b) secretary   c) housewife.
2 Chris Bingham is a   a) doctor   b) policeman   c) reporter.

b) Hören Sie die Erzählungen noch einmal. Kreisen Sie die Verben ein, die vorkommen.

write	work	see	go to school
get up	make	ask	go to bed
cook	start	help	have breakfast
talk	read	finish work	have a shower

c) Ergänzen Sie die Sätze mit dem richtigen Namen und der richtigen Verbform.

1 _____ (have) _____ breakfast with her husband and daughter.
2 _____ (not have got) _____ a typical day.
3 _____'s day usually (start) _____ at 6.30.
4 _____ never (work) _____ in the evening.
5 _____ (work) _____ in many different places.
6 _____ usually (talk) _____ to teachers at work.

6 Wie sagt man es auf englisch?

1 Wie fragt man, was jemand beruflich macht? _____
2 Wie fragt man, wo jemand arbeitet? _____
3 Wie sagt man, daß man in einem Büro arbeitet? _____
4 Wie sagt man, daß eine Frau Ärztin ist? _____
5 Wie sagt man, daß man zu Hause arbeitet? _____
6 Wie sagt man, daß man nie frühstückt? _____

7 And you?

Beschreiben Sie einen für Sie typischen Samstag oder Sonntag.
Was machen Sie immer/gewöhnlich/oft/manchmal?

Aussprache: Wortbetonung

Hören Sie zu und streichen Sie in jeder Zeile das Wort mit dem abweichenden Betonungsmuster aus.

1	toilet	chemist	boutique	station	....
2	relax	concert	tennis	swimming	....
3	interviewing	information	exercising	supermarket	....

Nun tragen Sie das Betonungsmuster der Gruppen ein. Schreiben Sie O für eine betonte Silbe, o für eine unbetonte. Beispiel: *instrument* = Ooo.

 Aussprache: Satzbetonung

Unterstreichen Sie in jedem Satz die Wörter, die betont werden.

1 Do you like cycling?   2 Yes, I do.
3 Does Peter like cycling?   4 No, he doesn't.
5 Have you got your book?   6 Yes, I have.
7 Have you got your book?   8 Yes, here it is.
9 Are you English?   10 No, I'm not, I'm German.

 Wann verwendet man das Hilfsverb *do*?

Das Hilfsverb *do* verwendet man:
- bei Fragen und bei der Kurzantwort auf eine Frage mit *do*

    Do you like hiking?   Yes, I do. / No, I don't.
    Does she know his name?   Yes, she does. / No, she doesn't.

    Aber: Wenn *be* oder ein anderes Hilfsverb außer *do/does* im Satz vorkommt, braucht man kein *do/does*.

    Are you from Germany?   Yes, I am. / No, I'm not.
    Have you got a brother?   Yes, I have. / No, I haven't.
    Can I phone you?   Yes, you can. / No, you can't.

- in verneinten Aussagesätzen

    I don't like hiking.
    She doesn't know his name.

    Aber:
    I'm not from Germany.
    I haven't got a brother.
    I can't phone you tonight.

3 like + -ing; Fragen mit does

Bilden Sie Sätze.

4 Verneinung mit und ohne don't/doesn't

Bilden Sie verneinte Sätze nach dem vorgegebenem Muster.

1 I often fly. (go by train) I OFTEN FLY BUT I DON'T OFTEN GO BY TRAIN.
2 I like cycling. (like gardening) _____
3 He lives in the USA. (live in New York) _____
4 I'm from England. (be from London) _____
5 I can speak English. (write it well) _____
6 Ted works with computers. (design software) _____
7 She's very outgoing. (be very romantic) _____
8 We play tennis. (play squash) _____

5 Hörverstehen

a) Hören Sie zu. Kreuzen Sie jeweils die richtige Lösung an.

	Man		Woman	
	Yes	No	Yes	No
flying	☐	☐	☐	☐
fruit	☐	☐	☐	☐
breakfast in bed	☐	☐	☐	☐
tennis	☐	☐	☐	☐
horror films	☐	☐	☐	☐

b) Beantworten Sie nun die Fragen mit *Yes, he/she does* oder *No, he/she doesn't*.

1 Does the woman like tennis? _____
2 Does the man like fruit? _____
3 Does the man like flying? _____
4 Does the man like breakfast in bed? _____
5 Does the woman like breakfast in bed? _____
6 Does she like horror films? _____
7 Does the man like them? _____
8 Does the woman like flying? _____

6 Übersetzung

Übertragen Sie folgende Sätze ins Englische.

1 Ich schwimme gern. _____
2 Schwimmst du gern? Nein (ich schwimme nicht gern). _____
3 Mag sie London? _____
4 Der Zug braucht den ganzen Tag. _____
5 Ich trinke keinen Kaffee. _____
6 Er arbeitet nicht in einem Büro. _____
7 Kann er gut kochen? – Nein (er kann es nicht). _____
8 Spielt er ein Instrument? – Nein (er spielt kein Instrument). _____

7 And you?

Sehen Sie sich die Bilder an und schreiben Sie, was Sie gern tun und was Sie nicht gern tun.
Beispiele:
I like going to the cinema but I don't like going to the theatre.
I don't like cooking but I like going to restaurants.

Aussprache: Wortbetonung

Hören Sie die Wörter von der Cassette. Wie werden sie betont?
Tragen Sie die Wörter in die richtige Spalte ein. (Benutzen Sie Ihre Pausetaste, wenn nötig!)

O o	o O	O o o	o O o	o o O o
___	___	___	___	___
___	___	___	___	___
___	___	___	___	___
___	___	___	___	___

 Aussprache: *w* im Englischen

Kreisen Sie in jeder Zeile das Wort ein, das keinen *w*-Laut enthält.

1	women	was	very	we
2	who	weekend	wife	which
3	where	between	write	welcome

Der englische *w*-Laut wird mit gerundeten Lippen ausgesprochen.
Beim *v*-Laut dagegen berühren die oberen Zähne die untere Lippe.

SPRACH **TIP**

Verlaufsform der Gegenwart (*The present continuous*)

Form: Die Verlaufsform der Gegenwart wird gebildet aus einer Form von *be* zusammen mit einem Hauptverb + Endung *-ing*.

            I am
You/We/They are watching TV.
He/She/It is

Funktion: Die Verlaufsform der Gegenwart beschreibt Handlungen, die im Augenblick gerade ablaufen, noch andauern, nicht abgeschlossen sind – meistens das, was im Moment passiert.

Es gibt also im Englischen zwei Gegenwartsformen: die einfache Gegenwart (*present simple*), die Sie aus früheren Units schon kennen, und die Verlaufsform der Gegenwart, die Sie in dieser Unit neu gelernt haben.
Die einfache Gegenwartsform beschreibt Zustände (*He works at home*), allgemein gültige Aussagen (*In Germany people speak German*) und wiederkehrende Handlungen (*I get up at 7.00*). Oft stehen Wörter wie *usually*, *often*, usw. im Satz. Aber selbst wenn kein solches Wort im Satz steht, wird mit dieser Gegenwartsform ausgedrückt, daß etwas normalerweise so ist.

    I get up at 7 o'clock. = Ich stehe (in der Regel) um 7 Uhr auf.
    I watch television in the evening. = Ich schaue (in der Regel) abends fern.

Mit der Verlaufsform dagegen beschreibt man Handlungen, die im Moment gerade ablaufen. Zeitangaben wie *now* oder *at the moment* werden oft mit der Verlaufsform gebraucht. Aber selbst wenn keine solche Angabe im Satz steht, wird mit der Verlaufsform ausgedrückt, daß etwas momentan passiert.

    I'm looking for the Tourist Information Center. = Ich suche (gerade) das Fremdenverkehrsamt.

Vergleichen Sie: *She plays tennis* – Sie spielt (regelmäßig) Tennis. (= Es ist ihr Hobby.)
                 She's playing tennis. – Sie spielt (gerade) Tennis.

Einen weiteren Gebrauch der Verlaufsform lernen Sie in der nächsten Unit kennen.

3 Verlaufsform der Gegenwart

Wer macht was?

listen to Vivaldi
have a shower
read the newspaper
write a letter
shop
watch TV
play with the children
make dinner
sleep

1 (Richard)   RICHARD IS HAVING A SHOWER.
2 (Helen Thomas) _____
3 (Mr Henry) _____
4 (Bobby) _____
5 (Paula) _____
6 (Mr Mendez) _____
7 (Mike and Mary) _____
8 (Mr O'Malley) _____
9 (Tony Capelli) _____

4 Fragen in der Verlaufsform der Gegenwart

Wie lautet die passende Frage?

1 (Mr Mendez) IS MR MENDEZ WATCHING TV? — No, Bobby is doing that.
2 (Paula) _____ — No, Helen is doing that.
3 (Mike and Mary) _____ — No, Mr O'Malley is doing that.
4 (Richard and Helen) _____ — No, Mr Henry is doing that.
5 (Mr Henry) _____ — No, Tony Capelli is doing that.
6 Who _____ — Mr Mendez is doing that.
7 Who _____ — Richard is doing that.
8 What _____ — She's making dinner.
9 What _____ — They're playing with the children.
10 What _____ — The newspaper.

5 Hörverstehen

Hören Sie zu und ergänzen Sie die Sätze.

1 Mario is _____
2 Mario's wife is _____
3 Samantha is _____
4 Barbara is _____

6 Wie sagt man es auf englisch?

1 Wie fragt man auf der Straße nach der nächsten Bank?
_____

2 Wie sagt man, „Fahren Sie geradeaus und biegen Sie am Supermarkt rechts ab. Die Post ist auf der linken Seite."
_____

3 Wie sagt man, daß die Post gegenüber dem Bahnhof ist?
_____

4 Sie frühstücken gerade. Das Telefon klingelt. Ein amerikanischer Freund fragt, was Sie gerade machen. Was antworten Sie?
_____

5 Wie fragt man jemanden, ob er einen Stadtplan hat?
_____

6 Wie sagt man, daß man mit dem Fahrrad zur Arbeit fährt?
_____

7 Wie sagt man, daß man zu Fuß zur Arbeit geht?
_____

7 And you?

a) Kreisen Sie die Dinge ein, die Sie jetzt gerade machen!

> reading ◆ working for my English class ◆ standing ◆ eating ◆ having a drink
> listening to a cassette ◆ watching television ◆ travelling on a bus/train ◆ looking at a book

b) Schreiben Sie nun sechs Sätze, drei über Dinge, die Sie gerade machen, drei über Dinge, die Sie nicht gerade machen.

things I'm doing   things I'm not doing
_____   _____
_____   _____
_____   _____

1 Aussprache: Wortbetonung

Hören Sie folgende Wörter aus Unit 7 von der Cassette. Wie werden sie betont?
Tragen Sie die Wörter in die richtige Spalte ein.

O o	o O	o O o	O o o
___	___	___	___
___	___	___	___
___	___	___	___

 2 Aussprache: *b, d, g* am Wortende

Kreisen Sie jeweils das Wort ein, das Sie hören. Jedes Wort wird zweimal gesprochen.

1	bed	bet	5	ride	right
2	God	got	6	bag	back
3	bid	bit	7	clog	clock
4	bud	but	8	dog	dock

b, d, g am Wortende werden nicht (wie im Deutschen) als p, t, k ausgesprochen.

Über zukünftige Pläne sprechen

Im Deutschen sagt man z.B. „Ich fliege morgen nach Spanien" oder „Wir fahren
nach Österreich in Urlaub", und jeder versteht, daß Pläne oder feste Abmachungen
für die Zukunft gemeint sind, obwohl das Verb in der Gegenwart steht. Das ist auch
im Englischen so; hier nimmt man die Verlaufsform der Gegenwart:
I'm flying to Spain tomorrow.
We're driving to Austria on holiday.

Zeitangaben, die anzeigen, daß man über die Zukunft spricht, sind z.B.:

today	next year
tomorrow	this morning
next weekend	this afternoon
next week	this evening
next month	tonight

3 Einfache Gegenwart oder Verlaufsform der Gegenwart?

Lesen Sie die Postkarte und entscheiden Sie, ob die fehlenden Verben in der einfachen oder in der Verlaufsform stehen müssen.
Ergänzen Sie dann den Text mit den richtigen Formen der folgenden Verben (manche Verben werden mehrmals benutzt):

eat ◆ have ◆ get up ◆ go ◆ play ◆ relax ◆ stay

DEAR ELLEN,

I (1) _____ A WONDERFUL TIME HERE IN CALIFORNIA.
I (2) _____ IN A BEAUTIFUL HOTEL NEAR THE BEACH*
I (3) _____ AT 8 O'CLOCK AND (4) _____ TENNIS. THEN I (5) _____ A SHOWER AND (6) _____ MY BREAKFAST. AFTER THAT I USUALLY (7) _____ TO A MUSEUM OR TO THE BEACH, OR I (8) _____ SHOPPING. AT THE MOMENT I (9) _____ IN A PARK. I (10) _____ A PICNIC LUNCH. THREE PEOPLE WITH GUITARS (11) _____ MUSIC FOR THE PEOPLE WHO COME HERE TO HAVE THEIR LUNCH. I THINK THAT'S A GREAT IDEA.

SEE YOU NEXT WEEK,
WILMA

*STRAND

4 Fragen

Bilden Sie Fragen. Achten Sie auf die richtige Form des Verbs.

1 (where/you move) <u>WHERE ARE YOU MOVING? – TO AMSTERDAM.</u>
2 (it/be a big flat) _____
3 (it/have got more rooms) _____
4 (when/you move) _____
5 (I/can help you) _____
6 (who/come to your party tomorrow) _____
7 (Alan/know about it) _____
8 (he/always come to your parties) _____
9 (what/have at the party) _____ – Paella and red wine.
10 (you/cook the paella) _____ – Of course.

one hundred and nineteen

5 Hörverstehen

Hören Sie zu und ergänzen Sie die Sätze.

1 David _____ at the moment.
2 Lynn _____ at eight.
3 James _____ this evening.
4 David and Lynn _____ this weekend.

6 Übersetzung

Übertragen Sie folgende Sätze ins Englische.

1 Was machst du gerade? _____
2 Sie zieht in zwei Wochen nach Bern. _____
3 Ich fahre morgen nach Stockholm. _____
4 Was machen Sie heute abend? _____
5 Sie wohnt in einer Einzimmerwohnung. _____
6 Meine Schwester heiratet nächstes Jahr. _____
7 Kannst du mir mal helfen? _____
8 Könnt ihr kommen? – Leider nicht. _____
9 Sie ist geschäftlich hier. _____
10 Kommt ihr am 6. Juli? _____

7 And you?

Was machen Sie am kommenden Wochenende? Schreiben Sie fünf Sätze.

go to the cinema ◆ swim ◆ work ◆ go shopping ◆ visit friends
work in the garden ◆ fly to Spain ◆ relax at home ◆ eat out ◆ ...

120   one hundred and twenty

Aussprache: Wortbetonung

Hören Sie folgende Wörter von der Cassette. Ein Wort hat ein abweichendes Betonungsmuster. Kreisen Sie es ein.

starter	problem
salad	special
carrot	dessert
hungry	dirty
thirsty	waiter

 Aussprache: Wie viele Silben?

Hören Sie genau hin. Wie viele Silben haben die folgenden Wörter?

1	tired	1 ☐	2 ☐
2	bored	1 ☐	2 ☐
3	grilled	1 ☐	2 ☐
4	potatoes	3 ☐	4 ☐
5	vegetables	3 ☐	4 ☐
6	differences	3 ☐	4 ☐

Die Zukunft mit *will*

Form: Das Hilfsverb *will* steht in Verbindung mit der Grundform des Hauptverbs.

Funktion: Mit *will* + Grundform des Hauptverbs beschreibt man Handlungen, die in der Zukunft (wahrscheinlich) geschehen werden, wie z.B. bei spontanen Entscheidungen (*I'll have the moussaka*) and Vorhersagen (*You'll live a long life*).

some und *any*

Some und *any* stehen für eine unbestimmte Menge. *Some* gebraucht man in bejahten Aussagesätzen, *any* in echten Fragen und in verneinten Sätzen.

I'll have some of your sole.	Ich nehme etwas von deiner Seezunge.
There are some good restaurants in San Francisco.	Es gibt (mehrere) gute Restaurants in San Francisco.
Are there any potatoes with that?	Gibt es Kartoffeln dazu?
Do you know any Americans?	Kennst du (irgendwelche) Amerikaner?
No, there aren't any good restaurants here.	Nein, es gibt keine guten Restaurants hier.
I haven't got any money with me.	Ich habe kein Geld dabei.

Wie Sie sehen, fällt die Entsprechung im Deutschen ganz unterschiedlich aus; manchmal gibt es keine Entsprechung im Deutschen.

3 some – any

a) Sehen Sie sich Freddies Kühlschrank an und bilden Sie Fragen mit *any*. Beantworten Sie dann die Fragen.

1. (eggs) HAS HE GOT ANY EGGS? – NO, HE HASN'T.
2. (beer) HAS HE GOT ANY BEER? – YES, HE HAS.
3. (vegetables) _____ – _____
4. (milk) _____ – _____
5. (butter) _____ – _____
6. (yoghurt) _____ – _____
7. (fruit) _____ – _____
8. (jam) _____ – _____
9. (cheese) _____ – _____
10. (bread) _____ – _____

b) Bilden Sie nun Sätze mit *some* und *any* mit Hilfe der angegebenen Wörter.

1. (beer/milk) HE'S GOT SOME BEER BUT HE HASN'T GOT ANY MILK.
2. (vegetables/cheese) _____
3. (fruit/jam) _____
4. (bread/yoghurt) _____
5. (butter/sausages) _____

4 will

Ordnen Sie die Zeichnungen den Sätzen zu.

a I'll answer those for you.
b I'll have vanilla, please.
c I think I'll go in the water.
d I'll see you in an hour.
e Here, I'll help you!

5 Hörverstehen

Hören Sie ein Telefongespräch zwischen Glenn und seiner Schwester. Wie viele Wörter werden im Gespräch gebraucht, die mit Essen und Trinken zu tun haben? Schreiben Sie sie auf.

GARLIC* BREAD

*garlic = Knoblauch

6 Wie sagt man es auf englisch?

1 Wie sagt man dem Kellner, daß man die Seezunge nimmt?

2 Wie fragt man den Tischnachbarn, was er nimmt?

3 Wie fragt man einen Gast, was er zu trinken wünscht?

4 Wie sagt man, daß man ein Glas Wein haben möchte?

5 Wie fragt man in einem Restaurant nach der Rechnung?

6 Wie schlägt man jemandem einen Kinobesuch vor?

7 Wie sagt man, daß man morgen anrufen wird?

8 Wie fragt man jemanden, ob er (denn) nichts Neues probieren will?

9 Wie bietet man jemandem an, das Fenster für ihn zu öffnen?

7 And you?

Sie sind übers Wochenende mit einem Freund in der Schweiz.
Schlagen Sie ihm fünf Dinge vor, die man machen könnte.

LET'S

Aussprache: Vergangenheitsformen unregelmäßiger Verben

Hören Sie zu und sprechen Sie nach.

 Aussprache: Vergangenheitsformen regelmäßiger Verben

Tragen Sie die Verben in die richtige Spalte ein.

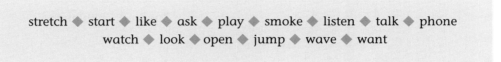

stretch ◆ start ◆ like ◆ ask ◆ play ◆ smoke ◆ listen ◆ talk ◆ phone
watch ◆ look ◆ open ◆ jump ◆ wave ◆ want

[t]	[d]	[ɪd]
work – worked	stop – stopped	paint – painted

Die Vergangenheitsform (*Simple past tense*)

Wenn es darum geht, die Vergangenheitsform auf englisch zu bilden, unterteilen sich die Verben – wie im Deutschen – in zwei Gruppen: die regelmäßigen und die unregelmäßigen Verben.

Form: Bei den regelmäßigen Verben hängt man *-ed* bzw. *-d* an die Grundform:

        look – looked
        wave – waved

    Bei den unregelmäßigen Verben gibt es besondere Formen, die neu gelernt werden müssen, z.B.:

        do – did
        go – went

    Eine Liste der wichtigsten unregelmäßigen Verben finden Sie auf Seite 147.

Funktion: Das *simple past tense* verwendet man, wenn man von abgeschlossenen Handlungen und Situationen spricht, die zu einem bestimmten Zeitpunkt geschehen bzw. eingetreten sind. Zeitangaben wie *yesterday, last week, on Tuesday* zeigen an, daß die Vergangenheitsform gebraucht werden sollte.

    Einfacher ausgedrückt: wenn man auf englisch eine Geschichte (wie z.B. das Gedicht auf S. 65) erzählt, verwendet man das *simple past tense*. Eine andere Vergangenheitsform ist hier nicht möglich.

3 Die Vergangenheitsform

Vervollständigen Sie die folgenden Sätze mit einem Verb in der Vergangenheit.

1 She usually gets up at 7.00, but this morning she _____ at 8.00.
2 Usually he says yes, but today he _____ no.
3 I usually take the train to work, but last week I _____ the bus.
4 I go to lunch at 12.00, but today I _____ at 1.00.
5 I never think about work, but yesterday I _____ about it all day.
6 Usually she comes at 8.00, but this morning she _____ at 9.00.
7 I usually do my housework on Saturday, but last weekend I _____ it on Friday afternoon.
8 Jack doesn't like flying, but he _____ to the USA last year.

4 Fragen in der Vergangenheit

Was hat *er* gestern gemacht?

1 She got up at 6.30. – (when/he get up)
   WHEN DID HE GET UP?

2 She ate breakfast. – (he/eat breakfast)
   DID HE EAT BREAKFAST?

3 She drove to work. – (how/he go to work)
   _____

4 She had a meeting. – (he/have a meeting)
   _____

5 She went out to lunch. – (where/he have lunch)
   _____

6 She took a coffee break at 3.15. – (when/he take a coffee break)
   _____

7 She went swimming after work. – (where/he go)
   _____

8 She had dinner at 7.00. – (he/have dinner at 7.00)
   _____

9 She went to bed at 11.00. – (when/he go to bed)
   _____

5 Hörverstehen

Hören Sie, was ein Mann über sein Wochenende erzählt, und bringen Sie die Bilder in die richtige Reihenfolge, indem Sie die Ziffern 1–9 in die Kästchen schreiben.

6 Übersetzung

Übertragen Sie folgende Sätze ins Englische.

1 Ich stehe gewöhnlich um 6.00 auf, aber heute bin ich um 7.00 aufgestanden.

2 Ich habe Oliver heute morgen angerufen. ___
3 Er hat „nein" gesagt! ___
4 Gestern bin ich schwimmen gegangen. ___
5 Am Sonntag sind wir ins Kino gegangen. ___
6 Wann hast du gefrühstückt? ___
7 Wie bist du heute morgen zur Arbeit gefahren? ___
8 Ich bin 1960 geboren. ___
9 Ich bin 1978 von der Schule abgegangen. ___
10 Wann habt ihr geheiratet? ___

7 And you?

Schreiben Sie fünf Sätze über Ihren gestrigen Tag.

Aussprache: *bed/bad* – [e] / [æ] im Englischen

a) Kreisen Sie jeweils das Wort ein, das Sie hören. Jedes Wort wird zweimal gesprochen.

1	bed	bad	8	Ellen	Alan
2	bed	bad	9	men	man
3	Ken	can	10	men	man
4	Ken	can	11	set	sat
5	said	sad	12	set	sat
6	said	sad	13	ten	tan
7	Ellen	Alan	14	ten	tan

b) Sprechen Sie nun alle Wörter nach. Achten Sie dabei auf die Länge der Vokale und die unterschiedlichen Mundstellungen. Der englische [æ]-Laut ist nicht identisch mit dem deutschen ä.

 Aussprache: Unbetonte Silben und Wörter

Zur Erinnerung: Unbetonte Silben schwächen im Englischen ab. Das kann man deutlich anhand von Wörtern hören, die einmal für sich stehen und dann als Teil zusammengesetzter Wörter vorkommen.

a) Hören Sie folgende Wörter und unterstreichen Sie die betonten Silben in dem jeweils zweiten Wort.

table   vegetable   son   Thompson   fast   breakfast   Don   London   day   Monday

b) Wie wir schon gesehen haben, gilt dieses Prinzip auch für unbetonte Wörter im Satz. Das Wort *was* z. B. hat eine betonte [wɒːz] und eine unbetonte [wəz] Form. Hören Sie folgende Sätze und kreuzen Sie den Satz an, in dem die volle Form von *was* zu hören ist.

What was nice about the kitchen?
It was sunny and hot.
Was Iris's room very big?
Yes, it was.
Was there a table in your room?

c) Hören Sie die Sätze noch einmal und sprechen Sie sie nach.

Die Vergangenheitsform von *do* ist *did*. Wie in der Gegenwart verwendet man dieses Hilfsverb bei der Bildung von Fragen und verneinten Sätzen, wenn kein anderes Hilfsverb vorhanden ist. Vergleichen Sie:

Gegenwart   Vergangenheit
  Do you have your own room?   *Did you have your own room?*
  I don't like tomatoes.   *I didn't like tomatoes.*

Aber:
  She's very outgoing.   *She was very outgoing as a child.*
  Can you read the menu?   *Could you read the menu?*

3 Wortschatz

Was stimmt hier nicht? Die Larkins ziehen in ein neues Haus ein.
Die Möbelpacker haben aber die Möbel in die falschen Zimmer gestellt.
Sagen Sie, wo die Möbelstücke hinkommen (= *go*) sollen.

1 THE SOFA GOES IN THE LIVING ROOM.
2 _____
3 _____
4 _____
5 _____
6 _____
7 _____

4 Fragen und Kurzantworten in der Vergangenheit

Ordnen Sie die Antworten den Fragen zu.

1 Did you fly to Paris last week? ☐
2 Did you hear that? ☐
3 Good morning! Did you sleep well? ☐
4 Did you like the film? ☐
5 Did you like the concert? ☐
6 Was Helen Riley at the meeting? ☐
7 Were there many people there? ☐
8 Why were you late? ☐

a) No, I didn't. I drank too much coffee last night.
b) Yes, she was, but she had to go before the end.
c) No, there weren't. When Helen went there were only six of us.
d) No, I didn't. What was it?
e) Yes, I did, but I didn't like the happy end.
f) Well, the weather was bad, so the plane didn't take off on time.
g) No, we didn't. Our French partners came here.
h) Yes, I did, but I couldn't hear very well.

5 Hörverstehen

a) Hören Sie das Gespräch zwischen Nick und Ellen auf der Cassette und beantworten Sie folgende Frage:

Where did Nick find his keys (= Schlüssel)? _____

b) Hören Sie das Gespräch noch einmal und beantworten Sie die folgenden Fragen mit *Yes, (s)he was/did* oder *No, (s)he wasn't/didn't*.

1 Did Nick have his keys when he came home? _____
2 Did he have them when he spoke to Emily? _____
3 Was Ellen at home when Emily phoned? _____
4 Did Emily want to speak to Ellen? _____
5 Did Ellen phone Emily? _____
6 Was Emily at home when Ellen phoned her? _____
7 Did Emily say the name of the film? _____

6 Wie sagt man es auf englisch?

1 Wie fragt man jemanden, wo er als Kind gelebt hat?

_____

2 Wie fragt man jemanden, ob er einen Fernseher gehabt hat, als er klein war?

_____

3 Wie fragt man jemanden, ob er einen Lieblingslehrer gehabt hat?

_____

4 Wie sagt man, daß man eine große Familie gewesen ist?

_____

5 Wie fragt man, wie viele Personen es in der Familie gab?

_____

6 Wie sagt man, daß man in der Kindheit auf dem Land lebte?

_____

7 Wie sagt man, daß es immer sehr windig war?

_____

7 And you?

Schreiben Sie fünf Sätze über das Haus, in dem Sie als Kind wohnten.

_____
_____
_____
_____
_____

Aussprache: Wortbetonung

Hören Sie folgende Wörter aus Unit 11 von der Cassette. Wie werden sie betont?
Tragen Sie die Wörter in die richtige Spalte ein.

because ◆ larger ◆ jacket ◆ pullover ◆ Europe ◆ customer ◆ fabric ◆ famous ◆ decide

O o	o O	O o o

2 Aussprache: *cheap/jeans* – [ts] / [dʒ] im Englischen

Sprechen Sie folgende Wörter nach. Achten Sie dabei auf den Unterschied zwischen [ts] und [dʒ].

cheap	jeans
cheese	juice
sandwich	sausage
Chinese	German
lunch	large
choose	June

3 Wortschatz

Was tragen die Leute?

1 SHE'S WEARING JEANS AND A SWEATSHIRT AND WHITE SHOES.
2 _____ and black shoes.
3 _____ and _____ shoes.
4 _____
5 _____

SPRACH TIP
Die Steigerung von Eigenschaftswörtern

Die Faustregel lautet: kurzen, einsilbigen Eigenschaftswörtern wird die Endung *-er* bzw. *-r* angehängt; mehrsilbige Eigenschaftswörter bilden ihre Steigerungsform durch Voranstellen von *more*:

    cheap   cheaper
    expensive   more expensive

Eine kleine Gruppe zweisilbiger Eigenschaftswörter, die auf *-y* enden, bilden ihre Steigerungsform so:

    noisy   – y + ier = noisier

Die zweite Steigerungsstufe wird bei den einsilbigen Eigenschaftswörtern durch Anhängen von *-est*, bei den mehrsilbigen durch Voranstellen von *most* gebildet:

    cheap   (the) cheapest
    expensive   (the) most expensive.

Zweisilbige Eigenschaftswörter auf *-y* erhalten anstelle des Buchstaben *y* die Endung *-iest*:

    noisy   – y + iest = (the) noisiest.

4 Redewendungen beim Einkaufen

Eine Frau kauft in einem Kaufhaus ein. Bringen Sie die folgenden Sätze in die richtige Reihenfolge, indem Sie die Ziffern 1–8 in die Kästchen schreiben. Der Dialog beginnt mit *Can I help you, madam?*

- [ ] Thirty-eights are over here. What colour are you looking for?
- [ ] Yes, I'm looking for a winter coat.
- [1] Can I help you, madam?
- [ ] Something dark; dark blue or black, I think.
- [ ] I'd like to try this one on, please. It looks very nice.
- [ ] These are all dark.
- [ ] Of course, Madam. There's a mirror (= Spiegel) over there.
- [ ] Thirty-eight.
- [ ] What size are you?

5 Steigerung von Adjektiven

Ergänzen Sie die Sätze mit der richtigen Form der folgenden Eigenschaftswörter:

> bad ◆ hot ◆ interesting ◆ long ◆ good ◆ big ◆ funny

1. Yesterday was hot, but today is even _____ .
2. New York is the _____ city in the United States.
3. The Nile is the _____ river in Africa.
4. Andy is a very funny person, but his wife is even _____ .
5. The Savoy is very good, but I think the Ritz is _____ .
6. "The Escape" was interesting, but "The Woman in Green" was the _____ film of the festival.
7. The restaurant we went to last week was bad, but this is the _____ restaurant in the city!

6 Hörverstehen

Die Polizei fahndet nach einem Verbrechertrio. Welche der drei abgebildeten Gruppen ist es?

7 Übersetzung

Übertragen Sie folgende Sätze ins Englische.

1 Ich schaue nur, danke. _____
2 Ich glaube, es ist zu klein. _____
3 Ich nehme dieses. _____
4 Was kostet es? _____
5 Nehmen Sie Eurocard? _____
6 Diese Jacke ist teurer. _____
7 Sie ist älter als ich. _____
8 Macy's ist das größte Kaufhaus in New York.
_____

8 And you?

Was werden Sie kaufen, wenn Sie zu Harrods gehen?

winter clothing   summer clothing

1 Aussprache: Ländernamen

Hören Sie folgende Ländernamen und sprechen Sie sie genau nach. Heben Sie die betonten Silben deutlich hervor. Damit werden sich die restlichen Silben automatisch abschwächen.

Austria	England	Hungary	Spain
Canada	France	Ireland	Sweden
China	Germany	Italy	Switzerland
the Czech Republic	Greece	Japan	the United Kingdom
Denmark	Holland	Russia	the United States

2 Aussprache: Satzbetonung

Hören Sie folgende Sätze und kreuzen Sie an, ob *have/has* betont [hæv/hæz] oder unbetont [həv/həz] ist.

		Betont	Unbetont
1	Has Jennifer ever been to the United States?	☐	☐
2	No, she hasn't.	☐	☐
3	Have you ever been to Canada?	☐	☐
4	Yes, I have.	☐	☐
5	Has Jennifer ever been to Canada?	☐	☐
6	I think she has.	☐	☐
7	Have you ever had Indonesian food?	☐	☐

SPRACHTIP

Das Perfekt (*The present perfect tense*)

Form: Das englische Perfekt besteht aus *have* bzw. *has* + Partizip Perfekt des Hauptverbs:
I have seen/heard/worked.
Das Partizip Perfekt von regelmäßigen Verben gleicht der Vergangenheitsform (*simple past*):
worked – worked
helped – helped.
Das Partizip Perfekt von unregelmäßigen Verben muß nach der Grundform (*infinitive*) und der Vergangenheit (*simple past*) als dritte Form extra gelernt werden. Auf Seite 147 finden Sie eine Liste der wichtigsten unregelmäßigen Verben.

Funktion: In Unit 9 haben Sie die Vergangenheitsform gelernt. Wann wird das *present perfect* nun gebraucht? Man gebraucht das *present perfect*, wenn:

a) der Zeitpunkt einer Handlung unbekannt oder unwichtig ist, z.B.
Have you ever been to Portugal?

b) der Zeitraum, in dem die Handlung passiert ist, noch nicht abgeschlossen ist, z.B.
I've played tennis once this week, but I want to play again before the weekend.

Wörter wie *ever, never* (jemals, niemals) werden oft mit dem *present perfect* gebraucht.
Wörter wie *yesterday, last year, when I was a child* bestimmen den konkreten Zeitpunkt bzw. den Zeitraum einer Handlung und zeigen an, daß die Vergangenheitsform gebraucht werden muß. Ein Satz wie **I have gone to the cinema last night* ist nicht möglich, weil der Zeitpunkt der Handlung genannt wird. Der Satz muß heißen:
I went to the cinema last night.

3 Das Perfekt

a) Einer der folgenden Sätze ist im Englischen nicht möglich. Welcher?

1. ☐ Have you seen the doctor?
2. ☐ I haven't found a babysitter.
3. ☐ Has she spoken to her mother?
4. ☐ Alan has found a new job last week.
5. ☐ She hasn't booked her flight. Have you?

b) Muß das Verb in den folgenden Sätzen durch das *simple past* oder das *present perfect* wiedergegeben werden?

		Simple past	Present perfect
1	Ich habe ihn gestern gesehen.	☐	☐
2	Hast du mit ihr diese Woche telefoniert?	☐	☐
3	Hat sie dich [schon einmal] in deiner Wohnung besucht?	☐	☐
4	Was hat er dir letzte Woche gesagt?	☐	☐
5	Ich habe ihn heute nicht gesehen.	☐	☐

4 Kurzantworten

Beantworten Sie folgende Fragen mit *Yes, I have/No, I haven't*.

1. Have you ever been to India? _____
2. Have you ever spent Christmas where it's warm? _____
3. Have you read the newspaper today? _____
4. Have you had more than three jobs in your life? _____
5. Have you ever broken your arm or leg? _____

5 Hörverstehen

Fill in the correct answer.

		Yes, he/she has.	No, he/she hasn't.
Has he ever …			
1	had moussaka?	☐	☐
2	been to Greece?	☐	☐
3	been to a Greek restaurant?	☐	☐
Has she ever			
4	been to Greece?	☐	☐
5	taken a class in Greek?	☐	☐
6	made moussaka?	☐	☐

6 Ergänzen Sie die richtige Form.

1	be	Has she ever __BEEN__ there?
2	see	I've never _____ that film.
3	say	He's already _____ that.
4	give	Has she _____ you an answer?
5	make	I've _____ dinner!
6	tell	She hasn't _____ me why.
7	have	I've _____ no time.
8	write	She's _____ to some of her friends.
9	read	Have you _____ the article?
10	come	Has she ever _____ with you?
11	take	We've _____ the smaller flat.
12	get	Have you _____ the time?
13	do	Has he _____ his homework?
14	drive	She's _____ to the country.
15	go	Has he _____ to the doctor's?

7 Übersetzung

Übertragen Sie die Sätze aus Übung 3b ins Englische.

1 _____
2 _____
3 _____
4 _____
5 _____

8 And you?

Nennen Sie fünf Dinge, die Sie in Ihrem Leben noch nicht gemacht haben, aber irgendwann machen möchten.

UNIT 12

Grammatik im Überblick

Inhalt

1		**Grammatikterminologie**
1.1		Wortarten
1.2		Satzteile
2		**Fürwörter**
2.1		Persönliche Fürwörter
2.2		Besitzanzeigende Fürwörter
2.3		Hinweisende Fürwörter
2.4		Fragefürwörter
3		**Bestimmter und unbestimmter Artikel**
4		**Hauptwörter**
4.1		Mehrzahlformen
4.2		Hauptwort + besitzanzeigendes *s*
5		**Steigerung von Eigenschaftswörtern**
5.1		Steigerungsformen
5.2		Vergleichskonstruktionen
6		**Mengenbezeichnungen**
6.1		*a lot of, lots of, much, many*
6.2		*some, any*
7		**Stellung von Umstandswörtern der Häufigkeit**
8		**Verben**
8.1		Das Verb *be*
8.2		Vollverben: einfache Gegenwart
8.3		Vollverben: Verlaufsform der Gegenwart
8.4		Vollverben: Vergangenheit
8.5		Vollverben: Perfekt
8.6		Vollverben: Zukunft
8.7		Modale Hilfsverben
9		**Satzmuster**
9.1		Bejahte Sätze
9.2		Verneinte Sätze
9.3		Entscheidungsfragen
9.4		Fragen mit Fragewörtern
10		**Unregelmäßige Verben**

GRAMMAR

Grammatik im Überblick

1 Grammatikterminologie

1.1 Wortarten

Deutsche Bezeichnung(en)	Englische Bezeichnung	Beispiele
Fürwort, Pronomen	pronoun	I, my, me, this
Geschlechtswort, Artikel	article	the, a
Hauptwort, Substantiv, Nomen	noun	Alan, coffee, friend
Eigenschaftswort, Adjektiv	adjective	big, smaller, best
Mengenbezeichnung	quantifier	much, some, a lot of
Umstandswort, Adverb	adverb	well, quickly, yesterday
Zeitwort, Tätigkeitswort, Verb	verb	is, drink, spoke, will go
Hilfszeitwort, Hilfsverb	auxiliary (verb)	have, will, can
Verhältniswort, Präposition	preposition	in, on, at, under

1.2 Satzteile

Ein Satz besteht zunächst aus einem Satzgegenstand (auch: Subjekt; englisch: *subject*) und einem Verb. Der Satzgegenstand ist die Person oder Sache, die etwas macht. Das Verb beschreibt das, was gemacht wird.

Das Verb kann allein stehen oder durch eine Satzergänzung (auch: Objekt; englisch: *object*) ergänzt werden. Die Satzergänzung ist die Person oder Sache, mit der etwas gemacht wird:

Satzgegenstand	Verb	Satzergänzung	
I	smoke.		(Ich rauche.)
I	drink	coffee.	(Ich trinke Kaffee.)

Außerdem kann dem Verb oder der Satzergänzung eine Umstandsbestimmung angeschlossen werden, die besagt, wo, wann, wie oder warum etwas gemacht wird:

Satzgegenstand	Verb	Satzergänzung	Umstandsbestimmung	
I	smoke		outside.	(Ich rauche draußen.)
I	drink	coffee	regularly.	(Ich trinke regelmäßig Kaffee.)

Alle diese Satzteile (Satzgegenstand, Verb, Satzergänzung, Umstandsbestimmung) können auch aus mehreren Wörtern bestehen:

Satzgegenstand	Verb	Satzergänzung	Umstandsbestimmung
My best friend	doesn't drink	much coffee	now in the evenings.

(Mein bester Freund trinkt jetzt abends nicht viel Kaffee.)

Im letzten Beispielsatz sind alle Wortarten aus Abschnitt 1.1 vertreten:

my	Fürwort	*doesn't*	Hilfsverb	*coffee*	Hauptwort	*the*	Artikel
best	Eigenschaftswort	*drink*	Vollverb	*now*	Umstandswort	*evenings*	Hauptwort
friend	Hauptwort	*much*	Mengenbezeichnung	*in*	Verhältniswort		

Grammatik im Überblick

2 Fürwörter/*Pronouns*

2.1 Persönliche Fürwörter/*Personal pronouns*

Als Satzgegenstand/*Subject pronoun* z.B. *I live in Berlin.*		Als Satzergänzung/*Object pronoun* z.B. *Alan loves **me**.*	
I	ich	me	mir/mich
you	du/Sie (Einzahl)	you	dir, dich, Ihnen, Sie (Einzahl)
he	er	him	ihm, ihn
she	sie	her	ihr, sie
it	es, er, sie (bei Sachen)	it	ihm, ihr, es, ihn, sie (bei Sachen)
we	wir	us	uns
you	ihr, Sie (Mehrzahl)	you	euch, Ihnen, Sie (Mehrzahl)
they	sie	them	ihnen, sie

- Es gibt im Englischen keinen Unterschied zwischen „du" und „Sie" oder „ihr" und „Sie". Das Wort *you* ist neutral.
- *you* entspricht auch dem deutschen „man":
  You can get information here = Man kann hier Auskünfte bekommen.
- In Vergleichssätzen steht nach *than* ein Objektpronomen (*me, him, her* usw):
  Mark is taller than me = Mark ist größer als ich.

GRAMMAR

2.2 Besitzanzeigende Fürwörter/*Possessive adjectives, possessive pronouns*

Vor einem Hauptwort/*Possessive adjective* Beispiel: *Is **your** name Julia?*		Alleinstehend/*Possessive pronoun* Beispiel: *Is this **yours**?*	
my	mein(e)	mine	meine(r/s)
your	dein(e), Ihr(e)	yours	deine(r/s), Ihre(r/s)
his	sein(e)	his	seine(r/s)
her	ihr(e)	hers	ihre(r/s)
its	sein(e), ihr(e)	its	seine(r/s), ihre(r/s)
our	unser(e)	ours	unsere(r/s)
your	euer, eure, Ihr(e)	yours	eure(r/s), Ihre(r/s)
their	ihr(e)	theirs	ihre(r/s)

2.3 Hinweisende Fürwörter/*Demonstrative adjectives, Demonstrative pronouns*

Vor einem Hauptwort/*Demonstrative adjective*		Alleinstehend/*Demonstrative pronoun*	
This coffee is hot.	diese(r/s)	**This** is hot coffee.	dies
That coffee is cold.	jene(r/s)	**That** is cold coffee.	das
These pullovers are expensive.	diese	**These** are expensive pullovers.	dies, diese
Those pullovers are cheap.	jene	**Those** are cheap pullovers.	das, jene

Grammatik im Überblick

2.4 Fragefürwörter/*Question words*

who	wer	Who was that? – Alan.
whose	wessen	Whose pen is that? – It's mine.
what	was	What's this? – It's my new computer.
which	welche(r/s)	Which word is correct?
where	wo	Where's Julia? – In the garden.
when	wann	When is breakfast?
why	warum	I don't want to go. – Why not?
how	wie	How are you?
how much	wieviel	How much milk is there?
how many	wieviel, wie viele	How many children are there?

3 Bestimmter und unbestimmter Artikel/*Definite and indefinite article*

	Bestimmter Artikel	Unbestimmter Artikel
Vor Mitlauten (*b, d, g* usw.)	the [ðə] friend, the friends	a [ə] friend
Vor Selbstlauten (*a, e, i* usw.)	the [ðɪ] office, the offices	an [ən] office

- In folgenden Fällen benutzt man den bestimmten Artikel im Englischen <u>nicht</u>:
  by + Verkehrsmittel: *by bicycle/car/bus/train/plane* = mit dem Fahrrad/Auto/Bus/Zug/Flugzeug
  on + Wochentage: *on Monday/Tuesday/Wednesday/...* = am Montag/Dienstag/Mittwoch/...
  Straßennamen: *Oxford Street, in London Road, to/on Madison Avenue* = die Oxfordstraße, in der Londoner Straße, zum/auf dem Madisonboulevard
- Den unbestimmten Artikel benutzt man im Englischen vor Berufsbezeichnungen:
  *My father is **an** engineer* = Mein Vater ist Ingenieur.

4 Hauptwörter/*Nouns*

4.1 Mehrzahlformen/*Plural forms*

Einzahl	Mehrzahl	Aussprache
book	books	[s], wie in „muß"
bag	bags	[z], wie in „Sommer"
address	addresses	[ɪz]

- Schreibweise. Die meisten Hauptwörter bilden ihre Mehrzahlform durch Anhängen von *-s*. Bei Hauptwörtern, die auf *s, ch, x, sh* oder *o* enden, wird *-es* angehängt: *address – address**es**, beach* (Strand) *– beach**es**, box – box**es**, dish* (Gericht) *– dish**es**, potato – potato**es***. Ausnahmen: *photo – photos, radio – radios*.
- Endet ein Hauptwort auf einem Mitlaut + *y*, wird die Mehrzahl mit Mitlaut + *ies* gebildet: *baby – bab**ies***.
- Unregelmäßige Mehrzahlformen:
  man – men, woman [wʊmən] *– women* [wɪmɪn]*, child – children, foot – feet*
- Die Wörter *jeans* und *trousers* (Hose) stehen immer in der Mehrzahl.

Grammatik im Überblick

4.2 Hauptwort + besitzanzeigendes s/Noun + possessive s

Einzahl	Hauptwort + '+ s	The teacher's name is Sally.
Mehrzahl	Hauptwort + s + '	The teachers' names are Sally and Helga.

- Besitzanzeigendes *s* wird an Hauptwörter angehängt, die Personen bezeichnen.
  Bei Sachen wird in der Regel eine *of*-Fügung gebraucht: *the name **of** the hotel*.

5 Steigerung von Eigenschaftswörtern/Comparison of adjectives

5.1 Steigerungsformen/Comparative and superlative forms

Grundform	1. Steigerungsstufe/Comparative	2. Steigerungsstufe/Superlative
new	new**er**	(the) new**est**
big	big**ger**	(the) big**gest**
noisy	nois**ier**	(the) nois**iest**
modern	**more** modern	(the) **most** modern

- Die Steigerungsstufen kurzer, d.h. einsilbiger Eigenschaftswörter werden durch Anhängen von *-er* bzw. *-est* gebildet. Eine kleine Gruppe von zweisilbigen Eigenschaftswörtern, die auf *-y* enden, werden auch so gesteigert: *noisy – noisier – (the) noisiest*.
- Längere, d.h. mehrsilbige Eigenschaftswörter bilden ihre Steigerungsstufen durch Voranstellen von *more* und *most*.
- Unregelmäßige Formen: *good   better   best*
  bad   worse   worst

5.2 Vergleichssätze/Comparisons

She's **as** big **as** her brother. He's **not as** old **as** his sister.	(not) as + Eigenschaftswort + as = „(nicht) so" + Eigenschaftswort + „wie"
You're funn**ier than** she is. She's **more** famous **than** him.	Komparativform + *than* = 1. Steigerungsstufe + „als"

Grammatik im Überblick

6 Mengenbezeichnungen / *Quantifiers*

6.1 *a lot of, lots of, much, many*

Bejahter Satz	Verneinter Satz	Fragesatz
I've got **a lot/lots of** time. I've got **a lot/lots of** friends.	I haven't got **a lot/lots of** money. I haven't got **a lot/lots of** relatives. I haven't got **much** money. I haven't got **many** relatives.	Have you got **a lot/lots of** money? Have you got **a lot/lots of** relatives? Have you got **much** money? Have you got **many** relatives?

- *a lot of/lots of* steht vor Hauptwörtern in der Einzahl und Mehrzahl; *a lot of /lots of* kann in bejahten wie verneinten Sätzen stehen.
- *much* steht vor einem Hauptwort in der Einzahl, *many* vor einem Hauptwort in der Mehrzahl. *much* und *many* werden in der Regel nur in verneinten Sätzen und in Fragen gebraucht.

6.2 *some, any*

Bejahter Satz *some*	Verneinter Satz *any*	Fragesatz *any*
I'll have **some** salmon. (Ich nehme etwas Lachs.) I'll have **some** carrots. (Ich nehme ein paar Karotten.)	I don't want **any** meat. (Ich möchte kein Fleisch.) I don't want **any** peas. (Ich möchte keine Erbsen.)	Is there **any** bread? (Gibt es Brot?) Are there **any** potatoes? (Gibt es Kartoffeln?)

- *some* und *any* bezeichnen eine unbestimmte Menge. Sie haben unterschiedliche Entsprechungen im Deutschen („etwas", „ein paar", „einige"), oder auch gar keine Entsprechung.
- *some* wird in bejahten, *any* in verneinten und in Fragesätzen gebraucht. In Fragesätzen, bei denen man die Antwort „ja" erwartet (z.B. wenn man jemandem etwas anbietet oder jemanden höflich um etwas bittet), wird aber *some* gebraucht:
*Would you like **some** wine? Can I have **some** water, please?*

7 Stellung von Umstandswörtern der Häufigkeit / *Position of adverbs of frequency*

> I **always/usually/often/sometimes/never** drive to work.
> **Usually/Often/Sometimes** I go by bus.
> I go by bus **usually/often/sometimes**.

- Umstandswörter der Häufigkeit stehen meistens vor dem Vollverb.
- *usually*, *often* und *sometimes* können auch am Satzanfang oder -ende stehen.

Grammatik im Überblick

8 Verben/Verbs

8.1 Das Verb be/The verb be

Bejahte Form		Verneinte Form	
Vollform	Kurzform	Vollform	Kurzform
<u>Gegenwart</u>		<u>Gegenwart</u>	
I am	I'm	I am **not**	I'm **not**
you are	you're	you are **not**	you're **not**/you aren't
he is	he's	he is **not**	he's **not**/he isn't
she is	she's	she is **not**	she's **not**/she isn't
it is	it's	it is **not**	it's **not**/it isn't
we are	we're	we are **not**	we're **not**/we aren't
you are	you're	you are **not**	you're **not**/you aren't
they are	they're	they are **not**	they're **not**/they aren't
<u>Vergangenheit</u>		<u>Vergangenheit</u>	
I was	–	I was **not**	I wasn't
you were	–	you were **not**	you weren't
he was	–	he was **not**	he wasn't
she was	–	she was **not**	she wasn't
it was	–	it was **not**	it wasn't
we were	–	we were **not**	we weren't
you were	–	you were **not**	you weren't
they were	–	they were **not**	they weren't

8.2 Vollverben: einfache Gegenwart/Full verbs: simple present

Bejahter Satz	Verneinter Satz	Frage	Kurzantworten
I eat fish.	I **don't** eat meat.	**Do** I eat eggs?	Yes, I **do**./No, I **don't**.
You eat fish.	You **don't** eat meat.	**Do** you eat eggs?	Yes, you **do**./No, you **don't**.
He eat**s** fish.	He **doesn't** eat meat.	**Does** he eat eggs?	Yes, he **does**./No, he **doesn't**.
She eat**s** fish.	She **doesn't** eat meat.	**Does** she eat eggs?	Yes, she **does**./No, she **doesn't**.
It eat**s** fish.	It **doesn't** eat meat.	**Does** it eat eggs?	Yes, it **does**./No, it **doesn't**.
We eat fish.	We **don't** eat meat.	**Do** we eat eggs?	Yes, we **do**./No, we **don't**.
You eat fish.	You **don't** eat meat.	**Do** you eat eggs?	Yes, you **do**./No, you **don't**.
They eat fish.	They **don't** eat meat.	**Do** they eat eggs?	Yes, they **do**./No, they **don't**.

- In bejahten Sätzen wird in der dritten Person Einzahl (*he, she, it*) *-s* an das Verb angehängt.
- Verneinte Sätze, Fragen und Kurzantworten werden mit *do* und *does* gebildet.
- Mit der einfachen Gegenwart beschreiben wir eine Handlung, die immer, regelmäßig oder routinemäßig ausgeführt wird, bzw. eine Dauersituation, die besteht.

Grammatik im Überblick

8.3 Vollverben: Verlaufsform der Gegenwart/*Full verbs: present progressive*

Bejahter Satz	Verneinter Satz	Frage	Kurzantworten
I'm read**ing**.	I'm not eat**ing**.	Am I work**ing**?	Yes, I am./No, I'm not.
You're read**ing**.	You aren't eat**ing**.	Are you work**ing**?	Yes, you are./No, you aren't.
He's read**ing**.	He isn't eat**ing**.	Is he work**ing**?	Yes, he is./No, he isn't.
She's read**ing**.	She isn't eat**ing**.	Is she work**ing**?	Yes, she is./No, she isn't.
We're read**ing**.	We aren't eat**ing**.	Are we work**ing**?	Yes, we are./No, we aren't.
You're read**ing**.	You aren't eat**ing**.	Are you work**ing**?	Yes, you are./No, you aren't.
They're read**ing**.	They aren't eat**ing**.	Are they work**ing**?	Yes, they are./No, they aren't.

- Die Verlaufsform der Gegenwart besteht aus einer Form von *be* und der Grundform des Vollverbs + Endung *-ing*.
  - read → read**ing**   + ing   carry → carry**ing**   + ing
  - make → mak**ing**   – e + ing   get → get**ting**   Mitlaut wird verdoppelt + ing
- Mit der Verlaufsform der Gegenwart wird eine Handlung oder Situation beschrieben, die vorübergehend, noch nicht abgeschlossen, im Verlauf begriffen ist.
- Die Verlaufsform der Gegenwart wird auch gebraucht, um auszudrücken, daß etwas in der Zukunft geschehen wird – etwas, das fest geplant, verabredet oder ausgemacht wurde: *We're going to Amsterdam this weekend.*

8.4 Vollverben: Vergangenheit/*Full verbs: simple past*

Bejahter Satz	Verneinter Satz	Frage	Kurzantworten
I need**ed** time.	I **didn't** need money.	**Did** I need help?	Yes, I **did**./No, I **didn't**.
You need**ed** time.	You **didn't** need money.	**Did** you need help?	Yes, you **did**./No, you **didn't**.
He need**ed** time.	He **didn't** need money.	**Did** he need help?	Yes, he **did**./No, he **didn't**.
She need**ed** time.	She **didn't** need money.	**Did** she need help?	Yes, she **did**./No, she **didn't**.
We need**ed** time.	We **didn't** need money.	**Did** we need help?	Yes, we **did**./No, we **didn't**.
You need**ed** time.	You **didn't** need money.	**Did** you need help?	Yes, you **did**./No, you **didn't**.
They need**ed** time.	They **didn't** need money.	**Did** they need help?	Yes, they **did**./No, they **didn't**.

- Die Vergangenheit von regelmäßigen Verben besteht aus der Grundform des Verbs mit der Endung *-(e)d*. Unregelmäßige Verben haben eine besondere Form: s. Liste auf S. 147.
  - need → need**ed**   + ed   carry → carr**ied**   y → i + ed
  - like → lik**ed**   + d   jog → jog**ged**   Mitlaut wird verdoppelt + ed
- Verneinte Sätze, Fragen und Kurzantworten werden für alle Verben (regelmäßige und unregelmäßige) mit *did(n't)* gebildet.
- Die Vergangenheit wird im Englischen für Handlungen und Situationen gebraucht, die zu einem bestimmten Zeitpunkt in der Vergangenheit abgeschlossen wurden. Diese Vergangenheitsform ist die übliche Erzählform, nicht das Perfekt.

GRAMMAR

Grammatik im Überblick

8.5 Vollverben: Perfekt/*Full verbs: present perfect*

Bejahter Satz	Verneinter Satz	Frage	Kurzantworten
I've asked Jack.	I haven't asked Jill.	Have I asked Ann?	Yes, I have./No, I haven't.
You've asked Jack.	You haven't asked Jill.	Have you asked Ann?	Yes, you have./No, you haven't.
He's asked Jack.	He hasn't asked Jill.	Has he asked Ann?	Yes, he has./No, he hasn't.
She's asked Jack.	She hasn't asked Jill.	Has she asked Ann?	Yes, she has./No, she hasn't.
We've asked Jack.	We haven't asked Jill.	Have we asked Ann?	Yes, we have./No, we haven't.
You've asked Jack.	You haven't asked Jill.	Have you asked Ann?	Yes, you have./No, you haven't.
They've asked Jack.	They haven't asked Jill.	Have they asked Ann?	Yes, they have./No, they haven't.

- Das Perfekt besteht aus einer Form von *have* (*has* oder *have*) + Partizip Perfekt des Vollverbs.
- Das Partizip Perfekt von regelmäßigen Verben ist identisch mit der Vergangenheit. Unregelmäßige Verben haben eine besondere Form: s. Liste auf S. 147.
- Die Kurzform *'s = has* nicht verwechseln mit der Kurzform *'s = is*!
- Das Perfekt wird gebraucht für Handlungen, die zu einem <u>unbestimmten</u> Zeitpunkt in der Vergangenheit abgeschlossen wurden, d.h. irgendwann vor dem jetzigen Zeitpunkt. Das englische Perfekt kann nicht mit Zeitbestimmungen wie *ago, last week, yesterday* usw. gebraucht werden, die einen bestimmten Zeitpunkt in der Vergangenheit nennen. Wichtig für den Gebrauch des englischen Perfekts ist nicht die Frage, wann etwas geschehen ist, sondern nur, ob es irgendwann geschehen ist und ob es möglicherweise Auswirkungen für die Gegenwart hat.

8.6 Vollverben: Zukunft/*Full verbs: future*

Bejahter Satz	Verneinter Satz	Frage	Kurzantworten
I'll tell him.	I won't ask him.	Will I see him?	Yes, I will./No, I won't.
You'll tell him.	You won't ask him.	Will you see him?	Yes, you will./No, you won't.
He'll tell him.	He won't ask him.	Will he see him?	Yes, he will./No, he won't.
She'll tell him.	She won't ask him.	Will she see him?	Yes, she will./No, she won't.
We'll tell him.	We won't ask him.	Will we see him?	Yes, we will./No, we won't.
You'll tell him.	You won't ask him.	Will you see him?	Yes, you will./No, you won't.
They'll tell him.	They won't ask him.	Will they see him?	Yes, they will./No, they won't.

- Die Zukunft ist für alle Personen gleich. Bejahte Aussagen werden mit *'ll* (= *will*) gebildet, verneinte mit *won't* (= *will not*).
- Mit *will* wird ausgesagt, was in der Zukunft geschehen wird; *will* wird auch für spontane Entscheidungen gebraucht: *The phone's ringing. I'll answer it.*
- Auch die Verlaufsform der Gegenwart wird gebraucht, um zukünftige Geschehen auszudrücken. Vgl. Abschnitt 8.3.

Grammatik im Überblick

8.7 Modale Hilfsverben/*Modal auxiliaries*

Es gibt Hilfsverben wie *do, have, be*, die gebraucht werden, um bestimmte Zeitformen von Vollverben zu bilden. Modale Hilfsverben werden nicht gebraucht, um Zeitformen zu bilden, sondern sie werden gebraucht, um Fähigkeit, Notwendigkeit, Erlaubnis, Rat usw. auszudrücken. „Können" und „müssen" sind zwei modale Hilfsverben, die im Deutschen gebraucht werden.

can, can´t (cannot)	„können" *I can (can't) speak Italian.* *You can (can't) swim here.* *Can I help you?*
could	„könnte(n)" *Could we have some water, please?* *We could go to the theatre.*
shall	Mit *shall* kann man einen Vorschlag oder ein Angebot machen: „sollen" *Shall we go?* *Shall I help you?*
have to	Mit *have to* drückt man aus, daß etwas gemacht werden muß bzw. notwendig ist: „müssen" *We have to go soon, I'm afraid.* *I have to get up at 5 o'clock.*

9 Satzmuster/*Sentence patterns*

9.1 Bejahte Sätze/*Affirmative sentences*

Satzgegenstand	(Hilfsverb)	Vollverb	Satzergänzung
I		swim.	
I		drink	tea.
I	'm	flying	to Amsterdam.
I		cooked	spaghetti.
I	've	cooked	it often.
I	'll	see	you tomorrow.
I	can	speak	English.

one hundred and forty-five 145

Grammatik im Überblick

9.2 Verneinte Sätze/*Negative sentences*

Satzgegenstand	Hilfsverb + *not/n't*	Vollverb	Satzergänzung
I	don't	like	camping.
I	'm not	coming	with you.
I	didn't	meet	Alan.
I	haven't	met	his wife.
I	won't	see	him tomorrow.
I	can't	swim.	

- In verneinten Sätzen wird *not/n't* an das Hilfsverb *be, have, will* oder *can* angeschlossen. Steht kein Hilfsverb im bejahten Satz, wird *not/n't* an eine Form von *do* angeschlossen.

9.3 Entscheidungsfragen/*Yes/No-questions*

Hilfsverb	Satzgegenstand	Vollverb	Satzergänzung	Kurzantwort
Do	you	like	spaghetti?	Yes, I **do**./No, I **don't**.
Are	you	learning	English?	Yes, I **am**./No, I'm **not**.
Did	it	rain?		Yes, it **did**./No, it **didn't**.
Have	you	seen	Ann?	Yes, I **have**./No, I **haven't**.
Can	she	sing?		Yes, she **can**./No, she **can't**.

9.4 Fragen mit Fragewörtern/*Questions with question words*

Fragewort	Hilfsverb	Satzgegenstand	Vollverb	Satzergänzung
Where	do	you	play	tennis?
How	is	she	making	it?
What	did	they	discuss?	
When	have	I	met	her?

Grammatik im Überblick

10 Unregelmäßige Verben/*Irregular verbs*

Grundform	Vergangenheit	Perfekt
be sein	was/were	have been
break zerreißen	broke	have broken
bring (mit)(herbringen)	brought	have brought
buy kaufen	bought	have bought
choose auswählen, aussuchen	chose	have chosen
come kommen	came	have come
do tun, machen	did	have done
drink trinken	drank	have drunk
drive betreiben	drove	have driven
eat aufessen	ate	have eaten
find besorgen	found	have found
fly fliehen	flew	have flown
get bekommen, erhalten	got	have got
give übergeben, übermitteln	gave	have given
go gehen	went	have gone
have haben	had	have had
hear hören	heard	have heard
keep behalten	kept	have kept
know wissen, kennen	knew	have known
leave abreisen	left	have left
meet treffen, begegnen	met	have met
put setzen, stellen, legen	put	have put
read [ri:d] lesen	read [red]	have read [red]
ride reiten	rode	have ridden
ring läuten, klingen	rang	have rung
say [seɪ] sagen	said [sed]	have said [sed]
see sehen	saw	have seen
sit sitzen, sich setzen	sat	have sat
sleep schlafen	slept	have slept
speak sprechen	spoke	have spoken
stand	stood	have stood
swim schwimmen	swam	have swum
take nehmen	took	have taken
tell erzählen	told	have told
think denken, glauben, meinen	thought	have thought
wear tragen	wore	have worn
write schreiben	wrote	have written

GRAMMAR

SCHLÜSSEL

Unit 1

1
O o: morning, twenty, English, people, welcome, evening, listen
o O: goodbye, address, hello, repeat

3
1 Good morning.
2 Nice to meet you.
3 Good afternoon.
4 Goodbye.
5 Good evening.

4
1 is, is   2 Are, am   3 is
4 m, are   5 is   6 s, s   7 are

5
1 in, from, near   2 of   3 at
4 from   5 at

6
1 What's your name?
2 What's your telephone number?
3 What's your address?
4 Where are you from?
5 Are you English? / Are you from England?
6 How are you?

7
Dennings
Roberta
204 Whelm Street
London SW9 4AF
081 746 4987

Tapescript
A: ... and your name?
B: Dennings.
A: Can you spell that please?
B: Yes, it's D-e-n-n-i-n-g-s.
A: And your first name?
B: Roberta.
A: R-o-b-e-r-t-a?
B: Yes, that's right.
A: And what's your address, please?
B: Two oh four Whelm Street, London SW9 4AF.
A: London SW9 4AF. Can you spell Whelm Street, please?
B: W-h-e-l-m.
A: OK. And your telephone number?
B: 081 746 4987.
A: 081 746 4987. OK. I'll send you that information straight away, Ms Dennings.

8
1 My name's Schmitz.
2 I'm from Germany.
3 Where are you from?
4 This is Nina.
5 Nice to meet you.
6 How are you?
7 Fine, thanks. And you?
8 Thank you.
9 You're welcome.
10 See you next week!

9
1 My name's …
2 Yes, I am. / No, I'm not.
3 I'm from …
4 I'm fine. /…

Unit 2

1
o O o   O o o   o o O o
romantic   family   optimistic

2
verschieden: 1, 2, 5, 6

3
2 Barbara and Brenda are beautiful/blond.
3 Fran is funny.
4 Greg and George are good-looking.
5 Harry is heavy/handsome.
6 Nick is nice/not very athletic/new.
7 Owen is outgoing/optimistic.
8 Paula and Pamela are pessimistic/pretty.
9 Ruth is reserved/realistic/romantic.
10 Sam is short/shy/serious.
11 Tina and Tanja are tidy/tall/thin.
12 Ursula is untidy.

4
a)

b)
2 Larry isn't Sam and Wendy's son. He's Rita and Frank's son.
3 Rita isn't Jennifer's mother. She's Larry's mother.
4 Frank isn't Rita's wife. He's Rita's husband.
5 Jennifer isn't Frank's daughter. She's Sam's daughter.

Tapescript
Hello. My name's Larry. I've got a brother – his name is Sam – and a sister – her name is Wendy. Sam's wife's name is Barbara. Sam and Barbara's daughter is Jennifer. My mother and father are Rita and Frank.

5
2 No, it isn't.   6 No, he isn't.
3 Yes, it is.   7 Yes, they are.
4 No, they aren't.   8 No, he isn't.
5 No, she isn't.

6
3 She's got long hair.
4 He wears glasses.
5 He's heavy and has got a moustache.
6 He's bald.
7 She's got short hair.

7
2 He/She isn't very romantic.
3 Are you from Canada?
4 No, I'm not.
5 This is my husband/wife.
6 Who's on the (tele)phone?
7 They're from (a place) near Berlin.
8 Can I phone you?
9 They're my best friends.

8
Beispiel:
I'm tall and rather thin. I've got brown hair and blue eyes. I think I'm an optimistic, untidy and athletic person. My best friend is my boyfriend.

SCHLÜSSEL

Unit 3

1 b
thirty, fourteen, fifty, sixty, seventeen, eighty, nineteen

2

[s]	[z]	[ɪz]
weeks	wives	offices
streets	girls	addresses
states	friends	classes
tests	eyes	glasses

3
2 There is an/one alarm clock.
3 There are two photos.
4 There is a/one handbag.
5 There are two films.
6 There is a/one computer.
7 There is a/one portable (tele)phone.
8 There are two newspapers.
9 There is a/one cat.

4
1 Where 2 What 3 How 4 How
5 Who 6 What 7 Where
8 What 9 When

5
A 10 (3.00) B 1 (4.30) C 4 (9.10)
D 7 (6.25) E 2 (2.40) F 8 (5.55)
G 6 (4.45) H 5 (11.05) I 3 (10.20)
J 9 (12.15)

6
1 Excuse me.
2 What time is it/What's the time?
3 It's a quarter past eight.
4 When is the next train to Paris?
5 There are two trains.
6 Have you got time now?
7 I haven't got children.
8 She has a cat.
9 There are fifty states in the USA.
10 How many people are there in your class?

7
Beispiel:
I've got a brother and two sisters. I've got lots of friends, too. I haven't got a pet.
My brother has two children, a boy and a girl. My sister has two boys. Their names are Colleen and Kevin, Ben and Scott. They live in Philadelphia and in Charlottesville, Virginia.

Unit 4

1
1 cornflakes 'n milk
2 tea 'n coffee
3 toast and jam
4 ham and egg
5 milk 'n honey
6 milk 'n cheese

2
[s] works, writes, helps, cooks
[z] repairs, has, goes, phones, cleans, reads, does
[ɪz] finishes

3
gets up, get up, goes, make, eat, has, is, do, start, have, work, cooks, do, finish, finishes

4
2 Sarah often has toast for breakfast.
3 Sarah never starts work after 8.30.
4 In her job Sarah sometimes talks to people with problems.
5 Sarah usually has lunch in a restaurant.
6 After lunch Sarah often reads and writes reports.
7 Sarah sometimes goes shopping after work.
8 On Monday evening Sarah usually goes to a dance class.

5
a) 1 b, 2 c

b) write, work, see, get up, make, ask, start, have breakfast, talk, finish work

c)
1 Ruth has breakfast with her husband and daughter.
2 Chris hasn't got a typical day.
3 Ruth's day usually starts at 6.30.
4 Ruth never works in the evening.
5 Chris works in many different places.
6 Ruth usually talks to teachers at work.

Tapescript
Woman:
My name is Ruth Cohen, I'm 39 years old and I live in York. A typical day for me starts at 6.30. I'm always the first out of bed. The rest of the family gets up in the next half hour. I make coffee, then my husband and I and our daughter, Rebecca, have breakfast. We all go to work together. You see, my husband and I work at Rebecca's school. My husband is a teacher, and I'm the school secretary.
Man:
I'm Chris Bingham. I haven't got a typical day. Sometimes I work in the morning, sometimes in the afternoon. I usually work in the evening, and I finish work at 10 or 11 o'clock. I go to many different places and I meet and talk to many different people. I ask them questions and then I write my articles. I'm a newspaper reporter.

6
1 What do you do?
2 Where do you work?
3 I work in an office.
4 She's a doctor.
5 I work at home.
6 I never eat/have breakfast.

7
Beispiel:
On Saturday I always go shopping in the morning. I usually go to the shop in the next street. I usually clean in the afternoon. In the evening I usually have dinner with my boyfriend and sometimes we go to the cinema after that.

Unit 5

1
1 boutique   Oo
2 relax   Oo
3 information Oooo

2
1 Do you like <u>cycling</u>?
2 Yes, I <u>do</u>.
3 Does <u>Peter</u> like cycling?
4 No, he <u>doesn't</u>.
5 Have you got your <u>book</u>?
6 Yes, I <u>have</u>.
7 Have you <u>got</u> your book?
8 Yes, <u>here</u> it is.
9 Are you <u>English</u>?
10 No, I'm <u>not</u>, I'm <u>German</u>.

one hundred and forty-nine 149

SCHLÜSSEL

3
2 She likes shopping, but does he (like shopping)?
3 She likes going to concerts, but does he (like going to concerts)?
4 He likes relaxing, but does she (like relaxing)?
5 He likes hiking, but does she (like hiking)?
6 She likes swimming, but does he (like swimming)?
7 She likes gardening, but does he (like gardening)?

4
2 I like cycling, but I don't like gardening.
3 He lives in the USA, but he doesn't live in New York.
4 I'm from England, but I'm not from London.
5 I can speak English, but I can't write it well.
6 Ted works with computers, but he doesn't design software.
7 She's very outgoing, but she's not very romantic.
8 We play tennis, but we don't play squash.

5
a)

	Man	Woman
1	No	Yes
2	Yes	Yes
3	Yes	Yes
4	No	Yes
5	No	No

b)
1 Yes, she does.
2 Yes, he does.
3 No, he doesn't.
4 Yes, he does.
5 Yes, she does.
6 No, she doesn't.
7 No, he doesn't.
8 Yes, she does.

Tapescript
Man 1: Do you like flying?
Woman: Yes, I do.
Man 1: Do you like flying?
Man 2: No, I don't.

Man 1: Do you like fruit?
Woman: Yes, I do.
Man 1: Do you like fruit, too?
Man 2: Yes, I like fruit. I eat fruit for breakfast.
Man 1: Do you like breakfast in bed?
Man 2: Oh yes. But I don't usually have it.
Man 1: Do you like breakfast in bed?
Woman: Yes, of course. Who doesn't.

Man 1: Do you like tennis?
Woman: Yes, I do.
Man 1: And you?
Man 2: No, I don't, not really. I play squash. I like that.

Man 1: Do you watch horror films?
Man 2: No, never. I hate them.
Man 1: And you? Do you like them?
Woman: No, I really don't like them.

6
1 I like swimming.
2 Do you like swimming? No, I don't.
3 Does she like London?
4 The train takes all day.
5 I don't drink coffee.
6 He doesn't work in an office.
7 Can he cook well? - No, he can't.
8 Does he play an instrument? - No, he doesn't.

7
Beispiele:
I like cooking and I like eating in a restaurant, too.
I like watching a film at the cinema and I like watching a play at the theatre, too.
I like going to museums but I don't like going to the zoo.
I like flying and I like going by train, too.
I don't like hiking but I like cycling.

Unit 6

1

O o	o O	O o o	o O o	o o O o
honey	relax	opposite	directly	information
toilet	boutique	family		situation
concert		bicycle		
shopping		telephone		
swimming				

2
1 very   2 who   3 write

3
2 Helen Thomas is reading the newspaper.
3 Mr Henry is listening to Vivaldi.
4 Bobby is watching TV.
5 Paula is making dinner.
6 Mr Mendez is sleeping.
7 Mike and Mary are playing with the children.
8 Mr O'Malley is shopping.
9 Tony Capelli is writing a letter.

4
2 Is Paula reading the newspaper?
3 Are Mike and Mary shopping?
4 Are Richard and Helen listening to Vivaldi?
5 Is Mr Henry writing a letter?
6 Who is sleeping?
7 Who is having a shower?
8 What is Paula doing?
9 What are Mike and Mary doing?
10 What is Helen reading?

5
1 Mario is working in San Francisco.
2 Mario's wife is looking for a job.
3 Samantha is relaxing/on holiday.
4 Barbara is helping Robert/working in the garden.

Tapescript
Barbara: In San Francisco.
Angie: So – Mario's working in San Francisco; what's his wife doing?
B: She's looking for a job. She wants to work as a kindergarten teacher.
A: And Samantha – what's she doing?
B: Sam's relaxing for two weeks – she's on holiday – in Hawaii.
A: Hawaii?
B: Yes, Hawaii.

SCHLÜSSEL

A: Well, we can't go there tonight, can we Barbara? Would you like to go to the cinema?
B: Sorry, Angie. I'm helping Robert in the garden.

6
1 Excuse me, where's the nearest bank?
2 Go straight on and turn right at the supermarket. The post office is on the left.
3 The post office is opposite the station.
4 I'm having breakfast.
5 Have you got a map?
6 I go to work by bicycle.
7 I go to work on foot.

7
Beispiel:
I'm working for my English class. I'm not watching television.

Unit 7

1
O o   o O   o O o   O o o
kitchen   because   November   balcony
modern   upstairs   expensive   probably
bedroom   tomorrow

2
1 bed   2 God   3 bit   4 but
5 right   6 back   7 clock   8 dog

3
1 'm having   2 'm staying
3 get up   4 play tennis   5 have
6 eat/have   7 go   8 go
9 'm relaxing   10 'm eating/having
11 are playing

4
2 Is it a big(ger) flat?
3 Has it got more rooms?
4 When are you moving?
5 Can I help you?
6 Who is coming to your party tomorrow?
7 Does Alan know about it?
8 Does he always come to your parties?
9 What are you having at the party?
10 Are you cooking the paella?

5
1 David is making dinner at the moment.
2 Lynn is coming home at eight.
3 James is going to the cinema this evening.
4 David and Lynn are going to Lynn's sister and her family's this weekend.

Tapescript
David: Hello?
James: Hello, David. James here.
D: Hi, James.
J: What are you doing?
D: Making dinner.
J: You're making dinner? Why?
D: It's Lynn's birthday.
J: Oh really? Is she there? Can I say hello?
D: It's her dance class tonight. She's coming home at eight.
J: Oh, I see.
D: What are you doing tonight, James?
J: I'm going to the cinema. I thought we could perhaps meet for a drink after the film.
D: Sorry, old chap.
J: Well, perhaps we can do something this weekend?
D: Sorry, Lynn and I are going to her sister and family's for the weekend.
J: OK, phone me next week when you have time. Good luck with the cooking – and have a good weekend.
D: Thanks, James. Bye.
J: Bye-bye.

6
1 What are you doing (at the moment)?
2 She is moving to Bern in two weeks.
3 I'm going/driving/flying to Stockholm tomorrow.
4 What are you doing tonight?
5 She lives in a bed-sitter.
6 My sister is getting married next year.
7 Can you help me/give me a hand?
8 Can you come? – I'm afraid not./I'm afraid we can't.
9 She's here on business.
10 Are you coming on July 6th?

7
Beispiel:
I'm going to the cinema and …

Unit 8

1
dessert

2
1 tired   2
2 bored   1
3 grilled   1
4 potatoes   3
5 vegetables   3
6 differences   3

3
3 Has he got any vegetables?
 – No, he hasn't.
4 Has he got any milk?
 – No, he hasn't.
5 Has he got any butter?
 – No, he hasn't.
6 Has he got any yoghurt?
 – No, he hasn't.
7 Has he got any fruit?
 – No, he hasn't.
8 Has he got any jam?
 – Yes, he has.
9 Has he got any cheese?
 – Yes, he has.
10 Has he got any bread?
 – Yes, he has.

b)
2 He hasn't got any vegetables but he's got some cheese.
3 He hasn't got any fruit but he's got some jam.
4 He's got some bread but he hasn't got any yoghurt.
5 He hasn't got any butter but he's got some sausages.

4
1 e   2 b   3 d   4 a   5 c

5
vegetable soup, dessert, coffee cream cake, fruit salad, wine

Tapescript
Woman: Are you doing anything this evening?
Brother: No, why?
W: Well, I'm making vegetable soup and Tony and I can't eat it all. You know how much vegetable soup I always make!
B: Are you having garlic bread, too?
W: Would you like garlic bread

SCHLÜSSEL

B: Would I? I love garlic bread!
W: Then I'll make that, too.
B: What's for dessert – coffee cream cake?
W: No, we're having fresh fruit salad. Coffee cream cake's too heavy after my soup. Is fruit salad OK with you?
B: Super. What time shall I come?
W: About 7.30?
B: Fine. Shall I bring a bottle of wine?
W: That would be nice. And why don't you bring your new girlfriend?
B: Oh, I see... I'll phone her. Can I still come if Rebecca can't?

6
1 I'll have the sole.
2 What are you having?
3 What would you like to drink?
4 I'd like a glass of wine.
5 Can I have the bill, please?
6 Let's go to the cinema./Shall we go to the cinema?
7 I'll phone you tomorrow.
8 Don't you want to try anything new?
9 I'll open the window.

7
Beispiele:
Let's go hiking in the mountains.

Unit 9

2

[t]	[d]	[ɪd]
stretched	played	started
liked	listened	wanted
asked	phoned	
smoked	opened	
talked	waved	
watched		
looked		
jumped		

3
1 got up   2 said   3 took   4 went
5 thought 6 came   7 did   8 flew

4
3 How did he go to work?
4 Did he have a meeting?
5 Where did he have lunch?
6 When did he take a coffee break?
7 Where did he go after work?
8 Did he have dinner at 7.00?
9 When did he go to bed?

5
a 2, b 7, c 1, d 5, e 9, f 8, g 4, h 6, i 3

Tapescript
What did I do last weekend? Let me think. Well, the first thing was that I went shopping. I never have time to go shopping during the week. Then on Saturday afternoon I played tennis with a friend; the weather was beautiful. Then I went home and slept. In the evening I went out to dinner with my girlfriend. That's right, we went to an Indian restaurant. We both like eating Indian food. After that we went to see the new Steven Spielberg film at the cinema. I liked it but, my girlfriend didn't.
On Sunday we had some friends to lunch. We often have people to lunch on Sunday. Then, in the afternoon, I just relaxed and read the paper. That's how I like to spend Sunday afternoon – just relaxing! I went to bed early on Sunday because I had to get up at 5.30 on Monday morning and fly to Paris.

6
1 I usually get up at 6.00 but today I got up at 7.00.
2 I phoned Oliver this morning.
3 He said no!
4 Yesterday I went swimming.
5 On Sunday we went to the cinema.
6 What did you have for breakfast?
7 How did you go to work this morning?
8 I was born in 1960.
9 I left school in 1978.
10 When did you get married?

7
Beispiel:
Yesterday I got up at 7.00 and made breakfast for my family. Then I had a shower and got dressed. After that I took the bus to work. I had a meeting before lunch. Then I ...

Unit 10

1
a)
1 bed   2 bad   3 can   4 Ken
5 said 6 sad   7 Alan 8 Alan
9 man   10 men 11 sat 12 set
13 ten 14 tan

2 a)
ve<u>ge</u>table, <u>Thomp</u>son, <u>break</u>fast
<u>Lon</u>don, <u>Mon</u>day

b) Yes, it was.

3
2 The lamp goes in the living room.
3 The armchair goes in the living room.
4 The bed goes in the bedroom.
5 The desk goes in the study.
6 The wardrobe goes in the bedroom.
7 The TV goes in the living room.

4
1 g   2 d   3 a   4 e   5 h   6 b
7 c   8 f

5
a) On the kitchen table.

b)
1 Yes, he did.
2 No, he didn't.
3 No, she wasn't.
4 Yes, she did.
5 Yes, she did.
6 Yes, she was.
7 No, she didn't.

Tapescript
Ellen: Well, where did you put them when you came home?
Nick: I don't know! If I ...
E: OK, what did you do when you came in?
N: Well, first I answered the telephone.
E: Who was it?
N: Emily.
E: What did she say?
N: She wanted to go to the cinema with you this evening.
E: Thanks for telling me!
N: I still don't know where my keys are.
E: They're not next to the telephone?

SCHLÜSSEL

N: No.
E: Well, what did you do after Emily phoned?
N: I went into the living room, sat down and read the paper. Then you came home.
E: Perhaps they're on the sofa. Why don't you look?
N: Don't forget. You have to phone Emily!
E: I will - right now. Are we doing anything tonight?
N: I have some work to do. Why don't you do something with Emily.
E: I think I will.

E: Emily, hi, it's Ellen. Nick told me you phoned about the cinema.
Emily: Yes, the new Woody Allen film is on at the Palladium.
E: That sounds great. What time?
Emily: Eight o'clock.
E: OK. I'll meet you there at quarter to.
Emily: Great. See you then. Bye.
E: Bye.

N: I've got them!
E: Where were they?
N: On the kitchen table. I forgot I made a sandwich before Emily phoned.

6
1 Where did you live when you were a child?
2 Did you have a television when you were small/a child?
3 Did you have a favourite teacher?
4 We were a big family.
5 How many people were there in your family?
6 We lived in the country when I was a child.
7 It was always very windy.

7
When I was a child ...

Unit 11

1

O o	o O	O o o
larger	because	pullover
jacket	decide	customer
Europe		
fabric		
famous		

3
2 He's wearing a suit, a tie and black shoes.
3 She's wearing a dress, a hat and black shoes.
4 He's wearing jeans, a T-shirt, a white hat and white shoes.
5 She's wearing a coat and gloves with black shoes.

4
Can I help you, madam?
Yes, I'm looking for a winter coat.
What size are you?
Thirty-eight.
Thirty-eights are over here. What colour are you looking for?
Something dark; dark blue or black, I think.
These are all dark.
I'd like to try this one on, please. It looks very nice.
Of course, Madam. There's a mirror over there.

5
1 hotter   2 biggest/most interesting
3 longest   4 funnier   5 better
6 best/most interesting   7 worst

6 Nr. 2

Tapescript
Policeman: What did they look like, madam?
Woman: Well, the woman was wearing a white blouse with a dark skirt and black shoes. And she had blond hair.
P: Was she tall or short, madam?
W: Tall, taller than me.
P: Would you say she was thin or heavy?
W: Thin, very thin.
P: And the two men, madam?
W: Ummm, one had a suit on, a black suit.
P: Can you describe him?
W: Well, he had dark hair and ...
P: Long or short hair?
W: Short hair, and he wore glasses.
P: And the other man?
W: The other man wore jeans and a jeans jacket.
P: What did he look like?
W: He had dark hair, too, I think – and a moustache.
P: Were the men tall or short?
W: Well, the one in the suit was short and the one in the jeans was tall; he was the tallest of the three.
P: OK, madam; anything else you can tell me about them?
W: No, I don't think so; it happened so fast, you know.

7
1 I'm just looking, thank you.
2 I think it's too small.
3 I'll take this (one).
4 How much is it?
5 Do you take Eurocard?
6 This jacket is expensive.
7 She's older than me.
8 Macy's is the biggest department store in New York.

8
I think I'll buy ...

Unit 12

2
Betont: 2, 4, 6

3
a) 4
b) Simple past: 1, 4

5
1 No, he hasn't
2 No, he hasn't.
3 Yes, he has.
4 Yes, she has.
5 No, she hasn't.
6 Yes, she has.

6

1 been	6 told	11 taken
2 seen	7 had	12 got
3 said	8 written	13 done
4 given	9 read	14 driven
5 made	10 come	15 gone

7
1 I saw him yesterday.
2 Have you phoned him this week?
3 Has he ever visited you at your flat?
4 What did he tell you last week?
5 I haven't seen him today.

8
Beispiel: I haven't been to Australia.

Wörterverzeichnis nach Units

Lautschrift

[ʌ]	but [bʌt], run [rʌn]	[i:]	evening ['i:vnɪŋ], see [si:]	[ʒ]	television ['telɪvɪʒn]
[ɑ:]	park [pɑ:k], class [klɑ:s]	[ɒ]	not [nɒt], long [lɒŋ]	[v]	very ['veri], love [lʌv]
[aɪ]	my [maɪ], nice [naɪs]	[ɔɪ]	boy [bɔɪ], noisy ['nɔɪzi]	[w]	when [wen], always ['ɔ:lweɪz]
[aʊ]	out [aʊt], how [haʊ]	[ɔ:]	all [ɔ:l], call [kɔ:l]	[tʃ]	cheese [tʃi:z], match [mætʃ]
[æ]	and [ænd], can [kæn]			[dʒ]	Germany ['dʒɜ:məni], page [peɪdʒ]
[e]	egg [eg], well [wel]	[ʊ]	book [bʊk] good [gʊd]		
[eɪ]	name [neɪm], they [ðeɪ]	[u:]	who [hu:] school [sku:l]		
[eə]	where [weə], their [ðeə]	[ŋ]	thing [θɪŋ], greetings ['gri:tɪŋz]	**Zeichenerklärung**
[ə]	about [ə'baʊt], grammar ['græmə]	[r]	right [raɪt], friend [frend]	' Dieses Zeichen bedeutet, daß die nach-
[əʊ]	no [nəʊ], phone [fəʊn]	[s]	say [seɪ], Miss [mɪs]	folgende Silbe stark betont wird.
[ɜ:]	first [fɜ:st], word [wɜ:d]	[z]	busy ['bɪzi], please [pli:z]	: Dieses Zeichen bedeutet, daß der voran-
[ɪ]	it [ɪt], live [lɪv]	[θ]	thing [θɪŋ], month [mʌnθ]	gegangene Laut lang ist.
[ɪə]	near [nɪə], here [hɪə]	[ð]	this [ðɪs], father [fɑ:ðə]	
		[ʃ]	she [ʃi:], fresh [freʃ]	

T = Titel, FW = First words, F = Focus, FU = Follow-up, SF = Special focus, S = Summary
= bedeutet: hat (etwa) die gleiche Bedeutung wie ...
<—> bedeutet: ist das Gegenstück zu/Gegenteil von ...

Unit 1

T	Nice to meet you.	Nett, Sie kennenzulernen.	Nice to ~ you.
FW	first words ['fɜ:st 'wɜ:dz]	erste Wörter	
	greetings ['gri:tɪŋz]	Begrüßungen	
FW1	(to) match [mætʃ]	zuordnen	
	the [ðə]	der/die/das	
	to [tə, tʊ, tu:]	zu	
	picture ['pɪktʃə]	Bild	
	match ... to the pictures	ordnen Sie ... den Bildern zu	
	Good morning. [gʊd 'mɔ:nɪŋ]	Guten Morgen.	
	Good afternoon. [gʊd 'ɑ:ftə'nu:n]	Guten Tag.	~ afternoon.
	afternoon ['ɑ:ftə'nu:n]	Nachmittag	morning - ~ - evening
	Good evening. [gʊd 'i:vnɪŋ]	Guten Abend.	Good morning. - Good afternoon. - ~.
	Good night. [gʊd 'naɪt]	Gute Nacht.	Good morning. <—> ~
F	focus ['fəʊkəs]	Brennpunkt, Fokus	
	saying hello [seɪɪŋ hə'ləʊ]	guten Tag sagen	
	Hello. [hə'ləʊ]	Hallo. Tag.	
F1	dialogue ['daɪəlɒg]	Dialog, Gespräch	
	my name's [maɪ neɪmz]	ich heiße	Hello. ~ Janet. - Nice to meet you, Janet.
	my [maɪ]	mein/meine	
	name [neɪm]	Name	
	's = is	ist	
	Julia ['dʒu:ljə]	(Frauenname)	
	that [ðæt]	das	
	sounds [saʊndz]	klingt	Helmut? That ~ German.
	German ['dʒɜ:mən]	deutsch; Deutsch; Deutsche(r)	Heinz is a ~ name.
	are you [ɑ: ju:]	sind Sie/bist du/seid ihr	I'm John. ~ Barbara?

154 one hundred and fifty-four

	from [frɒm]	aus; von	Heinz is ~ Germany.
	Germany ['dʒɜ:mənɪ]	Deutschland	
	Yes, I am. [aɪ'æm]	Ja (ich bin es).	Are you from Berlin? - ~.
	I am	ich bin	My name is Heinz. ~ from Berlin.
	where [weə]	wo; wohin	~ is Ohlerath?
	in [ɪn]	in	Ohlerath is ~ Germany.
	well [wel]	nun	
	I'm = I am [aɪm]	ich bin	~ = I am
	a [ə]	ein/eine	Heinz is ~ German name.
	place [pleɪs]	Ort; Platz; Stelle	Ohlerath is a ~ in Germany.
	near [nɪə]	in der Nähe von, nahe	Essen is ~ Düsseldorf.
	Hanover ['hænəʊvə]	Hannover	
	but [bʌt]	aber	Heinz is from Berlin, ~ I'm from Hanover.
	(to) live [lɪv]	leben; wohnen	I ~ in Ohlerath.
	Berlin [bɜː'lɪn]	Berlin	
	Where are you from?	Wo kommen Sie her?	I'm from Germany. ~?
F2	and [ænd]	und	Berlin ~ Hanover are in Germany.
	Austria ['ɒstrɪə]	Österreich	Salzburg is in ~.
	Switzerland ['swɪtsələnd]	die Schweiz	Zurich is in ~
	town [taʊn]	Stadt	Paderborn is a ~ in Germany.
F3	this [ðɪs]	dies; das	~ <—> that
	How are you? [haʊ 'ɑː juː?]	Wie geht es Ihnen/Dir/Euch?	
	Fine, thanks. ['faɪn θæŋks.]	Gut, danke.	How are you? - ~.
	not bad [nɒt 'bæd]	nicht schlecht	How are you? - ~.
	Anne [æn]	(Frauenname)	
	wife [waɪf]	(Ehe-)Frau	I'm Alan Taylor and this is my ~, Janet.
	Kim [kɪm]	(Frauenname)	
	Mundy ['mʌndɪ]	(Familienname)	
F4	Mr (Smith) ['mɪstə]	Herr (Schmidt)	
	Mrs (Smith) ['mɪsɪz]	Frau (Schmidt)	Not Mr Smith, but ~ Smith.
	Ms (Smith) [mɪz]	Frau (= Frau/Fräulein) (Smith)	Mr, Mrs, ~
	husband ['hʌzbənd]	(Ehe-)Mann	<—> wife
	friend [frend]	Freund/Freundin	
	colleague ['kɒliːg]	Kollege/Kollegin	
	too [tuː]	auch	Anne is a colleague, but a friend, ~.
F5	Goodbye! [gʊd'baɪ]	Auf Wiedersehen!	<—> hello
	See you next week! [wiːk]	Bis nächste Woche!	Goodbye. ~!
	(to) see [siː]	sehen	
	Bye! [baɪ]	Wiedersehen! Tschüs!	= Goodbye!
FU1	follow-up ['fɒləʊ ʌp]	Nachfassen, Weiterverfolgen, Fortsetzung	
	(to) follow ['fɒləʊ]	(ver)folgen	
	your [jɔː]	dein(e)/ihr(e)/Ihr(e)	Are you from Germany? ~ name sounds German.
	no [nəʊ]	nein	<—> yes
FU2	Listen and repeat. [lɪstn ənd rɪ'piːt]	Hören Sie zu und sprechen Sie nach.	
FU3	Listening ['lɪsnɪŋ]	Hören	
	Are they friends?	Sind sie Freunde/befreundet?	Janet and Anne are colleagues, but ~?
	Yes, they are. [ðeɪ]	Ja (sie sind es).	Are they from Germany? - Yes, ~.
	No, they aren't.	Nein (sie sind es nicht).	Are they from Germany? - No, ~.
	Sue, William [suː, 'wɪljəm]	(Vornamen)	
	Tim, Mr Hewitt [tɪm, 'hjuːɪt]	(Namen)	
	Dunn, Court [dʌn, kɔːt]	(Familiennamen)	
	Meg, David [meg, 'deɪvɪd]	(Vornamen)	
	Listen again. [lɪsn ə'gen]	Hören Sie nochmal/wieder zu.	
	Circle the items you hear. ['sɜːkl]	Kreisen Sie die Dinge/Punkte/(hier:) Wendungen ein, die Sie hören.	
FU4	Fill in. [fɪl 'ɪn]	Ergänzen Sie.	
FU5	number ['nʌmbə]	Nummer, Zahl, Ziffer	1, 2 and 3 are ~s.
FU6	gate [geɪt]	Flugsteig; Tor	
	gate number ['geɪt nʌmbə]	Flugsteignummer	The ~ for the Lufthansa flight is number 32.
	departure [dɪ'pɑːtʃə]	Abflug; Abreise	
	flight [flaɪt]	Flug	Lufthansa ~ number 234 from Frankfurt

VOCAB

	to	nach	<—> from
	time [taɪm]	(Uhr-)Zeit	The ~ is 5.35.
FU7	Make a list. [meɪk ə 'lɪst]	Machen Sie eine Liste.	
	a list of people ['pi:pl]	eine Liste von Personen/Menschen/Leuten	Sue, William, Tim, Meg is a ~.
	class [klɑːs]	Klasse	
	with [wɪð]	mit	Janet is ~ my husband.
	their [ðeə]	ihr(e)	They are from Germany. ~ name is Schmidt.
	telephone ['telɪfəʊn]	Telefon	
	Can I phone you? [kæn]	Kann/Darf ich Sie anrufen?	~? - Yes, my telephone number is 4376521.
	of course [əv 'kɔːs]	natürlich	Can I phone you? - Yes, ~.
	Sorry, ... ['sɒrɪ]	(Es) Tut mir leid, ...; Leider ...	Can I phone you? - No, ~.
	I haven't got a phone. [hævnt 'gɒt]	Ich habe kein Telefon.	Andrea's telephone number is 4376521, but ~.
	What's your name?	Wie ist Ihr Name?	My name's Alan. ~?
	what? [wɒt]	was? wie?	~ is your phone number? - 5769354.
	at work [wɜːk]	in/bei der Arbeit	
	at home [həʊm]	zu Hause	<—> at work
	Thank you. ['θæŋk jʊ]	Danke.	= Thanks.
	You're welcome. ['welkəm]	Bitte schön. Bitte sehr.	Thank you. - ~.
SF	special focus [speʃl 'fəʊkəs]	besonderer Schwerpunkt	
	alphabet ['ælfəbet]	Alphabet	
SF3	these [ðiːz]	diese	this name, ~ names
	English ['ɪŋglɪʃ]	englisch; Englisch	
	abbreviation [əbriːvɪ'eɪʃn]	Abkürzung	VW is the ~ of "Volkswagen".
SF4	(to) spell [spel]	buchstabieren	Can you ~ your name? - Yes, of course. F-O-X.
	please [pliːz]	bitte	<—> thank you
	surname ['sɜːneɪm]	Familienname	My name is Anne Fox. Fox is my ~.
	it's (= it is) [ɪts]	es ist	What's your surname? - ~ Fox.
	address [ə'dres]	Adresse	My ~ is Boltenstraße 34b, 40627 Düsseldorf.
	street [striːt]	Straße	The name of the ~ is Boltensternstraße.
S	summary ['sʌmərɪ]	Zusammenfassung	
	grammar ['græmə]	Grammatik	
	phrases ['freɪzɪz]	(Rede-)Wendungen	
	Hey, how's it going?	Na, wie geht's?	

Unit 2

T	she [ʃiː]	sie	
	What's she like? [laɪk]	Wie ist sie?	That is my colleague Ann. - ~? - She's nice.
FW1	untidy [ʌn'taɪdɪ]	unordentlich	
	shy [ʃaɪ]	schüchtern	
	athletic [æθ'letɪk]	athletisch, sportlich	
	romantic [rəʊ'mæntɪk]	romantisch	
	pessimistic [pesɪ'mɪstɪk]	pessimistisch	
	funny ['fʌnɪ]	lustig; komisch	
	now [naʊ]	jetzt, nun	Ask a partner. ... And ~ report to the class.
FW2	he [hiː]	er	<—> she
	(to) think [θɪŋk]	denken; glauben	Is she OK? - Yes, I ~ she's nice.
	isn't (= is not)	ist nicht	He's from Germany, he ~ from the USA.
	very ['verɪ]	sehr	Is she nice? - Yes, she's ~ nice.
F	describing people [dɪ'skraɪb]	Leute beschreiben	
F1	Do this personality test. [pɜːsə'nælətɪ]	Machen Sie diesen Persönlichkeitstest.	
	tidy ['taɪdɪ]	ordentlich	<—> untidy
	outgoing [aʊt'gəʊɪŋ]	aus sich herausgehend, extravertiert	<—> shy
	optimistic [ɒptɪ'mɪstɪk]	optimistisch	<—> pessimistic
	realistic [rɪə'lɪstɪk]	realistisch	
	reserved [rɪ'zɜːvd]	reserviert	= shy
	serious ['sɪərɪəs]	ernst(haft)	<—> funny
F2	an [ən]	ein(e)	John is ~ English name.
	person ['pɜːsn]	Person	one ~, two people
	rather ['rɑːðə]	ziemlich	She's not outgoing, she's ~ shy.

		No, I'm not.	Nein (ich bin es nicht).	<—> Yes, I am.
F3		Report to the class. [rɪ'pɔːt]	Berichten Sie der Klasse.	
		we [wiː]	wir	I'm tidy and you're tidy: ~'re tidy.
F4		office ['ɒfɪs]	Büro	Anne is at work in her ~.
		England ['ɪŋglənd]	England	London is in ~.
		Who was that? [huː]	Wer war das?	~? - That's my friend Anne.
		tall [tɔːl]	groß (gewachsen)	She's 1 meter 80 ~.
		girl [gɜːl]	Mädchen; junge Frau	Who is that ~? - Janet Smith.
		long [lɒŋ]	lang	Margaret Mary is a ~ name.
		blond [blɒnd]	blond	
		hair [heə]	Haare	Who is the person with the short blond ~?
		new [njuː]	neu	This is my ~ address and phone number.
		her [hɜː]	ihr	That's Alan's wife. ~ name is Janet.
		Chris Wilson ['krɪs 'wɪlsn]	(Name)	
		Devon ['devn]	(Grafschaft in Südwest-England)	
		Exeter ['eksɪtə]	(Stadt in Devon)	
		Yes, she is.	Ja (sie ist es).	Is she Alan's wife? - ~.
		a bit [bɪt]	ein bißchen	I'm not very shy, but I'm ~ shy.
		People are when they're new.	Die Leute sind so, wenn sie neu sind.	
		when [wen]	wenn; als	Phone Alan ~ you have time.
		Right! [raɪt]	Richtig!	He's not very romantic. - ~!
F5		Quick check [kwɪk 'tʃek]	Schnellkontrolle	
FU1		best [best]	beste(r/s)	My ~ friend is my colleague Ingrid.
		(to) ask [ɑːsk]	(be)fragen	What's their name? - ~ Ann.
		partner ['pɑːtnə]	Partner/Partnerin	Husband and wife are ~s.
		boyfriend ['bɔɪfrend]	Freund	He is Janet's new ~.
		girlfriend ['gɜːlfrend]	Freundin	<—> boyfriend
		school [skuːl]	Schule	She's in class 6A at Kahlenberg ~.
		old [əʊld]	alt	<—> new
		former ['fɔːmə]	ehemalige(r/s), frühere(r/s)	
		neighbour ['neɪbə]	Nachbar/Nachbarin	My address is Grünstraße 6. My ~'s address is Grünstraße 8.
		member ['membə]	Mitglied	She's a ~ of a golf club.
		family ['fæməlɪ]	Familie	
		mother ['mʌðə]	Mutter	My ~'s name is Jill and my name is Jill, too.
		father ['fɑːðə]	Vater	<—> mother
		sister ['sɪstə]	Schwester	
		brother ['brʌðə]	Bruder	<—> sister
		son [sʌn]	Sohn	Bernard is the father. Alan is Bernard's ~.
		daughter ['dɔːtə]	Tochter	<—> son
		his [hɪz]	sein(e)	Bernard is Alan's father. Bernard is ~ father.
FU2		information [ɪnfə'meɪʃn]	Information/Informationen, Auskunft/Auskünfte	
FU3		student ['stjuːdənt]	Lernende(r); Student/Studentin	She's a new ~ in my class.
FU5		(to) find out [faɪnd 'aʊt]	herausfinden	~ his address. You can ask his colleague.
		Look at this page. [peɪdʒ]	Sehen Sie sich diese Seite an.	
		at TV International [tiː viː ɪntə'næʃnl]	bei TV International	She's the boss ~ TV International.
		Ask your partner questions. ['kwestʃənz]	Stellen Sie Ihrem Partner/Ihrer Partnerin Fragen.	
		complete the table [kəm'pliːt]	vervollständigen Sie die Tabelle	
		only ['əʊnlɪ]	nur	My phone number is ~ three numbers - 561.
		first name ['fɜːst neɪm]	Vorname	My ~ is Andrea. My surname is Smith.
		Ask about ... [ɑːsk ə'baʊt]	Fragen Sie nach ...; Stellen Sie Fragen über ...	Ask questions. ~ her family.
FU6		Answer with a partner. [ɑːnsə]	(Be-)Antworten Sie mit einem Partner/einer Partnerin.	
		both [bəʊθ]	beide	I'm from Essen. My wife is from Essen. We're ~ from Essen.
		Make two more sentences like this. ['sentənsɪz]	Bilden Sie zwei weitere Sätze wie diesen.	
FU7		or [ɔː]	oder	Is she English ~ German?
		Miriam ['mɪrɪəm]	(Name)	
		Ed Madison ['mædɪsən]	(Name)	
		at the hotel [həʊ'tel]	im Hotel	Where's Alan? - He's ~.

	Pisa ['piːzə]	(Stadt in Italien)	
	Laura Sands ['lɔːrə'sænz]	(Name)	
	Toronto [tə'rɒntəʊ]	(Großstadt in Kanada)	
	Canada ['kænədə]	Kanada	I'm from ~, not the USA.
	on the telephone ['telɪfəʊn]	am Telefon	She's ~ in her office.
SF	describing appearance [ə'pɪərəns]	Aussehen beschreiben	
	has got [həz 'gɒt]	hat	She ~ short blond hair.
	blue [bluː]	blau	
	brown [braʊn]	braun	
	eye [aɪ]	Auge	He has got blue ~s.
	thin [θɪn]	dünn; schlank	
	heavy ['hevɪ]	schwer	<—> thin
	dark [dɑːk]	dunkel	not blond hair, but ~ hair
	fair [feə]	hell	= blond
	grey [greɪ]	grau	not blue eyes or brown eyes, but ~ eyes
	long [lɒŋ]	lang	<—> short
	bald [bɔːld]	kahl(köpfig), glatzköpfig	Not long hair, not short hair - he's ~!
	moustache [mə'stɑːʃ]	Schnurrbart	
	beard [bɪəd]	Bart	
	wears glasses ['glɑːsɪz]	trägt eine Brille	
	good-looking [gʊd'lʊkɪŋ]	gutaussehend	
	handsome ['hænsəm]	gutaussehend (bei Männern)	= good-looking
	pretty ['prɪtɪ]	hübsch	= good-looking
	beautiful ['bjuːtɪfʊl]	schön	= very pretty
SF1	have got	haben	My sisters ~ short blond hair.
SF2	other ['ʌðə]	andere(r/s)	This is my sister Emma. I have got two ~ sisters.
	exercise ['eksəsaɪz]	Übung	
	I love your hair!	Dein Haar/Deine Frisur finde ich toll!	

Unit 3

T	keeping count ['kiːpɪŋ 'kaʊnt]	Zählen; die Übersicht behalten	
FW2	quiz [kwɪz]	Quiz	
	country ['kʌntrɪ]	Land	Germany is a ~ in Europe.
	how many? [haʊ 'menɪ]	wie viele?	~ sisters have you got? - Three.
	state [steɪt]	(Bundes-)Staat	Texas is a ~ in the USA.
	there are [ðeər'ɑː]	es gibt	~ 14 people in this class.
	the United States [juː'naɪtɪd]	die Vereinigten Staaten	= the USA
	the United Kingdom ['kɪŋdəm]	das Vereinigte Königreich	= England, Scotland, Wales and Northern Ireland
	island ['aɪlənd]	Insel	Sylt is a German ~.
	around [ə'raʊnd]	um (... herum)	
	(to) tell [tel]	sagen; erzählen	~ your partner your address and phone number.
	What about you? ['wɒt əbaʊt]	Und Sie? Und wie ist es mit Ihnen?	I'm from the USA. ~? - I'm from Germany.
F	talking about quantities ['kwɒntətɪ]	über Mengen/Quantitäten sprechen	
F1	true [truː]	richtig; wahr	= right
	false [fɔːls]	falsch	<—> true
	book [bʊk]	Buch	*Colours* is an English ~.
	in the picture ['pɪktʃə]	auf dem Bild	There are three people ~ on page 15.
	there is [ðeər ɪz]	es gibt	~ a quiz on page 20.
	flight attendant ['flaɪt ətendənt]	Flugbegleiter(in)	
	newspaper ['njuːspeɪpə]	Zeitung	*Die Zeit* and *Süddeutsche Zeitung* are ~s.
	handbag ['hændbæg]	Handtasche	My address book is in my ~.
	man, men [mæn, men]	Mann, Männer	There is one ~ in the photo on page 21.
	woman, women ['wʊmən, 'wɪmɪn]	Frau, Frauen	<—> man, men
	child, children [tʃaɪld, 'tʃɪldrən]	Kind, Kinder	My ~ are 4 and 6. I'm 39.
F2	American [ə'merɪkən]	amerikanisch; Amerikaner/in	He's from the USA. He's ~.
	here [hɪə]	hier	
	Excuse me. [ɪk'skjuːz]	Entschuldigen Sie. Entschuldigung.	~. What's your name?

	seat [siːt]	(Sitz-)Platz	23C? I think this is my ~.
	you're right [raɪt]	Sie haben recht	Is she German? - Yes, she is. ~.
	OK [əʊˈkeɪ]	in Ordnung	
	no problem [ˈprɒbləm]	kein Problem	
	Philadelphia [fɪləˈdelfjə]	(Großstadt im Bundesstaat Pennsylvania)	
	really [ˈrɪəlɪ]	wirklich	My name is Brüseke, too. - Oh, ~?
	It's a small world. [smɔːl wɜːld]	Die Welt ist doch klein.	
	Washington [ˈwɒʃɪŋtən]	(Bundeshauptstadt der USA)	
	just [dʒʌst]	nur; bloß; einfach	= only
	dog [dɒg]	Hund	
	Sam [sæm]	(Name)	
F3	cat [kæt]	Katze	<—> dog
F4	Find someone who … [ˈfaɪnd sʌmwʌn]	Finden Sie jemanden, der …	
	relative [ˈrelətɪv]	Verwandte(r)	The members of your family are your ~s.
	English-speaking [ˈɪŋglɪʃ spiːkɪŋ]	englischsprechend	I have an ~ friend. She's from the USA.
	cousin [ˈkʌzn]	Vetter, Cousine	My mother's sister's daughter is my ~!
	young, younger [jʌŋ, ˈjʌŋgə]	jung, jünger	<—> old
	boy [bɔɪ]	Junge	<—> girl
FU1	computer [kəmˈpjuːtə]	Computer	
	baby [ˈbeɪbɪ]	Baby	
	Read the list to a partner. [riːd]	Lesen Sie die Liste einem Partner/einer Partnerin vor.	
	each [iːtʃ]	jede(r/s) [einzeln]	~ person in the class can ask one question.
	pair [peə]	Paar	= two
	(to) tick [tɪk]	abhaken	Please ~ the right answer.
FU2	block [blɒk]	Block, Klotz, Klötzchen	
	pile [paɪl]	Stoß, Stapel	There is a ~ of old newspapers in my office.
FU3	(to) use [juːz]	benutzen, gebrauchen, verwenden	~ the word "please" in your sentence.
	Find out as much as you can. [əz ˈmʌtʃ ez]	Finden Sie soviel heraus, wie Sie können.	
	some [sʌm]	manche, einige	~ people have got blue eyes, ~ people have got brown eyes.
	idea [aɪˈdɪə]	Idee	What can I say? I haven't got any ~.
	big [bɪg]	groß	They've got 8 children. They've got a ~ family.
	small [smɔːl]	klein	<—> big
FU5	photo [ˈfəʊtəʊ]	Foto	
	different [ˈdɪfrənt]	andere(r/s); verschieden; anders	She and her brother are very ~.
	(to) write [rɒɪt]	schreiben	
SF	minute [ˈmɪnɪt]	Minute	
	second [ˈsekənd]	Sekunde	Sixty ~s are one minute.
	hour [ˈaʊə]	Stunde	Sixty minutes are one ~.
	day [deɪ]	Tag	Twenty-four hours are one ~.
	month [mʌnθ]	Monat	Four weeks are one ~.
	year [jɪə]	Jahr	Twelve months are one ~.
	What time is it? [wɒt ˈtaɪm]	Wie spät ist es? Wieviel Uhr ist es?	
	three o'clock [əˈklɒk]	drei Uhr	What time is it? - It's ~.
	a quarter past [ˈkwɔːtəˈpɑːst]	Viertel nach	3.15 = ~ three
	half past three [ˈhɑːf pɑːst]	halb vier	3.30 = ~
	a quarter to [ˈkwɔːtəˈtʊ]	Viertel vor	3.45 = ~ four
	almost [ˈɔːlməʊst]	fast, beinahe	3.58 is ~ 4 o'clock.
	to [tʊ]	vor	3.50 = ten minutes ~ four
	past [pɑːst]	nach	4.10 = ten minutes ~ four
	am [eɪ ˈem]	nachts, morgens, vormittags (zwischen 00.01 und 12.00 Uhr)	Good morning. It's 8 ~, sir.
	pm [piː ˈem]	nachmittags, abends, nachts (zwischen 12.01 und 24.00 Uhr)	<—> am
	Monday [ˈmʌndɪ]	Montag	The first day in the week is ~.
	Tuesday [ˈtjuːzdɪ]	Dienstag	The next day in the week is ~.
	Wednesday [ˈwenzdɪ]	Mittwoch	Monday, Tuesday, ~
	Thursday [ˈθɜːzdɪ]	Donnerstag	Tuesday, Wednesday, ~
	Friday [ˈfraɪdɪ]	Freitag	Wednesday, Thursday, ~
	Saturday [ˈsætədɪ]	Samstag, Sonnabend	I'm not at work on ~.

	Sunday ['sʌndɪ]	Sonntag	Saturday, ~, Monday
	on Monday	am Montag	My flight to New York is ~.
	at the weekend [wiːk'end]	am Wochenende	I'm at home ~.
	from 8 till 5 [frəm ... tɪl]	von 8 bis 5	I'm at work ~ 8 o'clock ~ 5 o'clock.
	from Monday to Friday	von Montag bis Freitag	I'm at work ~, but not at the weekend.
SF1	clock [klɒk]	(Wand-)Uhr	
	train to London ['lʌndən]	Zug nach London	
	at twenty-five past eleven [ət]	um fünf vor halb zwölf	The next train is ~.
	film [fɪlm]	Film	
	tonight [tə'naɪt]	heute abend, heute nacht	The party is at 8 o'clock ~.
SF3	correct [kə'rekt]	korrekt, richtig	= right
	open ['əʊpən]	offen; geöffnet	The supermarket is ~ from 8 am till 8pm.
	zoo [zuː]	Zoo	
	museum [mjuː'zɪəm]	Museum	

Unit 4

T	What do you do?	Was machen Sie beruflich?	~? - I'm a computer specialist.
FW	job [dʒɒb]	Arbeit(sstelle)	What's your ~? - I'm a computer specialist.
FW1	doctor ['dɒktə]	Arzt/Ärztin	
	policewoman [pə'liːswʊmən]	Polizistin	
	gardener ['gɑːdnə]	Gärtner/Gärtnerin	
	workman ['wɜːkmən]	Handwerker	
	teacher ['tiːtʃə]	Lehrer/Lehrerin	She's an English ~ at Ohlerath school.
	reporter [rɪ'pɔːtə]	Reporter/Reporterin	He's a ~ for a big newspaper.
	secretary ['sekrətrɪ]	Sekretär/Sekretärin	She's the boss. I'm her ~.
	shop assistant ['ʃɒp əsɪstənt]	Verkäufer/Verkäuferin	I'm a ~ at Kaufhof.
FW2	at the top [tɒp]	oben	The name Abbot is ~ of the list.
	on the left [left]	links	When you look at a clock, the numbers 7-11 are ~.
	in the middle ['mɪdl]	in der Mitte	Kassel is ~ of Germany.
	on the right [raɪt]	rechts	<—> on the left
	at the bottom ['bɒtəm]	unten	<—> at the top; The name Zwemmer is ~ of the list.
	next to [nekst]	neben	On a clock 1 is ~ 12.
	can't [kɑːnt]	kann nicht	I ~ see Ann. Where is she?
	her [hɜː]	sie; ihr	Where's Ann? Can you see ~?
F	routine [ruː'tiːn]	Routine; (Tages-)Ablauf	
F1	party ['pɑːtɪ]	Party	
	Alice ['ælɪs]	(Name)	
	Diana [daɪ'ænə]	(Name)	
	Patrick ['pætrɪk]	(Name)	
	Sharon ['ʃærən]	(Name)	
	Kane [keɪn]	(Name)	
	Ireland ['aɪələnd]	Irland	
	(to) work, works [wɜːk, wɜːks]	arbeiten, arbeitet	I ~ from 8 till 5 in an office.
	there [ðeə]	dort; da	<—> here
	I'm a gardener.	Ich bin Gärtner.	
	outside [aʊt'saɪd]	draußen	Gardeners work ~, not in an office.
	was [wɒz]	war	
	housewife ['haʊswaɪf]	Hausfrau	I work at home, I'm a ~.
	full-time ['fʊltaɪm]	Vollzeit-; vollzeit	I work 40 hours each week: I work ~.
	You can say that again!	Das können Sie nochmal laut sagen!	
F3	Where do they work?	Wo arbeiten sie?	
	hospital ['hɒspɪtl]	Krankenhaus	Some doctors work in a ~.
	factory ['fæktərɪ]	Fabrik	A ~ is a place where people make things.
	shop [ʃɒp]	Laden, Geschäft	You can buy film in a camera ~.
	restaurant ['restrɒnt]	Restaurant; Gaststätte	
F5	Put these activities in order. [pʊt ɪn 'ɔːdə]	Bringen Sie diese Tätigkeiten in die richtige Reihenfolge.	
	(to) start work [stɑːt]	anfangen zu arbeiten	When do you ~? - At 7.30.

	(to) finish work ['fınıʃ]	aufhören zu arbeiten	I ~ at 4 o'clock.
	(to) go to bed [bed]	ins Bett gehen	I ~ at 11 pm.
	(to) get up [get ˈʌp]	aufstehen	I ~ at 5.30 am.
	(to) have a shower [ˈʃaʊə]	(sich) duschen, eine Dusche nehmen	
	(to) have breakfast ['brekfəst]	frühstücken	I ~ - cornflakes, coffee, toast - at 7 am.
	first [fɜːst]	zuerst	
	then [ðen]	dann; damals	<—> now
	after that [ˈɑːftə]	danach	= then
F6	typical [ˈtɪpɪkl]	typisch	A ~ English name is Smith.
	working day [ˈwɜːkɪŋ deɪ]	Arbeitstag	I work from 8 till 4.30. = My ~ is from 8 till 4.30.
	never ['nevə]	nie, niemals	I ~ get up at 1.30 am.
	a cup of coffee [ˈkɒfɪ]	eine Tasse Kaffee	
	usually [ˈjuːʒəlɪ]	(für) gewöhnlich, normalerweise	On Monday to Thursday I work from 8 till 4. = I ~ work from 8 till 4.
	always [ˈɔːlweɪz]	immer	<—> never
	(to) have a coffee break [ˈkɒfɪ breɪk]	eine Kaffeepause machen	I usually ~ at 10.30 and at 2.30.
	(to) have lunch [lʌntʃ]	(zu) Mittag essen	You have breakfast at 7, but when do you ~? - At 12.30.
	sometimes [ˈsʌmtaɪmz]	manchmal	I usually finish work at 4, but ~ I finish at 3.
	often [ˈɒfn]	oft, häufig	always, ~, sometimes, never
	(to) go shopping [ˈʃɒpɪŋ]	einkaufen, einkaufen gehen	I ~ in the supermarket in Green Street.
F7	give them to a partner [gɪv]	geben Sie sie einem Partner/einer Partnerin	
	(to) correct [kəˈrekt]	korrigieren	~ the false sentences. = Make the false sentences right.
FU1	Who does what?	Wer macht was?	
	talks to people	spricht mit Menschen/Leuten	A reporter often ~ in his or her job.
	(to) help [help]	helfen	I can't do this exercise. Can you ~ me, please?
	letter [ˈletə]	Brief	There's a ~ from your cousin in America.
	(to) cook [kʊk]	kochen	Can your husband ~? - Yes, omelettes and pizzas.
	(to) clean [kliːn]	putzen, saubermachen	
	thing [θɪŋ]	Ding, Sache	<—> person
	(to) repair [rɪˈpeə]	reparieren	
FU2	him [hɪm]	ihm; ihn	Tony is new here. Tell ~ where his office is.
FU3	When does ... do these things?	Wann macht ... diese Dinge?	
	housework [ˈhaʊswɜːk]	Hausarbeit(en)	A housewife works at home and does ~.
	(to) go to dance class [ˈdɑːns klɑːs]	zur Tanzstunde/zum Tanzkurs gehen	I ~ on Wednesday afternoon.
	dinner [ˈdɪnə]	Abendessen	breakfast, lunch, ~
SF	milk [mɪlk]	Milch	cornflakes with ~, coffee with ~
	muesli [ˈmjuːzlɪ]	Müsli	Breakfast is ~ and a cup of coffee.
	toast [təʊst]	Toast	
	ham [hæm]	Schinken	
	cornflakes [ˈkɔːnfleɪks]	Cornflakes	
	butter [ˈbʌtə]	Butter	You make ~ from milk.
	yoghurt [ˈjɒgət]	Joghurt	
	jam [dʒæm]	Marmelade	
	egg [eg]	Ei	
	tea [tiː]	Tee	~ or coffee?
	honey [ˈhʌnɪ]	Honig	
	roll [rəʊl]	Brötchen	Breakfast is ~ and butter and jam.
	cheese [tʃiːz]	Käse	You make butter and ~ from milk.
	bread [bred]	Brot	Rolls are ~ in a different form.
	fruit [fruːt]	Obst	Bananas are a sort of ~.
	sausage [ˈsɒsɪdʒ]	Wurst, Würstchen	bread and butter and cheese and ~
	juice [dʒuːs]	Saft	orange ~, fruit ~
SF1	what they have for breakfast	was sie zum Frühstück essen	
	weekday [ˈwiːkdeɪ]	Wochentag	Monday is a ~, but Sunday isn't a ~.
	table [ˈteɪbl]	Tisch	Breakfast is on the ~.

Unit 5

T	Do you like flying? [ˈflaɪɪŋ]	Fliegen Sie gern?	
FW1	reading [ˈriːdɪŋ]	Lesen	What's your hobby? ~, or sport, or ...?
	watching TV [ˈwɒtʃɪŋ]	Fernsehen	I like ~ in the evening.
	gardening [ˈgɑːdnɪŋ]	Gärtnern, Gartenarbeit	I often work in the garden. ~ is my hobby.
	swimming [ˈswɪmɪŋ]	Schwimmen	
	cycling [ˈsaɪklɪŋ]	Radfahren	
	playing tennis [pleɪŋ ˈtenɪs]	Tennisspielen	
	hiking [ˈhaɪkɪŋ]	Wandern	We really like ~ in the Alps.
	going to the cinema [ˈsɪnəmə]	ins Kino gehen	I like ~ and seeing new films.
	going to the theatre/concerts [ˈθɪətə/ˈkɒnsɜːts]	ins Theater/in Konzerte gehen	
	travelling [ˈtrævlɪŋ]	Reisen	Do you go to many different countries? Do you like ~?
	relaxing [rɪˈlæksɪŋ]	sich entspannen, sich erholen	I like ~ at the weekend.
FW2	I don't like gardening. [dəʊnt]	Ich mag Gärtnern/Gartenarbeit nicht.	Gardening isn't nice. ~.
F1	Yes, I do.	Ja (ich mag es).	Do you like yoghurt? - ~. It's very nice.
	No, I don't.	Nein (ich mag es nicht).	Do you like gardening? - ~.
F2	(he/she) doesn't like it [ˈdʌznt]	(er/sie) mag es nicht	
	football [ˈfʊtbɔːl]	Fußball	Bayern München and Borussia Dortmund are two ~ clubs.
	squash [skwɒʃ]	Squash	I play ~, not tennis.
	(to) eat [iːt]	essen	I ~ a sandwich and have a cup of coffee with it.
	by train [baɪ ˈtreɪn]	mit dem Zug	I travel to work ~.
	hobby [ˈhɒbɪ]	Hobby	
	I hate swimming. [heɪt]	Ich schwimme ungern/nicht gern. Ich hasse Schwimmen.	
F4	A reporter is interviewing people. [ˈɪntəvjuːɪŋ]	Eine Reporterin interviewt (gerade) Leute.	
	he wants to know [nəʊ]	er will wissen	
	(to) want to [wɒnt]	wollen	Who's that nice person? - Do you ~ meet her?
	(to) know	wissen; kennen	What's the English word for "Kolben"? - Sorry, I don't ~.
	answer [ˈɑːnsə]	Antwort	This is the question. What is the ~?
	Does your neighbour like flying?	Fliegt Ihr Nachbar/Ihre Nachbarin gern?	
	I don't mind. [maɪnd]	Ich habe nichts dagegen. Mir ist es egal.	I don't really like gardening, but ~ it.
F5	trip [trɪp]	Reise	How long is the ~ from here to London? - Ten hours.
	why [waɪ]	warum	I don't like going to the theatre. - Oh really? ~?
	the flight takes an hour [flaɪt teɪks]	der Flug dauert eine Stunde	How long is the flight to London? - ~
	panic [ˈpænɪk]	Panik	
	for [fɔː]	für	This book is ~ you. - Oh, thank you.
	me [miː]	mich	I know the answer. Ask ~.
	you [juː]	dich/dir; euch; Sie/Ihnen	You like him and he likes ~.
	all day [ɔːl ˈdeɪ]	den ganzen Tag	= the morning, afternoon and evening
	all	all/alle	I like the film, Susanne likes it, Frank likes it - we ~ like it.
	(to) sleep [sliːp]	schlafen	I go to bed at 11 and ~ till 6.
	(to) listen to music [ˈlɪsn tə ˈmjuːzɪk]	Musik hören	When you relax, you can read or watch TV or ~.
	on the plane [pleɪn]	im Flugzeug	On that flight they give you breakfast ~.
F6	long [lɒŋ]	lange	The flight doesn't take ~ - only one hour.
F7	(to) smoke [sməʊk]	rauchen	He ~s cigars, not cigarettes.
	(to) have a drink [drɪŋk]	etwas trinken	<—> I don't eat breakfast, but I ~.
	drink	Getränk	Tea, coffee, milk are all ~s.
FU1	well [wel]	gut	I know London ~. I often go there.
	discuss ... how your teacher will answer [dɪsˈkʌs]	besprechen Sie, wie Ihr Kursleiter/Ihre Kursleiterin antworten wird	
	(to) write down [raɪt ˈdaʊn]	aufschreiben	Can I ~ your address, please?
	(to) drive [draɪv]	(Auto) fahren	I ~ to work. I don't go by train.
	too fast [fɑːst]	zu schnell	
	a lot of [lɒt]	viel, viele	= much, many
	sweets [swiːts]	Süßigkeiten	

	(to) exercise ['eksəsaız]	Bewegung haben, Sport machen	Do you ~? - Yes, I play tennis and I swim.
	(to) take [teık]	nehmen; hinbringen	I have a shower. = I ~ a shower.
	public transport [pʌblık 'trænspɔːt]	öffentliche Verkehrsmittel	He doesn't drive, he takes ~.
	(to) go to parties	auf Partys gehen	Do you like ~ing ~?
	(to) get angry [get 'æŋgrı]	zornig/ärgerlich werden	I ~ when people drive too fast in streets where children play.
	(to) keep a secret ['siːkrıt]	ein Geheimnis bewahren	Jimmie can't ~. He always tells someone.
	(to) keep [kiːp]	behalten; (auf-)bewahren	Where do you ~ your coffee?
	instrument ['ınstrʊmənt]	Instrument	The piano, the trumpet or the guitar are ~s.
SF	bank [bæŋk]	Bank, Sparkasse	Deutsche Bank, Volksbank, Commerzbank are three German ~s.
	post office ['pəʊst ɒfıs]	Postamt	Can you take this letter to the ~ for me, please?
	chemist ['kemıst]	Apotheke; Drogerie	The ~ has aspirin.
	supermarket ['suːpəmɑːkıt]	Supermarkt	
	station ['steıʃn]	Bahnhof; Station	Can you take me to the ~? My train is in 20 minutes.
	travel agency ['trævl eıdʒənsı]	Reisebüro	The ticket for my flight is at the ~.
	toilet ['tɔılıt]	Toilette	
	boutique [buːˈtiːk]	Boutique	
SF1	(to) change money [tʃeındʒ 'mʌnı]	Geld wechseln	You can ~ at a bank.
	(to) buy [baı]	kaufen, erwerben	You can ~ aspirin at the chemist.
	food [fuːd]	Essen, Nahrung(smittel)	Bread, rolls, yoghurt and ham are all ~.
	medicine ['medsın]	Medizin	Aspirin is ~.
	(to) stay overnight [əʊvə'naıt]	über Nacht bleiben, übernachten	We can ~ at the George Hotel.
	T-shirt ['tiː ʃɜːt]	T-shirt	
	jeans [dʒiːnz]	Jeans	

Unit 6

	I'm looking for ['lʊkıŋ fə]	ich suche	~ a bank. - There's one on the left next to the post office.
FW	under ['ʌndə]	unter	not on the table, but ~ the table
	house [haʊs]	Haus	They live in a big ~ with a nice garden.
	at the door [dɔː]	an der Tür	There's someone ~. Can you go and open it, please.
	on [ɒn]	auf	Look at the quiz ~ page 20.
	between [bı'twiːn]	zwischen	Tuesday is ~ Monday and Wednesday.
	behind [bı'haınd]	hinter	My office is ~ that door.
	in front of [frʌnt]	vor	<—> behind
	opposite ['ɒpəzıt]	gegenüber	House number 2 is next to house number 4. They are ~ house number 3.
FW1	What is he saying?	Was sagt er (gerade)?	I can't hear him. ~?
	over there [əʊvəˈðeə]	da/dort drüben	not here, but ~
	on the corner ['kɔːnə]	an der Ecke	The hotel is ~ of George Street and Green Street.
	straight on [streıt]	geradeaus	The station is ~, at the other end of this street.
FW2	is thinking of an object ['ɒbdʒekt]	denkt (gerade) an einen Gegenstand	
	classroom ['klɑːsruːm]	Klassenraum/-zimmer	This is the ~ where our English class meets.
F	asking the way [weı]	nach dem Weg fragen	
F1	tourist ['tʊərıst]	Tourist/in	There are a lot of ~s in London in the summer.
	tourist information center ['sentə]	Fremdenverkehrsamt/-büro/-zentrale	You want some information about this town? Why don't you go to the ~?
	passer-by [pɑːsə 'baı]	Passant/in	
	on 42nd Street	an/in der 42. Straße	
	Times Square ['taımz 'skweə]	(berühmter Platz in New York)	
	map [mæp]	(Land-)Karte, (Stadt-)Plan	I can't find this street on our ~.
	(to) stand [stænd]	stehen	I can see him. He's ~ing on the corner of the next street.
	down [daʊn]	hinunter, herunter	Go ~ Green Street, and the bank is on the left.
	(to) turn right [tɜːn 'raıt]	nach rechts abbiegen	Go down here and ~ at the next corner.
	Grand Street ['grænd striːt]	(Straßenname)	
	subway ['sʌbweı]	U-Bahn	

	which line? [wɪtʃ 'laɪn]	welche Linie?	~? The blue line, or the orange line?
	going uptown ['ʌptaʊn]	der nach Manhattan fährt	
	orange ['ɒrɪndʒ]	orange	
	(to) change [tʃeɪndʒ]	umsteigen	Take this train, then ~ in Frankfurt to the ICE.
	Washington Square [skweə]	(Platz in New York City)	
	(to) get off [get 'ɒf]	aussteigen (aus)	Take the subway from here and ~ at 42nd Street.
	at 42nd Street	an der 42. Straße	
	one block east [wʌn blɒk 'i:st]	eine Straße/ein Häuserblock nach Osten	The tourist information center is ~.
	north [nɔ:θ]	(nach) Norden	Hamburg is in the ~ of Germany.
	south [saʊθ]	(nach) Süden	<—> north
	west [west]	(nach) Westen	<—> east
F2	on foot [ɒn 'fʊt]	zu Fuß	I don't drive to work, and I don't go by train. I go ~.
	foot, feet [fʊt, fi:t]	Fuß, Füße	He's a tall man with very big ~.
	directly [dɪ'rektlɪ]	direkt	The subway takes you ~ to your hotel.
F3	(to) mark [ma:k]	markieren, kennzeichnen	
	route [ru:t]	Route, Weg	= way
	stop [stɒp]	Haltestelle	Get off at the next stop.
F4	up [ʌp]	hinauf, herauf	<—> down
	(to) stop [stɒp]	(an-)halten	<—> start; = finish
	(to) get on [get 'ɒn]	einsteigen (in)	<—> get off
F5	interesting ['ɪntrəstɪŋ]	interessant	It's a super museum. They've got a lot of ~ things.
	best [best]	am besten	
	by car [ka:]	mit dem Auto	drive to work = go to work ~
	by bus [bʌs]	mit dem Bus	by car, by train, by subway, ~
	by bicycle ['baɪsɪkl]	mit dem Fahrrad	I don't drive and I don't use public transport. I go ~ or on foot.
F6	giving directions [dɪ'rekʃnz]	Wegbeschreibungen geben	A tourist asks the way. A passer-by gives ~.
	nearest ['nɪərest]	nächste(r/s)	The ~ bank is in this street.
	in Oxford Street ['ɒksfəd stri:t]	in der Oxford Street	
	(to) pass [pa:s]	passieren; vorbeigehen/-fahren (an)	You ~ a bank on the left. The hotel is then on the right.
F7	Midland Bank ['mɪdlənd 'bæŋk]	(Name einer Bank)	
	Parkview Hotel ['pa:kvju: həʊ'tel]	(Name eines Hotels)	
F8	(to) ask for [ɑ:sk fə]	bitten um	I can't do this exercise. I must ~ one of the other students ~ help.
	bookshop ['bʊkʃɒp]	Buchhandlung, -laden	a shop where you can buy books
	car park ['ka: pa:k]	Parkplatz	The ~ is full. Where can we park the car now?
FU1	(to) laugh [la:f]	lachen	The film is so funny. They're all ~ing.
	(to) speak [spi:k]	sprechen	I can ~ English, but I can't ~ Italian.
	French [frentʃ]	Französisch; französisch	Alain speaks ~. He's ~, from Paris.
	(to) ring [rɪŋ]	klingeln, läuten	The telephone is ~ing.
	situation [sɪtjʊ'eɪʃn]	Situation	
FU3	(to) mime [maɪm]	mimen	Can you ~ what a teacher or doctor does?
	action ['ækʃn]	Bewegung, Handlung	
SF	colour ['kʌlə]	Farbe	Blue and brown are two ~s.
	pink [pɪŋk]	pink	
	green [gri:n]	grün	Grass is ~.
	purple ['pɜ:pl]	violett, purpur	
	red [red]	rot	
	white [waɪt]	weiß	The British and American flags are red, ~ and blue.
	black [blæk]	schwarz	<—> white
	light blue [laɪt blu:]	hellblau	not dark blue, but ~ blue
	yellow ['jeləʊ]	gelb	You can find the telephone number on the ~ pages.
	beige [beɪʒ]	beige	a very light brown
SF1	parked [pa:kt]	geparkt	Is your car ~ in the car park?
	garage ['gæra:ʒ]	Garage	The car isn't outside, it's in the ~.
	tree [tri:]	Baum	

	tree [tri:]	Baum	
	pavement ['peɪvmənt]	Bürgersteig	You can't park on the ~! Park in the street!
SF2	favourite ['feɪvərɪt]	Lieblings-	I really like blue. It's my ~ colour.
	Which way to Lexington Avenue?	Wie komme ich zur Lexington Straße?	

Unit 7

T	We're moving [wɜ:ə 'mu:vɪŋ]	Wir ziehen um.	
FW	home [həʊm]	Zuhause, Heim, Haus, Wohnung	Houses, but not offices, are ~s.
FW1	the pictures above [ə'bʌv]	die Fotos oben	= the photos at the top of the page
	building ['bɪldɪŋ]	Gebäude	Houses, hotels and theatres are all ~s.
	bed-sitter ['bedsɪtə]	Einzimmerwohnung	I'm only one person so I don't want a house, just a ~.
	terraced house ['terəst haʊs]	Reihenhaus	
	attached [ə'tætʃt]	verbunden, verknüpft, angeschlossen	
	flat [flæt]	Wohnung	A bedsitter is a small ~.
	group [gru:p]	Gruppe	not just a pair, but a small ~
	including [ɪn'klu:dɪŋ]	einschließlich	= with
	kitchen ['kɪtʃɪn]	Küche	The ~ is where you cook in your home.
	bathroom ['ba:θru:m]	Bad(ezimmer)	The ~ is where you have a shower.
	block of flats [blɒk əv 'flæts]	Mietshaus, Wohnblock	A big building with a lot of flats is a ~.
	bedroom ['bedru:m]	Schlafzimmer	The ~ is where you go to bed and sleep.
	dining room ['daɪnɪŋ ru:m]	Eßzimmer	The ~ is where you eat - when you don't eat in the kitchen.
	entrance ['entrəns]	Eingang	The ~ to a flat or house is where the door is.
	living room ['lɪvɪŋ ru:m]	Wohnzimmer	The ~ in a flat or house is where the sofa and TV usually are.
	balcony ['bælkənɪ]	Balkon	Our flat has a ~, so we can eat outside sometimes.
FW2	modern ['mɒdə(r)n]	modern	= new; <—> old
	bright [braɪt]	hell	<—> dark; = light
	quiet ['kwaɪət]	ruhig, still	It's a ~ street - there aren't many cars.
	noisy ['nɔɪzɪ]	laut, lärmend	<—> quiet
	lift [lɪft]	Aufzug	It's a very tall building, so there's a ~.
FW3	cheap [tʃi:p]	preisgünstig, billig	not a lot of money
	expensive [ɪk'spensɪv]	teuer	<—> cheap
F	invitation [ɪnvɪ'teɪʃn]	Einladung	This letter is an ~ to Phil's party.
	plan [plæn]	Plan, Vorhaben	
F1	I'm busy. ['bɪzɪ]	Ich bin beschäftigt. Ich habe viel zu tun.	Can you help me? - Sorry, ~. I have a lot to do.
	(to) pack [pæk]	packen	She's ~ing. She's flying to New York at six o'clock!
	tomorrow [tə'mɒrəʊ]	morgen	It's Wednesday. ~ is Thursday.
	(to) move [mu:v]	umziehen	We are ~ing to our new house next week.
	upstairs [ʌp'steəz]	nach oben; oben	In a house the bedrooms are usually ~.
	bigger ['bɪgə]	größere(r/s)	I'm 1 metre 70, but Tony's ~. He's 1 metre 80.
	listen	hör mal	
	because [bɪ'kɒz]	weil	We want a bigger flat ~ we're having a baby.
	We're having some friends over for dinner.	Wir laden einige Freunde zum Abendessen ein.	It's not a party, but ~.
	Are you doing anything? ['enɪθɪŋ]	Habt ihr etwas vor?	Have you got plans for tonight? = ~ tonight?
	I'm afraid we are. [ə'freɪd]	Leider ja.	
	Simon is coming over. ['saɪmən]	Simon kommt vorbei.	
	(to) paint [peɪnt]	malen, anstreichen	We're ~ing our new flat first.
	next time	nächstes Mal	when we do it again = when we do it ~
F3	statement ['steɪtmənt]	Aussage(satz)	= sentence
	must [mʌst]	müssen	We ~ find a new flat - this flat is much too small.
F5	Making plans	Pläne machen	
	Who can give us a hand? [hænd]	Wer kann helfen/mit zugreifen?	= Who can help?
	let's see [lets]	laß mal sehen	~, what's the time now?
	at the moment ['məʊmənt]	im Moment, im Augenblick	= now
	Stephen's got a bad back. ['sti:vn]	Stephen hat's am Rücken.	

	at this time of year [jɪə]	zu dieser Jahreszeit	The tourist information centre isn't open ~, only in the summer.
	help [help]	Hilfe	
	perhaps [pə'hæps]	vielleicht, eventuell	She can't come on Monday. ~ she can come on Tuesday.
	(to) bring [brɪŋ]	bringen	Perhaps Cliff can come with him. = Perhaps he can ~ Cliff.
	(to) visit [vɪzɪt]	besuchen; zu Besuch sein	I always ~ my cousin when I'm in London.
	(to) get married ['mærɪd]	heiraten; sich verheiraten	She's ~ting ~ again. Her new husband is a man from Oxford.
	soon [suːn]	bald	not tomorrow, not next week, but ~
	wedding ['wedɪŋ]	Hochzeit	A ~ is when people get married.
F8	excuse [ɪk'skjuːs]	Ausrede	"I haven't got time" or "I'm very busy" is often just an ~ because someone doesn't want to do something.
FU1	Spain [speɪn]	Spanien	Madrid is in ~.
	on business ['bɪznɪs]	geschäftlich	He's in Spain ~. = He's working in Spain.
FU2	(to) go on holiday ['hɒlədeɪ]	in Urlaub/Ferien gehen/fahren	People usually ~ to Spain ~, not on business.
FU4	(to) eat out [iːt 'aʊt]	essen gehen	= to eat in a restaurant, not at home
	spaghetti [spə'getɪ]	Spaghetti	In Italy people eat a lot of ~.
	game show ['ɡeɪm ʃəʊ]	Spielshow	
	(to) go jogging ['dʒɒɡɪŋ]	joggen gehen	Do you exercise? - Yes, I ~.
	(to) go hiking ['haɪkɪŋ]	wandern gehen	I like hiking. I ~ in the Alps sometimes.
	(to) have a party ['pɑːtɪ]	eine Party feiern	Ellen and Nick are ~ing ~ in their new flat for all their friends.
SF	date [deɪt]	Datum	
SF1	second ['sekənd]	zweite(r/s)	Green Street is not the first street, but the ~ street.
	third [θɜːd]	dritte(r/s)	The next street after Green Street is the ~ street.
	the third of November [nəʊ'vembə]	der dritte November	
	November the third	der dritte November	
	January ['dʒænjʊərɪ]	Januar	
	February ['februərɪ]	Februar	
	March [mɑːtʃ]	März	
	April ['eɪprəl]	April	
	May [meɪ]	Mai	
	June [dʒuːn]	Juni	
	July [dʒuː'laɪ]	Juli	
	August ['ɔːɡəst]	August	
	September [sep'tembə]	September	
	October [ɒk'təʊbə]	Oktober	
	November [nəʊ'vembə]	November	
	December [dɪ'sembə]	Dezember	
SF2	When is your birthday? ['bɜːθdeɪ]	Wann haben Sie Geburtstag?	~? - Tomorrow! Come to my party.
	at one end [end]	am einen Ende	A is ~ of the alphabet, Z is at the other.
	on 2nd January	am 2. Januar	
	in July	im Juli	
SF3	Easter ['iːstə]	Ostern	~ is when children eat a lot of chocolate eggs.
	beginning [bɪ'ɡɪnɪŋ]	Beginn, Anfang	<—> end
	school holidays ['skuːl 'hɒlədeɪz]	Schulferien	The ~ are the time when there is no school.
	wedding anniversary [ænɪ'vɜːsərɪ]	Hochzeitstag	Our wedding was on 29th December, so our ~ is on 29th December.
	fair [feə]	Kirmes	

Unit 8

T	I'll have the moussaka. [muːˈsɑːkə]	Ich nehme die Moussaka.	
FW1	beef [biːf]	Rind(fleisch)	
	cake [keɪk]	Kuchen	On my birthday I have coffee and ~ in the afternoon with all my relatives.
	carrot [ˈkærət]	Karotte, Möhre, Mohrrübe	
	chicken [ˈtʃɪkɪn]	Huhn, Hühnerfleisch	~s give eggs.
	ice cream [aɪsˈkriːm]	Eis, Eiskrem	Italian and American ~ is very good.
	pea [piː]	Erbse	*Leipziger Allerlei* is ~s and carrots and asparagus (Spargel).
	potato, potatoes [pəˈteɪtəʊ]	Kartoffel, Kartoffeln	
	prawn cocktail [ˈprɔːn ˈkɒkteɪl]	Krabbencocktail	You can often eat ~ as a starter in a restaurant.
	salad [ˈsæləd]	Salat	
	soup [suːp]	Suppe	potato ~, pea ~
	vegetable(s) [ˈvedʒtəbl]	Gemüse	Peas, carrots and potatoes are all ~.
	wine [waɪn]	Wein	Red ~ or white ~?
	some [sʌm]	etwas; einige	There are ~ letters for you.
	meat [miːt]	Fleisch	Chicken and beef are ~.
	not ... any [nɒt ... ˈenɪ]	kein, keine; keins	There is no ice cream. = There is ~ ice cream.
	any	(in Fragen:) (irgend)welche(r/s)	Are there ~ good hotels in this town?
FW2	starter [ˈstɑːtə]	Vorspeise	what you eat first for lunch or dinner
	main course [ˈmeɪn ˈkɔːs]	Hauptgericht	what you eat after the starter
	dessert [dɪˈsɜːt]	Nachtisch, Dessert	what you eat at the end of lunch or dinner
F	decision [dɪˈsɪʒn]	Entscheidung, Entschluß, Beschluß	What do we do now? We must make a ~.
	prediction [prɪˈdɪkʃn]	Vorhersage, Voraussage	
F1	grilled salmon [ˈgrɪld ˈsæmən]	gegrillter Lachs	
	fresh [freʃ]	frisch	This bread isn't ~, it's old.
	you had that last time [hæd]	das hattest du letztes Mal	
	So? [səʊ]	(Na) Und?	
	(to) try [traɪ]	probieren; versuchen	~ this wine. It's really good.
	anything new [ˈenɪθɪŋ]	etwas Neues	You always have moussaka. Don't you want to try ~?
	not ... anything	nichts	We have ~ got - no bread, no butter, no milk.
	No, you won't (= will not). [wəʊnt]	Nein, das wirst du nicht.	I'll have some of your wine. - ~!
	What would you like to drink? [wʊd laɪk]	Was möchtest du trinken?	~? Tea? Coffee? Wine? Juice?
	a glass of white wine [glɑːs]	ein Glas Weißwein	~, or a glass of red wine?
	Me, too.	Ich auch.	I'll have salmon. - ~.
F3	tomato [təˈmɑːtəʊ]	Tomate	You eat ~s in a salad. They're red.
	melon [ˈmelən]	Melone	~s are yellow or green. You can eat yellow ~s with ham as a starter.
	roast beef [ˈrəʊst ˈbiːf]	Rinderbraten	
	sole [səʊl]	Seezunge	
	salad platter [ˈsæləd plætə]	Salatteller	a big salad = a ~
	side salad [ˈsaɪd sæləd]	Salat (als Beilage)	a small salad. You eat it with the main course.
	Italian [ɪˈtæljən]	italienisch; Italienisch	
	apple [ˈæpl]	Apfel	
	pie [paɪ]	Pie (= Pastete, Torte, gefüllter Kuchen)	Apple ~ is a typical English dessert.
F4	at a Chinese restaurant [tʃaɪˈniːz]	in einem chinesischen Restaurant	You can eat chop suey ~.
	Chinese	chinesisch; Chinesisch; Chinese/Chinesin	The Peking Dragon is a ~ restaurant.
	fortune cookie [ˈfɔːtʃuːn kʊki]	Glückskeks	In some Chinese restaurants they give you a ~ at the end of your dinner.
	you will live [lɪv]	du wirst leben	~ till you are 110!
	life [laɪf]	Leben	
	yours [jɔːz]	deine(r/s); Ihre(r/s); eure(r/s)	This is your book. It's ~.
	mine [maɪn]	meine(r/s)	<—> yours
	Let's swap. [swɒp]	Laßt uns tauschen.	~. = I'll give you mine and you give me yours.
	Shall we go? [ʃəl]	Sollen/Wollen wir gehen?	It's 11 pm. ~ home?
	waiter [ˈweɪtə]	Kellner; (Herr) Ober!	the man who brings your food in a restaurant
	bill [bɪl]	Rechnung	Dinner was expensive. The ~ is £63 for two.

VOCAB

F5	(to) exchange [ɪksˈtʃeɪndʒ]	aus-/ein-/umtauschen	= swap
F6	future [ˈfjuːtʃə]	Zukunft	the ~ = tomorrow, next week, next year
	(to) win [wɪn]	gewinnen; siegen	Borussia Dortmund will ~ 3-0!
	lots of [lɒts]	viel, viele	= a lot of
	(to) learn [lɜːn]	lernen	I'm ~ing English at the Volkshochschule.
	(to) be [biː]	sein	Where will I ~ at 3 a.m.? I'll ~ in bed!
FU1	for one minute	eine Minute lang	Look at the picture ~.
	not quite [kwaɪt]	nicht ganz	It's almost the same, but ~ the same.
	the same [seɪm]	der-, die-, dasselbe	You always eat moussaka. You always eat ~.
	difference [ˈdɪfrəns]	Unterschied	I'm bigger. That's the ~ between Gerd and me.
FU2	chain game [ˈtʃeɪn geɪm]	Kettenspiel, Reigen	
FU3	(to) get	besorgen, holen	When you go shopping, can you ~ some coffee, please?
	hot [hɒt]	heiß, warm	It's very ~ in the Sahara in the middle of the day.
	(to) open [ˈəʊpən]	öffnen, aufmachen	~ your books at page 40.
	window [ˈwɪndəʊ]	Fenster	From the ~ of my room I can see the bank opposite.
FU4	tired [ˈtaɪəd]	müde	Sometimes I watch TV till 2 a.m. I'm always ~ the next morning.
	cold [kəʊld]	kalt	<—> hot
	hungry [ˈhʌŋgrɪ]	hungrig	When is lunch? I'm very ~.
	bored [bɔːd]	gelangweilt	I'm ~. Have you got an interesting book for me?
	dirty [ˈdɜːtɪ]	dreckig, schmutzig	I'm very ~ after that work in the garden. I'll have a shower.
	thirsty [ˈθɜːstɪ]	durstig	<—> hungry
	(to) choose [tʃuːz]	wählen, auswählen	You can ~: I've got red wine and white wine.
	reaction [rɪˈækʃn]	Reaktion	What does he do? - His ~ is to laugh.
	pullover [ˈpʊləʊvə]	Pullover	
	something [ˈsʌmθɪŋ]	etwas	I'm hungry. I'd like ~ to eat.
	(to) go swimming	schwimmen gehen	It's so hot. Can we ~?
	hamburger [ˈhæmbɜːgə]	Hamburger	
FU5	(to) need [niːd]	brauchen, benötigen	For an omelette you ~ eggs and butter.
	reservation [rezəˈveɪʃən]	Reservierung	a hotel ~, a ticket ~
	ticket [ˈtɪkɪt]	Ticket, (Fahr-)Karte	How much is a ~ for the concert?
	guide (book) [gaɪd]	(Reise-)Führer	a book. It has information about a place.
	holiday flat [ˈhɒlədɪ flæt]	Ferienwohnung	a flat where you can stay on holiday
FU6	making suggestions [səˈdʒestʃən]	Vorschläge machen	
	phone for a pizza [ˈpiːtsə]	anrufen und eine Pizza kommen lassen	I'm hungry, but I don't want to eat out. Let's ~.
	bar [baː]	Bar	a place where you can drink alcohol
	(to) order [ˈɔːdə]	bestellen	Where's the waiter? I want to ~.
	a bottle of mineral water [ˈbɒtl]	eine Flasche Mineralwasser	I'm thirsty. Can I have ~, please?
	sandwich [ˈsænwɪdʒ]	belegtes Brot	a ham ~, a cheese ~
	(to) sit [sɪt]	sitzen	Let's ~ outside on the balcony and have our coffee.
SF1	customer [ˈkʌstəmə]	Kunde/Kundin	the person who buys something in a shop or restaurant
	waitress [ˈweɪtrɪs]	Kellnerin	<—> waiter; a woman who does the same job as a waiter
	Are you ready to order?	Haben Sie gewählt?	
	ready [ˈredɪ]	fertig, bereit	I'm ~ now. We can go.
	I'd like [aɪd laɪk]	ich möchte	~ the grilled salmon, please.
	could [kʊd]	könnte(n)	~ you say that again, please?
	menu [ˈmenjuː]	Speisekarte, Speiseplan	the list of food (and drinks) in a restaurant
	here you are	bitte schön (beim Überreichen von etwas)	This is your ticket. ~. - Thank you.
SF3	meal [miːl]	Essen, Mahlzeit	Breakfast, lunch and dinner are ~s.
S	negative statements [ˈnegətɪv]	verneinte Aussagesätze	= sentences with the word *not*

VOCAB

Unit 9

T	What did you do? [dɪd]	Was machten Sie? Was haben Sie gemacht?	
	yesterday ['jestədɪ]	gestern	Tomorrow is Tuesday. ~ was Sunday.
FW	past [pɑːst]	Vergangenheit; Vergangenheitsform	<—> present
FW1	have to [hæv tʊ]	müssen	= must
	made [meɪd]	Vergangenheit von *make*	I often make a pizza. I ~ one yesterday.
	took [tʊk]	Vergangenheit von *take*	I usually go on foot, but yesterday I ~ the car.
	went [went]	Vergangenheit von *go*	I go to bed late. Yesterday I ~ at 2.a.m.
	had to [hæd]	Vergangenheit von *have to*	I have to get up at 5. Yesterday I ~ get up at 4.30.
	worked [wɜːkt]	Vergangenheit von *work*	I don't usually work on Saturday, but I ~ last weekend.
FW2	caption ['kæpʃn]	Bildunterschrift, Legende	= the text under a photo
	cartoon [kɑːˈtuːn]	Cartoon, Karikatur	
	bowler (= bowler hat) ['bəʊlə]	Melone (Hut)	
	playgroup ['pleɪgruːp]	Spielgruppe	a place like a kindergarten
	What a day! ['wɒt ə]	Was für ein Tag!	
	(to) break [breɪk]	(zer)brechen, kaputtmachen, kaputtgehen	
	(to) break down [breɪk 'daʊn]	eine Panne haben	
	broke down [brəʊk]	Vergangenheit von *break down*	The car ~ and I had to go on foot.
	before [bɪˈfɔː]	bevor	~ you go, can you give me your address?
	us [ʌs]	uns	We like him and he likes ~.
	Mum [mʌm]	Mama, Mami, Mutti	Children say ~ to their mother.
	today [təˈdeɪ]	heute	yesterday, ~, tomorrow
	midnight ['mɪdnaɪt]	Mitternacht	12 o'clock in the night
F1	feeling ['fiːlɪŋ]	Gefühl, Empfindung	It's a nice ~ to know it is Friday afternoon.
	saw [sɔː]	Vergangenheit von *see*	I usually see Ann at work. I ~ her yesterday.
	was [wɒz]	Vergangenheit von *am* oder *is*	It's Tuesday today. Yesterday ~ Monday.
	late [leɪt]	spät; verspätet	I usually get up ~, at 9.30.
	got [gɒt]	Vergangenheit von *get*	I ~ on this train at 11.00. Now it's 11.30 and I'm almost in London.
	(to) get out of	aussteigen	(to) ~ bed = (to) get up
	out of	aus (... heraus)	Drive the car ~ the garage.
	which is something I hate [heɪt]	was etwas ist, das ich hasse	
	(to) stretch; stretched [stretʃ]	(sich) strecken; Vergangenheit von *stretch*	
	(to) yawn; yawned [jɔːn]	gähnen; Vergangenheit von *yawn*	Jimmie's ~ing. He must be tired.
	(to) scratch; scratched [skrætʃ]	kratzen; Vergangenheit von *scratch*	
	head [hed]	Kopf	the place where your eyes and hair are
	while [waɪl]	während	Have a cup of coffee ~ I go to the bookshop.
	little ['lɪtl]	klein	= small
	voice [vɔɪs]	Stimme	There are people here. I can hear ~s.
	told [təʊld]	Vergangenheit von *tell*	
	told me to go back [bæk]	sagte mir, daß ich zurückgehen sollte	
	(to) get dressed [drest]	sich anziehen	I get up, have a shower and ~. Then I have breakfast.
	mould [məʊld]	Schimmel	You can't eat that jam. There's ~ on it.
	flew [fluː]	Vergangenheit von *fly*	I often fly. I ~ last week.
	out (= out of) the door	zur Tür hinaus	
	(to) jump; jumped [dʒʌmp]	springen; Vergangenheit von *jump*	I ~ed over the gate.
	(to) wave; waved [weɪv]	winken; Vergangenheit von *wave*	When you go I'll ~ from the window.
	driver ['draɪvə]	Fahrer/in	the person who drives a bus or car
	he didn't wait [weɪt]	er wartete nicht	
	thought [θɔːt]	Vergangenheit von *think*	I ~ Jack is in London today.
	I thought to myself [maɪˈself]	ich dachte mir	
	cool [kuːl]	kühl	not cold, but ~
	so [səʊ]	also	I'm thirsty ~ I think I'll make some tea.
	sat [sæt]	Vergangenheit von *sit*	She ~ in the car while I went to the bank.
	(to) sit down [sɪt 'daʊn]	sich setzen	Come in and ~.
	paper (= newspaper) ['peɪpə]	Zeitung	= newspaper
	read [red]	Vergangenheit von *read*	I ~ that book last year.
	came [keɪm]	Vergangenheit von *come*	Who ~ to the door last night?

	could [kʊd]	Vergangenheit von *can*	I ~n't answer the last question. What was the answer?
	garage ['gærɑːʒ]	Tankstelle, Werkstatt	the place where they repair your car
	along [ə'lɒŋ]	entlang	up/down this street = ~ this street
	gave [geɪv]	Vergangenheit von *give*	Yes, he ~ me his address yesterday.
	gave me a ride [raɪd]	nahm mich mit	She ~. = She took me with her in her car.
	(to) push [pʊʃ]	schieben; schubsen; drücken	The car broke down and we had to ~ it.
	motor ['məʊtə]	Auto; Motor	
	(to) die; died [daɪ, daɪd]	sterben; Vergangenheit von *die*	My grandfather ~d in 1980.
	Things got worse. [wɜːs]	Es wurde schlimmer.	The day didn't get better - ~!
	as	(so) wie; als; während	~ you all know, Philip is in London at the moment.
	(to) go by [gəʊ 'baɪ]	vergehen	
	as the day went by	im Verlauf des Tages	
	did I ask myself [maɪ'self]	habe ich mich gefragt	
	said [sed]	Vergangenheit von *say*	When I saw her she ~ "Hello", but that was all.
	ever ['evə]	je(mals)	Do you ~ work on Sunday? - No, never.
	(to) get a feeling	ein Gefühl bekommen	
	(to) roll over [rəʊl]	(sich) herumdrehen, (sich) herumwälzen	
	(to) play sick [sɪk]	krank spielen	He's not really sick, he's just ~ing ~.
F2	verse [vɜːs]	Strophe	The poem has 9 ~s
F3	What does the poem say? ['pəʊɪm]	Was steht im Gedicht?	What is in the poem? = ~?
	(to) rhyme [raɪm]	sich reimen	"Bed" ~s with "red".
F4	what eight verbs? [vɜːbz]	welche acht Verben?	
FU1	(to) forget [fə'get]	vergessen	I always ~ her first name. What is it?
	Dad [dæd]	Papa, Vati	<—> Mum
	(to) tape [teɪp]	(auf Band) aufzeichnen/aufnehmen	I can't watch the film on TV tonight so I'll ~ it.
	TV programme ['prəʊgræm]	Fernsehsendung	*Tagesschau* and *Sportschau* are two ~s in Germany.
FU3	on time [ɒn 'taɪm]	pünktlich, rechtzeitig	Will the train be ~? - It's 10 minutes late, I'm afraid.
FU4	ending ['endɪŋ]	Endung	= the end of a word
	regular ['regjʊlə]	regelmäßig	~ verbs have the ending -ed.
	way [weɪ]	Art und Weise, Methode	Is this the right ~ to cook spaghetti?
	(to) pronounce [prə'naʊns]	aussprechen	= (to) say. I can write the word *beautiful* but I can't ~ it.
	(to) put [pʊt]	stecken, stellen, legen, tun	~ the bottle on the table, please.
	column ['kɒləm]	Spalte	This page has three ~s.
FU5	Who can tell the best lie? [laɪ]	Wer kann am besten lügen?	
	last night [lɑːst 'naɪt]	gestern abend; gestern nacht; letzte Nacht	~ we went to the theatre, had dinner and came home late.
FU6	(to) go sightseeing ['saɪtsiːɪŋ]	Sehenswürdigkeiten besichtigen	= (to) see the interesting things in a place
	(to) go fishing ['fɪʃɪŋ]	angeln gehen	Let's ~. Perhaps we'll get a salmon.
	(to) go camping ['kæmpɪŋ]	Camping machen	We're ~ing ~. We don't want to stay in a hotel.
	(to) go sailing ['seɪlɪŋ]	segeln gehen	
	(to) go riding ['raɪdɪŋ]	reiten gehen	
	golf [gɒlf]	Golf(spiel)	
	baseball ['beɪsbɔːl]	Baseball	
SF	I was born [bɔːn]	ich bin geboren	My birthday is 5th June. ~ on 5th June, 1970.
	in 1962	1962; im Jahre 1962	
	to school [skuːl]	zur Schule	I went ~ when I was five.
	(to) leave school ['liːv skuːl]	von der Schule abgehen	Young people usually ~ when they are 16-18.
	(to) train [treɪn]	eine Ausbildung machen; trainieren	
	as [əz]	als	She works at the hospital, ~ a doctor.
	local ['ləʊkl]	örtlich, einheimisch; Lokal-	There was a report about my daughter's school in the ~ paper.
	suburb ['sʌbɜːb]	Vorort, Vorstadt	We don't live in the centre of London, but in one of the ~s.
	(to) get divorced [dɪ'vɔːst]	sich scheiden lassen	They aren't married now. They got ~ last year.
	(to) have a baby ['beɪbɪ]	ein Baby bekommen	When did Janet ~? - Last week. It's a boy.

Unit 10

FW	furniture ['fɜːnɪtʃə]	Möbel, Möbelstücke	Tables and beds are ~.
	lamp [læmp]	Lampe	
	chest of drawers [tʃest əv 'drɔːəz]	Kommode	The pullovers are in that ~ over there.
	desk [desk]	Schreibtisch	An office? But where's the ~?
	sofa ['səʊfə]	Sofa	
	chair [tʃeə]	Stuhl	An office always has a desk and a ~.
	bookshelf, bookshelves ['bʊkʃelf]	Bücherregal, -regale	Where can I put this book? The ~ are full.
	wardrobe ['wɔːdrəʊb]	Kleiderschrank	There was a bed and a big ~ in the bedroom.
	armchair ['ɑːmtʃeə]	Sessel, Lehnstuhl	In their living room they've got a sofa and two big ~.
FW1	Label the drawing ['leɪbl ðə 'drɔːɪŋ]	Beschriften Sie die Zeichnung.	= Write the words on the picture.
F	childhood ['tʃaɪldhʊd]	Kindheit	
F1	text [tekst]	Text	
	opposite ['ɒpəzɪt]	gegenüberliegend	The ~ page is page number 169.
	except that [ɪk'sept]	außer daß	= but
	(to) love [lʌv]	lieben	= (to) like very much. I ~ you, darling.
	musician [mjuː'zɪʃn]	Musiker/in	She's a ~. She plays the violin.
	full of ['fʊl əv]	voller/voll von	The shelves are ~ books. = There are a lot of books on the shelves.
	record ['rekɔːd]	Schallplatte	I've got a lot of old Elvis Presley ~s.
	(to) spend [spend]	verbringen	We often ~ Sunday morning in bed.
	spent [spent]	Vergangenheit von *spend*	
	dishwasher ['dɪʃwɒʃə]	Spülmaschine	A modern kitchen usually has a ~.
	fridge [frɪdʒ]	Kühlschrank	There's some nice cold beer in the ~.
	light [laɪt]	Licht	It was dark. = There was no ~.
	we each had [iːtʃ]	wir hatten jede(r)	
	our own room [əʊn ruːm]	unser eigenes Zimmer	We each had ~.
	parents ['peərənts]	Eltern	= mother and father
	summer ['sʌmə]	Sommer	In the ~ people have parties outside.
	the whole family [həʊl]	die ganze Familie	= all the family
	used to sit outside [juːstə sɪt]	saß früher (immer) draußen	
	porch [pɔːtʃ]	Veranda	
	were [wɜː]	Vergangenheit von *are*	There ~ only three people at my class yesterday.
	no one ['nəʊwʌn]	niemand	~ knows where Jack is. Where can he be?
	another [ə'nʌðə]	ein/e andere(r/s); noch ein(e)	Her office isn't here. It's in ~ building.
	grandparents ['grænpeərənts]	Großeltern	Your parents' parents are your ~.
	smallest ['smɔːlɪst]	kleinste(r/s)	
	still [stɪl]	(immer)noch	It's old, but I ~ use it.
	hall [hɔːl]	(Haus-)Flur	the room where the entrance is
	tiffany lamp ['tɪfənɪ læmp]	Tiffany-Lampe	
	on the street (= BE in the street)	in der Straße	
	television ['telɪvɪʒn]	Fernsehgerät	= TV
	after school	nach der Schule	In the afternoon ~ children play and watch TV.
F2	what was nice about the kitchen?	was war schön an der Küche?	
	whose? [huːz]	wessen?	~ book is this? - It's mine.
	popular with ['pɒpjʊlə]	beliebt bei	Teachers liked her. = She was ~ teachers.
F3	city ['sɪtɪ]	Stadt, Großstadt	It's not just a town, it's a big ~.
	village ['vɪlɪdʒ]	Dorf	Ohlerath is just a small ~. Only 300 people live there.
	in the country ['kʌntrɪ]	auf dem Lande	<—> in the town or city
	plant [plɑːnt]	Pflanze	
	slept [slept]	Vergangenheit von *sleep*	I ~ ten hours last night.
	I did my homework ['həʊmwɜːk]	ich machte meine Hausaufgaben	After school I ~, then I played.
FU1	interview ['ɪntəvjuː]	Interview	
	cassette [kə'set]	Cassette	a music ~, a video ~
	the questions below [bɪ'ləʊ]	die Fragen unten	<—> the questions above
	a room of his own	ein eigenes Zimmer	My brother had his own room. = He had ~.
	together [tə'geðə]	zusammen	They live ~. = They have one flat, not two.
	in both their rooms	in ihren beiden Zimmern	They each had a TV in their room. = They had a TV ~.

FU3	sport [spɔːt]	Sport; Sportart	Tennis, squash and football are ~s.
	animal [ˈænɪml]	Tier	A dog or a cat is an ~.
	story [ˈstɔːrɪ]	Geschichte; Erzählung	Tell us a nice ~.
SF	weather [ˈweðə]	Wetter	We want to go hiking, but the ~ isn't very good.
	sunny [ˈsʌnɪ]	sonnig	It was a hot, ~ day in June.
	rainy [ˈreɪnɪ]	regnerisch	<—> sunny
	cloudy [ˈklaʊdɪ]	bewölkt, wolkig	You can't see much from a plane when it's ~.
	windy [ˈwɪndɪ]	windig	It's ~. Let's go sailing.
	foggy [ˈfɒgɪ]	neblig	It was very ~. We couldn't see ten metres.
	degree [dɪˈgriː]	Grad	It was a hot day, almost 30 ~s.
SF1	sun [sʌn]	Sonne	
	(to) shine [ʃaɪn]	scheinen	When the sun ~s in the summer, it gets very hot.
	shone [ʃɒn]	Vergangenheit von *shine*	
	(to) rain [reɪn]	regnen	It ~ed. = It was rainy.
	partly [ˈpɑːtlɪ]	teilweise	not totally cloudy, but ~ cloudy
	(to) blow [bləʊ]	blasen	The wind always ~s up here.
	blew [bluː]	Vergangenheit von *blow*	
	(to) snow [snəʊ]	schneien	When it ~s, it makes things white.
	warm [wɔːm]	warm	not cold, not cool, not hot, but ~
SF2	this morning	heute morgen	~ = today in the morning
	last Christmas [ˈkrɪsməs]	letztes Jahr (zu) Weihnachten; letztes Weihnachtsfest	= last year at Christmas
SF3	spring [sprɪŋ]	(der) Frühling	March, April and May are the months of ~.
	autumn [ˈɔːtəm]	(der) Herbst	September, October and November are the months of ~.
	winter [ˈwɪntə]	(der) Winter	December, January and February are the months of ~.
	season [ˈsiːzn]	Jahreszeit	Spring, summer, autumn and winter are the four ~s.

Unit 11

FW1	clothing [ˈkləʊðɪŋ]	Kleidung	what we wear
	tie [taɪ]	Krawatte, Schlips	
	jacket [ˈdʒækɪt]	Jacke, Jackett	
	dress [dres]	Kleid	When I go to the theatre or a concert I sometimes wear a long ~.
	glove [glʌv]	Handschuh	When it's cold in the winter I wear ~s ...
	coat [kəʊt]	Mantel	... and a warm ~.
	trousers [ˈtraʊzəz]	Hose	Jeans are ~.
	shirt [ʃɜːt]	Hemd	At the office he always wears a ~ and tie.
	hat [hæt]	Hut	You wear a ~ on your head.
	shoe [ʃuː]	Schuh	You wear ~s on your feet.
F1	try this one on [traɪ ˈɒn]	probier diese an	I like this jacket for you. ~.
	(to) suit [sjuːt]	stehen	Blue is a good colour for Ann. = Blue ~s Ann.
	What's the matter? [ˈmætə]	Was ist (los)?	You're all white. ~?
	sleeve [sliːv]	Ärmel	the clothing around your arm
	just right [dʒʌst ˈraɪt]	genau richtig	This coffee is not too hot, not too cold. It's ~.
	the last jacket looked better [lʊkt]	die letzte Jacke sah besser aus	
	longer [ˈlɒŋgə]	länger	The sleeves on that jacket are too short. The sleeves on this jacket are ~.
	(to) put on [pʊt ˈɒn]	anziehen	Before you go out of the house you always ~ your shoes ~.
F2	I'm just looking.	Ich schaue nur.	Assistant: Can I help you? - Customer: No, thank you, ~.
	(to) pay [peɪ]	(be-)zahlen	(to) give money to someone for something
	in a larger size [ˈlɑːdʒə saɪz]	in größer	This is too small. Have you got the same jacket ~?
	size	Größe	My shoes are ~ 39.
	changing room [ˈtʃeɪndʒɪŋ rʊm]	Umkleideraum, -kabine	the little room where you try something on in a shop

	those [ðəʊz]	jene (dort); diese	this - these; that - ~
F4	(to) shop [ʃɒp]	einkaufen	= (to) go shopping
	(to) decide [dɪˈsaɪd]	sich entscheiden; beschließen	It was a beautiful day so we ~d to go out.
	when you're finished [ˈfɪnɪʃ]	wenn Sie fertig sind	Do exercises 8, 9 and 10. ~, you can go home.
	(to) practise [ˈpræktɪs]	üben	When you learn an instrument like the piano or violin, you have to ~ regularly.
	(to) roleplay [ˈrəʊpleɪ]	als Rollenspiel aufführen; mit verteilten Rollen spielen	
F5	comparing things [kəmˈpeərɪŋ]	Dinge vergleichen	
	superlative [suːˈpɜːlətɪv]	Superlativ	
	the most famous [ˈfeɪməs]	der/die/das berühmteste	The Eiffel Tower is ~ thing in Paris.
	a hundred years ago	vor hundert Jahren	
	ago [əˈgəʊ]	vor	It's 10.15. Five minutes ~ it was 10.10.
	important [ɪmˈpɔːtənt]	wichtig, bedeutend	A car is usually very ~ when you live in the country.
	capital [ˈkæpɪtl]	Hauptstadt	Berlin is the ~ of Germany.
	in the world [wɜːld]	der Welt	There is a woman in France who is 120. She's the oldest woman ~.
	even [iːvn]	sogar; noch	It was cold yesterday, but it's ~ colder today.
	financial [faɪˈnænʃl]	finanziell; Finanz-	London and Frankfurt are two important ~ centres in Europe.
	the Houses of Parliament [ˈpɑːləmənt]	das Parlamentsgebäude	
	stock exchange [ˈstɒk ɪkstʃeɪndʒ]	(Aktien-)Börse	
	stock market [ˈstɒk mɑːkɪt]	(Aktien-)Börse	
	public transport system [ˈsɪstəm]	öffentliches Verkehrssystem	Buses, trains and subways are all part of a city's ~.
	(to) carry [ˈkærɪ]	befördern	This plane can ~ over 300 people.
	parkland [pɑːklænd]	Parklandschaft, Parkgelände	
	% = per cent [pɜːˈsent]	Prozent	Children under twelve pay only 50 ~.
	Greater London [ˈgreɪtəˈlʌndən]	Großlondon	the centre of London and all the suburbs
	department store [dɪˈpɑːtmənt stɔː]	Kaufhaus, Warenhaus	Kaufhof and Karstadt are two ~s in Munich.
	Europe [ˈjʊərəp]	Europa	Spain and France are the two biggest countries in ~.
	best known for its fabrics [ˈfæbrɪks]	am besten wegen seiner Stoffe bekannt	
	National Gallery [næʃnl ˈgælərɪ]	Nationalgalerie	
	collection [kəˈlekʃn]	(An-)Sammlung	The museum has a large ~ of old books.
	wax figure [ˈwæks fɪgə]	Wachsfigur	
	the list goes on and on	die Liste geht immer weiter	
FU1	than [ðæn]	als	I'm older ~ my wife. I'm 29, and she's 27.
	as tall as [tɔːl]	so groß wie	I'm ~ my brother. We're both 1 metre 75.
FU2	yourself [jɔːˈself]	(Sie) sich (selber)	
	than me	als ich	I'm 24 and you're 25, so you're older ~.
FU3	headline [ˈhedlaɪn]	Schlagzeile	The big words at the top of a newspaper article are the ~.
FU4	simply [ˈsɪmplɪ]	einfach	= just
	advert [ˈædvɜːt]	Anzeige, Annonce	On Saturday the newspaper is full of ~s.
	classmate [ˈklɑːsmeɪt]	Klassenkamerad(in)	The other people in your class are your ~s.
SF	parts of the body [pɑːts ... bɒdɪ]	Körperteile	The arms and head are ~.
SF1	nose [nəʊz]	Nase	
	mouth [maʊθ]	Mund	We speak and eat with our ~.
	ear [ɪə]	Ohr	We listen with our ~s.
	chin [tʃɪn]	Kinn	
	neck [nek]	Nacken	The part of the body between our head and the rest of our body is our ~.
	chest [tʃest]	Brust	
	arm [ɑːm]	Arm	
	hand [hænd]	Hand	He's got big feet and big ~s.
	finger [ˈfɪŋgə]	Finger	I wear my ring on this ~ here.
	waist [weɪst]	Taille	
	leg [leg]	Bein	He's got long arms and long ~s.
	toe [təʊ]	Zehe	The "fingers" on your feet are your ~s.
SF2	(to) move [muːv]	bewegen	I can't ~ this little finger. I think it's broken.

Unit 12

FW1	magazine [mægə'zi:n]	Zeitschrift	not a newspaper, but a ~. *Der Spiegel* and *Stern* are two German ~s.
	au-pair [əʊ'peə]	Au-Pair-Mädchen	
	go to see a film	(ins Kino gehen und) einen Film sehen	Let's go to the cinema. = Let's ~.
	listen to the news [nju:z]	die Nachrichten hören	
	on the radio ['reɪdɪəʊ]	im Radio	I didn't watch the news on TV, I listened to it ~.
	keep a diary ['daɪərɪ]	Tagebuch führen	When you ~, you write down what you do in a little book.
FW2	Yes, I have.	Ja (das habe ich).	
	No, I haven't.	Nein (das habe ich nicht).	
	have listened ['lɪsnd]	vollendete Gegenwart von *listen*	
	regularly ['regjʊlǝlɪ]	regelmäßig	I visit my parents ~ each Sunday.
	have kept [kept]	vollendete Gegenwart von *keep*	
	in English	auf englisch	The word *Zeitschrift* is *magazine* ~.
	have been [bi:n]	vollendete Gegenwart von *be*	
	have bought [bɔ:t]	vollendete Gegenwart von *buy*	
	English-language [ɪŋglɪʃ 'læŋgwɪdʒ]	englischsprachig	*The Herald Tribune* is a well-known ~ newspaper.
	language	Sprache	She can speak four ~s: German, English, French and Italian.
	have read [red]	vollendete Gegenwart von *read*	
F1	when?	wann?	~ did they move to London? - In 1991.
	have you been back since then?	bist du seit damals wieder dort gewesen?	
	back	zurück; wieder	I went to Argentina in 1992, and went ~ again in 1993.
	since [sɪns]	seit	I started work at IBF in 1989. I have been with them all the time ~ then.
	unfortunately [ʌn'fɔ:tʃnətlɪ]	leider; unglücklicherweise	= I'm afraid
F3	the Czech Republic [tʃek rɪ'pʌblɪk]	die tschechische Republik	Prague is the capital of ~.
	Denmark ['denmɑ:k]	Dänemark	Copenhagen is the capital of ~.
	France [frɑ:ns]	Frankreich	Paris is the capital of ~.
	Greece [gri:s]	Griechenland	Athens is the capital of ~.
	Holland ['hɒlənd]	Holland	Amsterdam is the most well-known city in ~.
	Hungary ['hʌŋgərɪ]	Ungarn	Budapest is the capital of ~.
	Italy ['ɪtəlɪ]	Italien	Rome is the capital of ~.
	Japan [dʒə'pæn]	Japan	Tokyo is the capital of ~.
	Russia ['rʌʃə]	Rußland	Moscow is the capital of ~.
	Scotland ['skɒtlənd]	Schottland	~ is part of the United Kingdom.
	Sweden ['swi:dn]	Schweden	Stockholm is the capital of ~.
	foreign ['fɒrən]	ausländisch; fremd	She has lived in six different ~ countries and speaks four ~ languages.
FU1	have had	vollendete Gegenwart von *have*	
	have spoken ['spəʊkən]	vollendete Gegenwart von *speak*	
	have flown [fləʊn]	vollendete Gegenwart von *fly*	
	have driven ['drɪvən]	vollendete Gegenwart von *drive*	
	have eaten ['i:tən]	vollendete Gegenwart von *eat*	
	have found [faʊnd]	vollendete Gegenwart von *find*	
	have heard [hɜ:d]	vollendete Gegenwart von *hear*	
	once [wʌns]	einmal	I haven't been there three times, only ~. That was in 1994.
	(to) call [kɔ:l]	rufen; anrufen	= (to) phone
	(to) happen ['hæpən]	geschehen, passieren	You're late. What ~ed? - The car broke down.
	Indonesian [ɪndə'ni:zjən]	indonesisch	
	Dutch [dʌtʃ]	holländisch, niederländisch; Holländisch, Niederländisch	My wife is from Holland. She's ~.
FU2	sports equipment ['spɔ:ts ɪkwɪpmənt]	Sportausrüstung(sgegenstände)	Skis and tennis balls are ~.
	bag [bæg]	Tasche	I can't find my ~ with all my money, my address book and my keys.
	passport ['pɑ:spɔ:t]	Reisepaß	You don't need a ~ now when you go from Germany to Belgium.

	tennis racket ['tenɪs rækɪt]	Tennisschläger	
FU3	ask someone to do something	jemanden bitten, etwas zu tun	You can't do it? Well, ~ help you.
	(to) water the plants [plɑːnts]	die Pflanzen gießen	Who can ~ while we're in France?
FU4	have seen [siːn]	vollendete Gegenwart von *see*	
	have met [met]	vollendete Gegenwart von *meet*	
FU7	course [kɔːs]	Kurs	an English ~, a computer ~
	(to) remember [rɪ'membə]	sich erinnern (an); denken (an)	<—> (to) forget
SF1	looking back	zurückschauen(d), -blicken(d)	~ at the end of the course I remembered a lot of nice things.
	happy ['hæpɪ]	glücklich; zufrieden	I'm going on holiday for three weeks. I'm very ~.
	progress ['prəʊgres]	Fortschritt, Fortschritte	Have you learned a lot? = Have you made a lot of ~?
	enough [ɪ'nʌf]	genug, ausreichend	We've got 12 bottles. Is that ~ for the party?
	What did you like best about the course?	Was gefiel Ihnen am besten am Kurs?	
SF2	ahead [ə'hed]	voraus	When you look ~, what are your plans for the future?
	(to) do a course	einen Kurs belegen	I don't know much about computers, so I've decided to ~ at the Volkshochschule.
	(to) go to a language school ['læŋwɪdʒ skuːl]	eine Sprachenschule besuchen	You can ~ in England and do an English course for three weeks.
	easy readers [iːzɪ 'riːdəz]	leichte/vereinfachte Lektürehefte	Books with stories in simple English are ~s.
	(to) go to ... for a holiday	nach ... in Urlaub fahren	= (to) go on holiday
	definitely ['defɪnɪtlɪ]	definitiv; (ganz) bestimmt	We'll perhaps go to France, but we haven't ~ decided.

Alphabetisches Wörterverzeichnis

Für jeden Eintrag ist angegeben, wo das Wort erstmalig vorkommt. Die erste Ziffer gibt die Unit an, die Buchstaben den betreffenden Unitteil: F = Focus, FU = Follow-up, FW = First words, S = Summary, SF = Special Focus, T = Titel.
Beispiel: 5 FU1 = Unit 5, Follow-up Übung 1

VOCAB

A

a	ein(e) 1 F1
a lot of	viel, viele 5 FU1
abbreviation	Abkürzung 1 SF3
about	über 3 FU6
nice about (the room)	schön an (dem Raum) 10 F2
what about ...?	und ...? und wie ist es mit ...? 3 FW2
What did you like about it?	Was hat Ihnen daran gefallen? 12 SF1
above	oben 7 FW1
action	Bewegung, Handlung 6 FU3
activity	Tätigkeit, Aktivität 4 F5
address	Adresse 1 SF4
advert	Anzeige, Annonce 11 FU4
afraid: I'm afraid	leider 7 F1
after	nach 4 F5
after school	nach der Schule 10 F1
after that	danach 4 F5
afternoon	1 FW Nachmittag
good afternoon	guten Tag 1 FW
again	noch einmal, wieder 1 FU3
You can say that again!	Das können Sie laut sagen! 4 F1
ago: a hundred years ago	vor hundert Jahren 11 F5
ahead	voraus 12 SF2
all	all 5 F5
all day	den ganzen Tag 5 F5
almost	fast, beinahe 3 SF
along	entlang 9 F1
alphabet	Alphabet 1 SF
always	immer 4 F6
am	bin 1 F1
a.m.	nachts, morgens, vormittags (zwischen 00.01 und 12.00 Uhr) 3 SF
American	amerikanisch; Amerikaner/in 3 F2
an	ein(e) 2 F2
and	und 1 F2
angry	zornig, ärgerlich 5 FU1
animal	Tier 10 FU3
another	ein/e andere(r/s); noch ein(e) 10 F1
answer	Antwort 5 F4
(to) answer	(be-)antworten 2 FU6
any	(in Fragen:) (irgend)welche(r/s) 8 FW1
not ... any	kein, keine; keins 8 FW1
anything	etwas 8 F1
Are you doing anything?	Habt ihr etwas vor? 7 F1
not ... anything	nichts 8 F1
appearance	Aussehen 2 SF
apple	Apfel 8 F3
April	April 7 SF1
are	sind/bist/seid 1 F1
aren't	sind/bist/seid nicht 1 FU3
arm	Arm 11 SF1
armchair	Sessel, Lehnstuhl 10 FW
around	um (... herum) 3 FW2
as	(so) wie; als; während 9 F1
	als 9 SF
as ... as	so ... wie 11 FU2
as ... as	so ... wie 3 FU3
(to) ask	(be-)fragen 2 FU1
ask about	fragen nach; Fragen stellen über 2 FU5
ask for	bitten um 6 FU8
ask questions	Fragen stellen 2 FU5
ask someone to do something	jemanden bitten, etwas zu tun 12 FU3
ask the way	nach dem Weg fragen 6 F
at: at 42nd Street	an der 42. Straße 6 F1
at home	zu Hause 1 FU7
at one end	am einen Ende 7 SF2
at the bottom	unten 4 FW2
at the door	an der Tür 6 FW
at the hotel	im Hotel 2 FU7
at the moment	im Moment, im Augenblick 7 F5
at a restaurant	in einem Restaurant 8 F4
at the top	oben 4 FW2
at the weekend	am Wochenende 3 SF
at this time of year	zu dieser Jahreszeit 7 F5
at TV International	bei TV International 2 FU5
at twenty-five past eleven	um fünf vor halb zwölf 3 SF1
at work	in/bei der Arbeit 1 FU7
athletic	athletisch, sportlich 2 FW1
attached	verbunden, verknüpft, angeschlossen 7 FW1
au-pair	Au-Pair-Mädchen 12 FW1
August	August 7 SF1
Austria	Österreich 1 F2
autumn	(der) Herbst 10 SF3

B

baby	Baby 3 FU1
have a baby	ein Baby bekommen 9 SF
back	zurück; wieder 12 F1
	Rücken 7 F5
have a bad back	es am Rücken haben 7 F5
bad	schlecht 1 F3
bag	Tasche 12 FU2
balcony	Balkon 7 FW1
bald	kahl(köpfig), glatzköpfig 2 SF
bank	Bank, Sparkasse 5 SF
bar	Bar 8 FU6
baseball	Baseball 9 FU6
bathroom	Bad, Badezimmer 7 FW1
(to) be	sein 8 FU6
be finished	fertig sein 11 F4
beard	Bart 2 SF
beautiful	schön 2 SF

because	weil 7 F1	bus	Bus 6 F5
bed	Bett 4 F5	business: on business	geschäftlich 7 FU1
to bed	ins Bett 4 F5	busy	beschäftigt 7 F1
bed-sitter	Einzimmerwohnung 7 FW1	I'm busy.	Ich habe viel zu tun. 7 F1
bedroom	Schlafzimmer 7 FW1	but	aber 1 F1
beef	Rind(fleisch) 8 FW1	butter	Butter 4 SF
been: have been	vollendete Gegenwart von *be* 12 FW2	(to) buy	kaufen, erwerben 5 SF1
		by: by train	mit dem Zug 5 F2
before	bevor 9 FW2	by: go by	vergehen 9 F1
beginning	Beginn, Anfang 7 SF3	bye	Wiedersehen! Tschüs! 1 F5
behind	hinter 6 FW		
beige	beige 6 SF	**C**	
below	unten 10 FU1		
best	beste(r/s) 2 FU1	cake	Kuchen 8 FW1
	am besten 6 F5	(to) call	rufen; anrufen 12 FU1
better	besser 11 F1	came	Vergangenheit von *come* 9 F1
between	zwischen 6 FW	camping	Camping 9 FU6
bicycle	Fahrrad 6 F5	go camping	Camping machen 9 FU6
big	groß 3 FU3	can	können, dürfen 1 FU7
bigger	größere(r/s) 7 F1	can't	nicht können 4 FW2
bill	Rechnung 8 F4	Canada	Kanada 2 FU7
birthday	Geburtstag 7 SF2	capital	Hauptstadt 11 F5
When is your birthday?	Wann haben Sie Geburtstag? 7 SF2	caption	Bildunterschrift, Legende 9 FW2
		car	Auto 6 F5
bit: a bit	ein bißchen 2 F4	car park	Parkplatz 6 F8
black	schwarz 6 SF	carrot	Karotte, Möhre, Mohrrübe 8 FW1
blew	Vergangenheit von *blow* 10 SF1	(to) carry	befördern 11 F5
block	Block, Klotz, Klötzchen 3 FU2	cartoon	Cartoon, Karikatur 9 FW2
	Straße, Häuserblock 6 F1	cassette	Cassette 10 FU1
block of flats	Mietshaus, Wohnblock 7 FW1	cat	Katze 3 F3
blond	blond 2 F4	center	Zentrum 6 F1
(to) blow	blasen 10 SF1	chain	Kette 8 FU2
blue	blau 2 SF	chair	Stuhl 10 FW
body	Körper 11 SF	(to) change	wechseln 5 SF1
book	Buch 3 F1		umsteigen 6 F1
bookshop	Buchhandlung, -laden 6 F8	changing room	Umkleideraum, -kabine 11 F2
bored	gelangweilt 8 FU4	cheap	preisgünstig, billig 7 FW3
born: I was born	ich bin geboren 9 SF	check	Kontrolle 2 F5
both	beide 2 FU6	cheese	Käse 4 SF
bottle	Flasche 8 FU6	chemist	Apotheke; Drogerie 5 SF
a bottle of water	eine Flasche Wasser 8 FU6	chest	Brust 11 SF1
bottom: at the bottom	unten 4 FW2	chest of drawers	Kommode 10 FW
bought: have bought	vollendete Gegenwart von *buy* 12 FW2	chicken	Huhn, Hühnerfleisch 8 FW1
		child, children	Kind, Kinder 3 F1
boutique	Boutique 5 SF	childhood	Kindheit 10 F
bowler (= bowler hat)	Melone (Hut) 9 FW2	chin	Kinn 11 SF1
boy	Junge 3 F4	Chinese	chinesisch; Chinesisch; Chinese/Chinesin 8 F4
boyfriend	Freund 2 FU1		
bread	Brot 4 SF	(to) choose	wählen, auswählen 8 FU4
break	Pause 4 F6	Christmas	Weihnachten, das Weihnachtsfest 10 SF2
(to) break	(zer)brechen, kaputtmachen, kaputtgehen 9FW2		
		cinema: go to the cinema	ins Kino gehen 5 FW1
break down	eine Panne haben 9 FW2	(to) circle	einkreisen 1 FU3
breakfast	Frühstück 4 F5	city	Stadt, Großstadt 10 F3
for breakfast	zum Frühstück 4 SF1	class	Klasse 1 FU7
have breakfast	frühstücken 4 F5		Kurs, Unterricht 4 FU3
have for breakfast	zum Frühstück essen 4 SF1	classmate	Klassenkamerad/in 11 FU4
bright	hell 7 FW2	classroom	Klassenraum/-zimmer 6 FW2
(to) bring	bringen 7 F5	(to) clean	putzen, saubermachen 4 FU1
broke	Vergangenheit von *break* 9 FW1	clock	(Wand-)Uhr 3 SF1
brother	Bruder 2 FU1	clothing	Kleidung 11 FW1
brown	braun 2 SF	cloudy	bewölkt, wolkig 10 SF
building	Gebäude 7 FW1		

coat	Mantel 11 FW1	did	Vergangenheit von *do* 9 T
coffee	Kaffee 4 F6	(to) die	sterben 9 F1
a cup of coffee	eine Tasse Kaffee 4 F6	difference	Unterschied 8 FU1
coffee break	Kaffeepause 4 F6	different	andere(r/s); verschieden; anders 3 FU4
have a coffee break	eine Kaffeepause machen 4 F6	dining room	Eßzimmer 7 FW1
cold	kalt 8 FU4	dinner	Abendessen 4 FU3
colleague	Kollege/Kollegin 1 F4	directions	Wegbeschreibungen 6 F6
collection	(An-)Sammlung 11 F5	directly	direkt 6 F2
colour	Farbe 6 SF	dirty	dreckig, schmutzig 8 FU4
column	Spalte 9 FU4	(to) discuss	besprechen 5 FU1
(to) come: come over	vorbeikommen 7 F1	dishwasher	Spülmaschine 10 F1
(to) compare	vergleichen 11 F5	divorced: get divorced	sich scheiden lassen 9 SF
(to) complete	vervollständigen 2 FU5	(to) do	machen, tun 2F1
computer	Computer 3F1	Are you doing anything?	Habt ihr etwas vor? 7 F1
concert	Konzert 5 FW1	do a course	einen Kurs belegen 12 SF2
concert: go to a concert	ins Konzert gehen 5 FW1	What do you do?	Was machen Sie beruflich? 4 T
(to) cook	kochen 4 FU1	doctor	Arzt/Ärztin 4 FW1
cool	kühl 9 F1	does	3. Person von *do* 4 FU1
corner	Ecke 6 FW1	dog	Hund 3 F2
cornflakes	Cornflakes 4 SF	door	Tür 6 FW
correct	korrekt, richtig 3 SF3	at the door	an der Tür 6 FW
(to) correct	korrigieren 4 F7	down	hinunter, herunter 6 F1
could	könnte(n) 8 SF1; Vergangenheit von *can* 9 F1	write down	aufschreiben 5 FU1
country	Land 3 FW2	drawer: chest of drawers	Kommode 10 FW
country: in the country	auf dem Lande 10 F3	drawing	Zeichnung 10 FW1
course	Gericht, Speise 8 FW2; Kurs 12 FU7	dress	Kleid 11 FW1
do a course	einen Kurs belegen 12 SF2	dressed: get dressed	sich anziehen 9 F1
course: of course	natürlich 1 FU7	drink	Getränk 5 F7
cousin	Vetter, Cousine 3 F4	have a drink	etwas trinken 5 F7
cup	Tasse 4 F6	(to) drive	(Auto) fahren 5 FU1
a cup of coffee	eine Tasse Kaffee 4 F6	driven: have driven	vollendete Gegenwart von *drive* 12 FU1
customer	Kunde/Kundin 8 SF1	driver	Fahrer/in 9 F1
(to) cycle	radfahren 5 FW1	Dutch	holländisch, niederländisch; Holländisch, Niederländisch 12 FU1
Czech: the Czech Republic	die Tschechische Republik 12 F3		

D

E

Dad	Papa, Vati 9 FU1	each	jede(r/s) 3 FU1
dance class	Tanzstunde, Tanzunterricht 4 FU3	ear	Ohr 11 SF1
go to dance class	zur Tanzstunde gehen 4 FU3	east	(nach) Osten 6 F1
dark	dunkel 2 SF	Easter	Ostern 7 SF3
date	Datum 7 SF	easy	leicht; vereinfacht 12 SF2
daughter	Tochter 2 FU1	(to) eat	essen 5 F2
day	Tag 3 SF	eat out	essen gehen 7 FU4
all day	den ganzen Tag 5 F5	eaten: have eaten	vollendete Gegenwart von *eat* 12 FU1
working day	Arbeitstag 4 F6	egg	Ei 4 SF
December	Dezember 7 SF1	end	Ende 7 SF2
(to) decide	sich entscheiden; beschließen 11 F4	at one end	am einen Ende 7 SF2
decision	Entscheidung, Entschluß, Beschluß 8 F	ending	Endung 9 FU4
definitely	definitiv; (ganz) bestimmt 12 SF2	England	England 2 F4
degree	Grad 10 SF	English	englisch; Englisch 1 SF3
Denmark	Dänemark 12 F3	in English	auf englisch 12 FW2
department store	Kaufhaus, Warenhaus 11 F5	English-language	englischsprachig 12 FW2
departure	Abflug, Abreise 1 FU6	English-speaking	englischsprechend 3 F4
(to) describe	beschreiben 2 F	entrance	Eingang 7 FW1
desk	Schreibtisch 10 FW	enough	genug, ausreichend 12 SF1
dessert	Nachtisch, Dessert 8 FW2	equipment	Ausrüstung(sgegenstände) 12 FU2
dialogue	Dialog, Gespräch 1 F1	Europe	Europa 11 F5
diary	Tagebuch 12 FW1	even	sogar; noch 11 F5
keep a diary	Tagebuch führen 12 FW1	evening	Abend 1 FW

VOCAB

ever	je(mals) 9 F1	foreign	ausländisch; fremd 12 F3
except that	außer daß 10 F1	(to) forget	vergessen 9 FU1
(to) exchange	aus-/ein-/umtauschen 8 F5	former	ehemalige(r/s), frühere(r/s) 2 FU1
excuse	Ausrede 7 F	fortune cookie	Glückskeks 8 F4
excuse me	entschuldigen Sie, Entschuldigung 3 F2	found: have found	vollendete Gegenwart von *find* 12 FU1
exercise	Übung 2 SF2	France	Frankreich 12 F3
(to) exercise	Bewegung haben, Sport treiben 5 FU1	French	Französisch; französisch 6 FU1
expensive	teuer 7 FW3	fresh	frisch 8 F1
eye	Auge 2 SF	Friday	Freitag 3 SF
		fridge	Kühlschrank 10 F1
F		friend	Freund/Freundin 1 F4
		from	aus; von 1 F1
fabric	Stoff 11 F5	Where are you from?	Wo kommen Sie her? 1 F1
factory	Fabrik 4 F3	front: in front of	vor 6 FW
fair	hell 2 SF	fruit	Obst 4 SF
fair	Kirmes 7 SF3	full	voll 4 F1
false	falsch 3 F1	full of	voller 10 F1
family	Familie 2 FU1	full-time	Vollzeit-; vollzeit 4 F1
famous	berühmt 11 F5	funny	lustig; komisch 2 FW1
fast	schnell 5 FU1	furniture	Möbel, Möbelstücke 10 FW
father	Vater 2 FU1	future	Zukunft 8 F6
favourite	Lieblings- 6 SF2		
February	Februar 7 SF1	**G**	
feeling	Gefühl, Empfindung 9 F1		
feet	Mehrzahl von *foot* 6 F2	gallery	Galerie 11 F5
(to) fill in	ergänzen 1 FU4	game	Spiel 7 FU4
film	Film 3 SF1	garage	Garage 6 SF1
financial	finanziell; Finanz- 11 F5		Tankstelle, Werkstatt 9 F1
(to) find	finden 3 F4	(to) garden	gärtnern, Gartenarbeit machen 5 FW1
find out	herausfinden 2 FU5	gardener	Gärtner/Gärtnerin 4 FW1
fine	gut 1 F3	gate	Flusteig; Tor 1 FU6
finger	Finger 11 SF1	gave	Vergangenheit von *give* 9 F1
(to) finish	aufhören (mit); (be-)enden 4 F5	German	deutsch; Deutsch; Deutsche(r) 1 F1
be finished	fertig sein 11 F4	Germany	Deutschland 1 F1
finish work	aufhören zu arbeiten 4 F5	(to) get	werden 5 FU1
first	erste(r/s) 1 FW		besorgen, holen 8 FU3
	zuerst 4 F5		bekommen 9 F1
first name	Vorname 2 FU5	get divorced	sich scheiden lassen 9 SF
(to) fish	angeln 9 FU6	get dressed	sich anziehen 9 F1
flat	Wohnung 7 FW1	get married	heiraten; sich verheiraten 7 F5
block of flats	Mietshaus, Wohnblock 7 FW1	get off	aussteigen (aus) 6 F1
flew	Vergangenheit von *fly* 9 F1	get on	einsteigen (in) 6 F4
flight	Flug 1 FU6	get out of	aussteigen 9 F1
flight attendant	Flugbegleiter(in) 3 F1	get up	aufstehen 4 F5
flown: have flown	vollendete Gegenwart von *fly* 12 FU1	girl	Mädchen; junge Frau 2 F4
(to) fly	fliegen 5T	girlfriend	Freundin 2 FU1
focus	Brennpunkt, Fokus 1 F	(to) give	geben 4 F7
foggy	neblig 10 SF	give someone a hand	jemandem helfen 7 F5
(to) follow	(ver)folgen 1 FU1	give someone a ride	jemanden (im Auto) mitnehmen 9 F1
follow-up	Nachfassen, Weiterverfolgen, Fortsetzung 1 FU1	glass	Glas 8 F1
food	Essen, Nahrung(smittel) 5 SF1	a glass of wine	ein Glas Wein 8 F1
foot, feet	Fuß, Füße 6 F2	glasses	eine Brille 2 SF
on foot	zu Fuß 6 F2	glove	Handschuh 11 FW1
football	Fußball 5 F2	(to) go	gehen 4 F5
for	für 5 F5	go by	vergehen 9 F1
for breakfast/lunch	zum Frühstück/Mittagessen 4 SF1	go jogging/hiking	joggen/wandern gehen 7 FU4
for one minute	eine Minute lang 8 FU1	go on (and on)	(immer) weitergehen 11 F5
ask for	bitten um 6 FU8	go shopping	einkaufen, einkaufen gehen 4 F6
go to ... for a holiday	nach ... in Urlaub fahren 12 SF2	go swimming	schwimmen gehen 8 FU4
		go to a language school	eine Sprachenschule besuchen 12 SF2

go to bed	ins Bett gehen 4 F5
go to dance class	zur Tanzstunde/zum Tanzkurs gehen 4 FU3
go to parties	auf Partys gehen 5 FU1
go to see a film	(ins Kino gehen und) einen Film sehen 12 FW1
golf	Golf(spiel) 9 FU6
good	gut 1 FW
good-looking	gutaussehend 2 SF
goodbye	auf Wiedersehen 1 F5
got	Vergangenheit von *get* 9 F1
grammar	Grammatik 1 S
grandparents	Großeltern 10 F1
Greater London	Großlondon 11 F5
Greece	Griechenland 12 F3
green	grün 6 SF
greeting	Begrüßung 1 FW
grey	grau 2 SF
grilled	gegrillte(r/s) 8 F1
group	Gruppe 7 FW1
guide (book)	(Reise-)Führer 8 FU5

H

had	Vergangenheit von *have* 9 FW1
have had	vollendete Gegenwart von *have* 12 FU1
hair	Haare 2 F4
half: half past three	halb vier 3 SF
hall	(Haus-)Flur 10 F1
ham	Schinken 4 SF
hamburger	Hamburger 8 FU4
hand	Hand 11 SF1
give someone a hand	jemandem helfen 7 F5
handbag	Handtasche 3 F1
handsome	gutaussehend (bei Männern) 2 SF
(to) happen	geschehen, passieren 12 FU1
happy	glücklich, zufrieden 12 SF1
has got	hat 2 SF
hat	Hut 11 FW1
(to) hate	ungern/nicht gern haben/tun; hassen 5 F2
(to) have (got)	haben 2 SF1
	essen, trinken 4 SF1
have a baby	ein Baby bekommen 9 SF
have a coffee break	eine Kaffeepause machen 4 F6
have a drink	etwas trinken 5 F7
have a party	eine Party feiern 7 FU4
have a shower	(sich) duschen, eine Dusche nehmen 4 F5
have breakfast	frühstücken 4 F5
have for breakfast	zum Frühstück essen 4 SF1
have lunch	(zu) Mittag essen 4 F6
I'll have the moussaka.	Ich nehme die Moussaka. 8 T
We're having some friends over.	Wir laden einige Freunde ein. 7 F1
(to) have to	müssen 9 FW1
he	er 2 FW2
head	Kopf 9 F1
headline	Schlagzeile 11 FU3
(to) hear	hören 1 FU3
heard: have heard	vollendete Gegenwart von *hear* 12 FU1
heavy	schwer 2 SF
Hello	Hallo, [guten] Tag 1 F
help	Hilfe 7 F5
(to) help	helfen 4 FU1
her	ihr 2 F4
	sie; ihr 4 FW2
here	hier 3 F2
here you are	bitte schön 8 SF1
(to) hike	wandern 5 FW1
him	ihm; ihn 4 FU2
his	sein(e) 2 FU1
hobby	Hobby 5 F2
holiday	Urlaub, Ferien 7 FU1
holidays	Ferien 7 SF3
holiday flat	Ferienwohnung 8 FU5
go to ... for a holiday	nach ... in Urlaub fahren 12 SF2
on holiday	in Urlaub/Ferien 7 FU2
Holland	Holland 12 F3
home	Heim, Zuhause, Wohnung 7 FW
at home	zu Hause 1 FU7
homework	Hausaufgaben 10 F3
honey	Honig 4 SF
hospital	Krankenhaus 4 F3
hot	heiß, warm 8 FU3
hotel	Hotel 2 FU7
at the hotel	im Hotel 2 FU7
hour	Stunde 3 SF
house	Haus 6 FW
house: Houses of Parliament	(das britische) Parlamentsgebäude 11 F5
housewife	Hausfrau 4 F1
housework	Hausarbeit(en) 4 FU3
how?	wie? 1 F3
how are you?	wie geht es Ihnen/Dir/Euch? 1 F3
how many?	wie viele? 3 FW2
hundred	hundert 3 FW
Hungary	Ungarn 12 F3
hungry	hungrig 8 FU4
husband	(Ehe-)Mann 1 F4

I

I	ich 1 F1
ice cream	Eis, Eiskrem 8 FW1
idea	Idee 3 FU3
important	wichtig, bedeutend 11 F5
in	in 1 F1
in 1962	1962; im Jahre 1962 9 SF
in English	auf englisch 12 FW2
in front of	vor 6 FW
in her arm	auf dem Arm 3 FU5
in July	im Juli 7 SF2
in Oxford Street	in der Oxford Street 6 F6
in the country	auf dem Lande 10 F3
in the picture	auf dem Bild 3 F1
in the world	(auf) der Welt 11 F5
including	einschließlich 7 FW1
Indonesian	indonesisch 12 FU1
information	Information/Informationen, Auskunft/Auskünfte 2 FU2
tourist information center	Fremdenverkehrsamt/-büro/

	-zentrale 6 F1	let's see	laß mal sehen 7 F5
instrument	Instrument 5 FU1	letter	Brief 4 FU1
interesting	interessant 6 F5	lie	Lüge 9 FU5
international	international 2 FU5	tell a lie	lügen 9 FU5
interview	Interview 10 FU1	life	Leben 8 F4
(to) interview	interviewen 5 F4	lift	Aufzug 7 FW2
invitation	Einladung 7 F	light	hell 6 SF
Ireland	Irland 4 F1		Licht 10 F1
is	ist 1 F1	like	wie 2 FU6
island	Insel 3 FW2	What's she like?	Wie ist sie? 2 T
isn't (= is not)	ist nicht 2 FW2	(to) like	mögen, gern tun/haben 5 T
it	es 1 SF4	What did you like about it?	Was hat Ihnen daran gefallen? 12 SF1
Italian	italienisch; Italienisch 8 F3	would like (to)	möchte/möchten/möchte(s)t 8 F1
Italy	Italien 12 F3	line	Linie 6 F1
item	Ding, Punkt, Wendung 1 FU3	list	Liste 1 FU7
		(to) listen	zuhören 1 FU2
J		listen	hör mal 7 F1
		listen to music	Musik hören 5 F5
jacket	Jacke, Jackett 11 FW1	listen to the news	die Nachrichten hören 12 FW1
jam	Marmelade 4 SF	listening	Hören 1 FU3
January	Januar 7 SF1	little	klein 9 F1
Japan	Japan 12 F3	(to) live	leben; wohnen 1 F1
jeans	Jeans 5 SF1	living room	Wohnzimmer 7 FW1
job	Arbeit(sstelle) 4 FW	local	örtlich, einheimisch; Lokal- 9 SF
jogging	Joggen 7 FU4	long	lang 2 SF
juice	Saft 4 SF		lange 5 F6
July	Juli 7 SF1	(to) look	aussehen 11 F1; (hin-/her-)schauen, blicken 12 SF1
(to) jump	springen 9 F1	I'm just looking.	Ich schaue nur. 11 F2
June	Juni 7 SF1	look at	(sich) ansehen 2 FU5
just	nur; bloß; einfach 3 F2	look for	suchen 6 T
just right	genau richtig 11 F1	lot: a lot of	viel, viele 5 FU1
		lots of	viel, viele 8 F6
K		(to) love	lieben 10 F1
		lunch	Mittagessen 4 F6
(to) keep	behalten; (auf-)bewahren 5 FU1	have lunch	(zu) Mittag essen 4 F6
keep a diary	Tagebuch führen 12 FW1		
keep count	zählen; die Übersicht behalten 3 T	**M**	
kept: have kept	vollendete Gegenwart von *keep* 12 FW2	made	Vergangenheit von *make* 9 FW1
kingdom	Königreich 3 FW2	magazine	Zeitschrift 12 FW1
kitchen	Küche 7 FW1	main	Haupt- 8 FW2
(to) know	wissen; kennen 5 F4	main course	Hauptgericht 8 FW2
known for	bekannt wegen 11 F5	(to) make	machen 1 FU7
		man, men	Mann, Männer 3 F1
L		many	viele 3 FW2
		map	(Land-)Karte, (Stadt-)Plan 6 F1
(to) label	beschriften 10 FW1	March	März 7 SF1
lamp	Lampe 10 FW	(to) mark	markieren, kennzeichnen 6 F3
language	Sprache 12 FW2	married: get married	heiraten; sich verheiraten 7 F5
large	groß 7 FW1	(to) match	zuordnen 1 FW
last	letzte(r/s) 8 F1	matter: What's the matter?	Was ist (los)? 11 F1
last night	gestern abend/nacht; letzte Nacht 9 FU5	May	Mai 7 SF1
late	spät; verspätet 9 F1	me	mich; mir 5 F5
(to) laugh	lachen 6 FU1	Me, too.	Ich auch. 8 F1
(to) learn	lernen 8 F6	meal	Essen, Mahlzeit 8 SF3
(to) leave: leave school	von der Schule abgehen 9 SF	meat	Fleisch 8 FW1
left: on the left	links 4 FW2	medicine	Medizin 5 SF1
turn left	nach links abbiegen 6 F1	(to) meet	kennenlernen 1 T
leg	Bein 11 SF1	Nice to meet you.	Nett, Sie kennenzulernen 1 T
let's	laßt uns 8 F4	melon	Melone 8 F3

member	Mitglied 2 FU1	next	nächste(r/s) 1 F5
menu	Speisekarte, Speiseplan 8 SF1	next to	neben 4 FW2
met: have met	vollendete Gegenwart von *meet* 12 FU4	nice	nett 1 T
		nice about (the room)	schön an (dem Raum) 10 F2
middle	Mitte 4 FW2	Nice to meet you.	1 T
midnight	Mitternacht 9 FW2	night	Nacht 1 FW
milk	Milch 4 SF	night: last night	gestern abend/nacht; letzte Nacht 9 FU5
million	Million 3 FW		
(to) mime	mimen 6 FU3	no	nein 1 FU1
(to) mind: I don't mind.	Ich habe nichts dagegen. Mir ist es egal. 5 F4		kein(e) 3 F2
		no one	niemand 10 F1
mine	meine(r/s) 8 F4	noisy	laut, lärmend 7 FW2
mineral water	Mineralwasser 8 FU6	north	(nach) Norden 6 F1
minute	Minute 3 SF	nose	Nase 11 SF11 SF1
modern	modern 7 FW2	not	nicht 1 F3
moment	Moment, Augenblick 7 F5	November	November 7 SF1
at the moment	im Moment, im Augenblick 7 F5	now	jetzt, nun 2 FW1
Monday	Montag 3 SF	number	Nummer, Zahl, Ziffer 1 FU5
money	Geld 5 SF1		
month	Monat 3 SF	**O**	
more	weitere(r/s); mehr 2 FU6		
morning	1 FW Morgen	o'clock: three o'clock	drei Uhr 3 SF
this morning	heute morgen 10 SF2	October	Oktober 7 SF1
most: the most famous	der/die/das berühmteste 11 F5	of	von 1 FU7
mother	Mutter 2 FU1	of course	natürlich 1 FU7
motor	Auto; Motor 9 F1	off: get off	aussteigen (aus) 6 F1
mould	Schimmel 9 F1	office	Büro 2 F4
moussaka	Moussaka 8 T	often	oft, häufig 4 F6
moustache	Schnurrbart 2 SF	OK	in Ordnung 3 F2
mouth	Mund 11 SF1	old	alt 2 FU1
(to) move	umziehen 7 F1	on	auf 6 FW
	bewegen 11 SF2	on 42nd Street	an/in der 42. Straße 6 F1
Mr	Herr 1 F4	on 2nd January	am 2. Januar 7 SF2
Mrs	Frau 1 F4	on business	geschäftlich 7 FU1
Ms	Frau 1 F4	on foot	zu Fuß 6 F2
much	viel 3 FU3	on holiday	in Urlaub/Ferien 7 FU2
muesli	Müsli 4 SF	on Monday	am Montag 3 SF
Mum	Mama, Mami, Mutti 9 FW2	on the left/right	links/rechts 4 FW2
museum	Museum 3 SF3	on the plane/train	im Flugzeug/Zug 5 F5
music	Musik 5 F5	on the radio	im Radio 12 FW1
musician	Musiker/in 10 F1	on the telephone	am Telefon 2 FU7
must	müssen 7 F3	on time	pünktlich, rechtzeitig 9 FU3
my	mein(e) 1 F1	get on	einsteigen (in) 6 F4
myself	mich, mir 9 F1	go on (and on)	(immer) weitergehen 11 F5
		straight on	geradeaus 6 FW1
N		once	einmal 12 FU1
		one: this one	diese(r/s) 11 F1
name	Name 1 F1	only	nur 2 FU5
first name	Vorname 2 FU5	open	offen; geöffnet 3 SF3
my name's	ich heiße 1 F1	(to) open	öffnen, aufmachen 8 FU3
national	national, National- 11 F5	opposite	gegenüber 6 FW
near	in der Nähe von, nahe 1 F1		gegenüberliegend 10 F1
nearest	nächste(r/s) 6 F6	optimistic	optimistisch 2 F1
neck	Nacken 11 SF1	or	oder 2 FU7
(to) need	brauchen, benötigen 8 FU5	orange	orange 6 F1
negative	verneinte(r/s) 8S	order	Reihenfolge 4 F5
neighbour	Nachbar/Nachbarin 2 FU1	(to) order	bestellen 8 FU6
never	nie, niemals 4 F6	Are you ready to order?	Haben Sie gewählt? 8 SF1
new	neu 2 F4	other	andere(r/s) 2 SF2
news	Nachricht, Nachrichten 12 FW1	out: eat out	essen gehen 7 FU4
listen to the news	die Nachrichten hören 12 FW1	out of	aus (... heraus) 9 F1
newspaper	Zeitung 3 F1	out of the door	zur Tür hinaus 9 F1

VOCAB

outgoing	aus sich herausgehend, extravertiert 2 F1	plane	Flugzeug 5 F5
outside	draußen 4 F1	on the plane	im Flugzeug 5 F5
over	über 5 SF1	plant	Pflanze 10 F3
over there	da/dort drüben 6 FW1	platter: salad platter	Salatteller 8 F3
come over	vorbeikommen 7 F1	(to) play	spielen 5 FW1
roll over	(sich) herumdrehen 9 F1	playgroup	Spielgruppe 9 FW2
overnight	über Nacht 5 SF1	please	bitte 1 SF4
stay overnight	über Nacht bleiben, übernachten 5 SF1	p.m.	nachmittags, abends, nachts (zwischen 12.01 und 24.00 Uhr) 3 SF
own	eigene(r/s) 10 F1	poem	Gedicht 9 F1
a room of his own	ein eigenes Zimmer 10 FU1	policeman	Polizist 4 FW1
		policewoman	Polizistin 4 FW1

P

		popular with	beliebt bei 10 F2
		porch	Veranda 10 F1
(to) pack	packen 7 F1	post office	Postamt 5 SF
page	Seite 2 FU5	potato, potatoes	Kartoffel, Kartoffeln 8 FW1
(to) paint	malen, anstreichen 7 F1	(to) practise	üben 11 F4
pair	Paar 3 FU1	prawn cocktail	Krabbencocktail 8 FW1
panic	Panik 5 F5	prediction	Vorhersage, Voraussage 8 F
paper (= newspaper)	Zeitung 9 F1	pretty	hübsch 2 SF
parents	Eltern 10 F1	problem	Problem 3 F2
parked	geparkt 6 SF1	programme	Sendung 9 FU1
parkland	Parklandschaft, Parkgelände 11 F5	progress	Fortschritt, Fortschritte 12 SF1
parliament	Parlament 11 F5	(to) pronounce	aussprechen 9 FU4
part	Teil 11 SF	public	öffentlich 5 FU1
partly	teilweise 10 SF1	public transport	öffentliche Verkehrsmittel 5 FU1
partner	Partner/Partnerin 2 FU1	pullover	Pullover 8 FU4
party	Party 4 F	purple	violett, purpur 6 SF
go to parties	auf Partys gehen 5 FU1	(to) push	schieben; schubsen; drücken 9 F1
have a party	eine Party feiern 7 FU4	(to) put	stecken, stellen, legen, tun 9 FU4
(to) pass	passieren; vorbeigehen/-fahren (an) 6 F6	put in order	in die richtige Reihenfolge bringen 4 F5
passer-by	Passant/in 6 F1	put on	anziehen 11 F1
passport	Reisepaß 12 FU2		
past	Vergangenheit; Vergangenheits- form 9 FW	**Q**	
five past ten	fünf nach zehn 3 SF	quantity	Menge, Quantität 3 F
half past three	halb vier 3 SF	quarter	Viertel 3 SF
pavement	Bürgersteig 6 SF1	a quarter past	Viertel nach 3 SF
(to) pay	(be-)zahlen 11 F2	a quarter to	Viertel vor 3 SF
pea	Erbse 8 FW1	question	Frage 2 FU5
people	Leute, Personen, Menschen 1 FU7	quick	schnell 2 F5
per cent	Prozent 11 F5	quiet	ruhig, still 7 FW2
perhaps	vielleicht, eventuell 7 F5	quite: not quite	nicht ganz 8 FU1
person	Person 2 F2	quiz	Quiz 3 FW2
personality	Persönlichkeit 2 F1		
pessimistic	pessimistisch 2 FW1	**R**	
phone	Telefon 1 FU7		
(to) phone	anrufen, telefonieren 1 FU7	radio	Radio 12 FW1
phone for a pizza	(anrufen und) eine Pizza kommen lassen 8 FU6	on the radio	im Radio 12 FW1
		(to) rain	regnen 10 SF1
photo	Foto 3 FU5	rainy	regnerisch 10 SF
phrase	(Rede-)Wendung 1 S	rather	ziemlich 2 F2
picture	Bild 1 FW	reaction	Reaktion 8 FU4
in the picture	auf dem Bild 3 F1	(to) read (to)	(vor)lesen 3 FU1
pie	Pie (= Pastete, Torte, gefüllter Kuchen) 8 F3	read	Vergangenheit von read 9 F1
		read: have read	vollendete Gegenwart von read 12 FW2
pile	Stoß, Stapel 3 FU2	reader	Lektüre(heft) 12 SF2
pink	pink 6 SF	ready	fertig, bereit 8 SF1
place	Ort; Platz; Stelle 1 F1	Are you ready to order?	Haben Sie gewählt? 8 SF1
plan	Plan, Vorhaben 7 F	realistic	realistisch 2 F1

really	wirklich 3 F2	Scotland	Schottland 12 F3
record	Schallplatte 10 F1	(to) scratch	kratzen 9 F1
red	rot 6 SF	season	Jahreszeit 10 SF3
regular	regelmäßig 9 FU4	seat	(Sitz-)Platz 3 F2
regularly	regelmäßig 12 FW2	second	Sekunde 3 SF
relative	Verwandte(r) 3 F4	second	zweite(r/s) 7 SF1
(to) relax	sich entspannen, sich erholen 5 FW1	secret	Geheimnis 5 FU1
(to) remember	sich erinnern (an), denken (an) 12 FU7	secretary	Sekretär/Sekretärin 4 FW1
(to) repair	reparieren 4 FU1	(to) see	sehen 1 F5
(to) repeat	nachsprechen 1 FU2	go to see a film	(ins Kino gehen und) einen Film sehen 12 FW1
(to) report (to)	berichten 2 F3	let's see	laß mal sehen 7 F5
reporter	Reporter/Reporterin 4 FW1	See you next week!	Bis nächste Woche! 1 F5
republic	Republik 12 F3	seen: have seen	vollendete Gegenwart von see 12 FU4
reservation	Reservierung 8 FU5	sentence	Satz 2 FU6
reserved	reserviert 2 F1	September	September 7 SF1
restaurant	Restaurant; Gaststätte 4 F3	serious	ernst(haft) 2 F1
at a restaurant	in einem Restaurant 8 F4	shall: Shall we go?	Sollen/Wollen wir gehen? 8 F4
(to) rhyme	sich reimen 9 F3	she	sie 2 T
ride: give someone a ride	jemanden (im Auto) mitnehmen 9 F1	shelf, shelves	Regal, Regale 10 FW
(to) ride	reiten 9 FU6	(to) shine	scheinen 10 SF1
right	richtig 2 F4	shirt	Hemd 11 FW1
just right	genau richtig 11 F1	shoe	Schuh 11 FW1
on the right	rechts 4 FW2	shone	Vergangenheit von shine 10 SF1
turn right	nach rechts abbiegen 6 F1	shop	Laden, Geschäft 4 F3
you're right	Sie haben recht 3 F2	shop assistant	Verkäufer/Verkäuferin 4 FW1
(to) ring	klingeln, läuten 6 FU1	(to) shop	einkaufen 11 F4
roast beef	Rinderbraten 8 F3	shopping	Einkaufen 4 F6
(to) roleplay	als Rollenspiel aufführen; mit verteilten Rollen spielen 11 F4	(to) go shopping	einkaufen, einkaufen gehen 4 F6
roll	Brötchen 4 SF	short	kurz 2 F4
(to) roll: roll over	(sich) herumdrehen 9 F1	show	Show 7 FU4
romantic	romantisch 2 FW1	shower	Dusche 4 F5
room	Raum, Zimmer 6 FW2	have a shower	(sich) duschen, eine Dusche nehmen 4 F5
changing room	Umkleideraum, -kabine 11 F2	shy	schüchtern 2 FW1
route	Route, Weg 6 F3	sick	krank 9 F1
routine	Routine; (Tages-)Ablauf 4 F	side: side salad	Salat (als Beilage) 8 F3
Russia	Rußland 12 F3	sightseeing: go sightseeing	Sehenswürdigkeiten besichtigen 9 FU6

S

		simply	einfach 11 FU4
said	Vergangenheit von say 9 F1	since	seit 12 F1
(to) sail	segeln 9 FU6	sister	Schwester 2 FU1
salad	Salat 8 FW1	(to) sit	sitzen 8 FU6
salad platter	Salatteller 8 F3	sit: sit down	sich setzen 9 F1
side salad	Salat (als Beilage) 8 F3	situation	Situation 6 FU1
salmon	Lachs 8 F1	size	Größe 11 F2
same: the same	der-, die-, dasselbe 8 FU1	skirt	Rock 11 FW1
sandwich	belegtes Brot 8 FU6	(to) sleep	schlafen 5 F5
sat	Vergangenheit von sit 9 F1	sleeve	Ärmel 11 F1
Saturday	Samstag, Sonnabend 3 SF	slept	Vergangenheit von sleep 10 F3
sausage	Wurst, Würstchen 4 SF	small	klein 3 FU3
saw	Vergangenheit von see 9 F1	It's a small world.	Die Welt ist doch klein. 3 F2
(to) say	sagen 1 F	(to) smoke	rauchen 5 F7
what does the poem say?	was steht im Gedicht? 9 F3	(to) snow	schneien 10 SF1
You can say that again!	Das können Sie laut sagen! 4 F1	so	also 9 F1
school	Schule 2 FU1	So?	(Na) Und? 8 F1
after school	nach der Schule 10 F1	sofa	Sofa 10 FW
leave school	von der Schule abgehen 9 SF	sold	Vergangenheit von sell 9 SF2
school holidays	Schulferien 7 SF3	sole	Seezunge 8 F3
to school	zur Schule 9 SF	some	einige 3 FU3
			etwas; einige 8 FW1

someone	jemand 3 F4	Switzerland	die Schweiz 1 F2
something	etwas 8 FU4	system	System 11 F5
sometimes	manchmal 4 F6		
son	Sohn 2 FU1	**T**	
soon	bald 7 F5		
sorry	(es) tut mir leid; leider 1 FU7	table	Tabelle 2 FU5
(to) sound	klingen 1 F1		Tisch 4 SF1
soup	Suppe 8 FW1	(to) take	nehmen; hinbringen 5 FU1
south	(nach) Süden 6 F1		dauern 5 F5
spaghetti	Spaghetti 7 FU4	(to) talk	reden 3 F
Spain	Spanien 7 FU1	talk to (people)	mit (Leuten) sprechen 4 FU1
(to) speak	sprechen 6 FU1	tall	groß (gewachsen) 2 F4
English-speaking	englischsprechend 3 F4	(to) tape	(auf Band) aufzeichnen/aufnehmen 9 FU1
special	besondere(r/s) 1 SF		
(to) spell	buchstabieren 1 SF4	tea	Tee 4 SF
(to) spend	verbringen 10 F1	teacher	Lehrer/Lehrerin 4 FW1
spent	Vergangenheit von spend 10 F1	telephone	Telefon 1 FU7
spoken: have spoken	vollendete Gegenwart von speak 12 FU1	on the telephone	am Telefon 2 FU7
		television	Fernsehgerät 10 F1
sport	Sport; Sportart 10 FU3	(to) tell	sagen; erzählen 3 FW2
sport: sports equipment	Sportausrüstung(sgegenstände) 12 FU2	tell someone to ...	jemandem sagen, daß er ... soll(te) 9 F1
spring	(der) Frühling 10 SF3	tennis	Tennis 5 FW1
squash	Squash 5 F2	tennis racket	Tennisschläger 12 FU2
(to) stand	stehen 6 F1	terraced house	Reihenhaus 7 FW1
(to) start	anfangen, beginnen 4 F5	test	Test 2 F1
start work	anfangen zu arbeiten 4 F5	text	Text 10 F1
starter	Vorspeise 8 FW2	than	als 11 FU1
state	(Bundes-)Staat 3 FW2	than me	als ich 11 FU3
statement	Aussage(satz) 7 F3	thanks	danke 1 F3
station	Bahnhof; Station 5 SF	thank you	danke 1 FU7
(to) stay	bleiben; wohnen 5 SF1	that	das 1 F1
stay overnight	über Nacht bleiben, übernachten 5 SF1	after that	danach 4 F5
		the	der/die/das 1 FW
still	(immer)noch 10 F1	theatre	Theater 5 FW1
stock exchange	(Aktien-)Börse 11 F5	go to the theatre	ins Theater gehen 5 FW1
stock market	(Aktien-)Börse 11 F5	their	ihr(e) 1 FU7
stop	Haltestelle 6 F3	them	sie 4 F7
(to) stop	(an-)halten 6 F4	then	dann; damals 4 F5
store: department store	Kaufhaus, Warenhaus 11 F5	there	dort; da 4 F1
story	Geschichte; Erzählung 10 FU3	there: over there	da/dort drüben 6 FW1
straight: straight on	geradeaus 6 FW1	there: there are	es gibt 3 FW2
street	Straße 1 SF4	there: there is	es gibt 3 F1
(to) stretch	(sich) strecken 9 F1	these	diese 1 SF3
student	Lernende(r); Student/in 2 FU3	they	sie 1 FU3
suburb	Vorort 9 SF	thin	dünn; schlank 2 SF
subway	U-Bahn 6 F1	thing	Ding, Sache 4 FU1
suggestion	Vorschlag 8 FU6	(to) think	denken; glauben 2 FW2
(to) suit	stehen 11 F1	think of	denken an 6 FW2
summary	Zusammenfassung 1 S	I thought to myself	ich dachte mir 9 F1
summer	Sommer 10 F1	third	dritte(r/s) 7 SF1
sun	Sonne 10 SF1	thirsty	durstig 8 FU4
Sunday	Sonntag 3 SF	this	dies; das 1 F3
sunny	sonnig 10 SF		diese(r/s) 2 F1
superlative	Superlativ 11 F5	this morning	heute morgen 10 SF2
supermarket	Supermarkt 5 SF	those	jene (dort); diese 11 F2
surname	Familienname 1 SF4	thought	Vergangenheit von think 9 F1
(to) swap	tauschen 8 F4	thousand	Tausend 3 FW
Sweden	Schweden 12 F3	Thursday	Donnerstag 3 SF
sweets	Süßigkeiten 5 FU1	(to) tick	abhaken 3 FU1
(to) swim	schwimmen 5 FW1	ticket	Ticket, (Fahr-)Karte 8 FU5
go swimming	schwimmen gehen 8 FU4	tidy	ordentlich 2 F1

tie	Krawatte, Schlips 11 FW1	upstairs	nach oben; oben 7 F1
tiffany lamp	Tiffany-Lampe 10 F1	uptown	stadtauswärts 6 F1
till	bis 3 SF	us	uns 9 FW2
time	(Uhr-)Zeit 1 FU6	(to) use	benutzen, gebrauchen 3 FU3
	Mal 7 F1	used to (do)	früher (immer) (tat) 10 F1
What time is it?	Wie spät ist es? Wieviel Uhr ist es? 3 SF	usually	(für) gewöhnlich, normalerweise 4 F6
on time	pünktlich, rechtzeitig 9 FU3		
time of year	Jahreszeit 7 F5	**V**	
tired	müde 8 FU4		
to	zu 1 FW, 1T	vegetable(s)	Gemüse 8 FW1
	nach 1FU6	verb	Verb, Tätigkeitswort 9 F4
five to ten	fünf vor zehn 3 SF	verse	Strophe 9 F2
from Monday to Friday	von Montag bis Freitag 3 SF	very	sehr 2 FW2
go to the cinema/	ins Kino/Theater/Konzert gehen	village	Dorf 10 F3
the theatre/a concert	5 FW1	(to) visit	besuchen; zu Besuch sein 7 F5
to school	zur Schule 9 SF	voice	Stimme 9 F1
toast	Toast 4 SF		
today	heute 9 FW2	**W**	
toe	Zehe 11 SF1		
together	zusammen 10 FU1	waist	Taille 11 SF1
toilet	Toilette 5 SF	waiter	Kellner; (Herr) Ober! 8 F4
told	Vergangenheit von *tell* 9 F1	waitress	Kellnerin 8 SF1
tomato	Tomate 8 F3	(to) want to	wollen 5 F4
tomorrow	morgen 7F1	warm	warm 10 SF1
tonight	heute abend, heute nacht 3 SF1	was	Vergangenheit von *am/is* 9 F1
too	auch 1 F4	(to) watch: watch TV	fernsehen 5 FW1
	zu 5 FU1	water	Wasser 8 FU6
took	Vergangenheit von *take* 9 FW1	(to) water: water the plants	die Pflanzen gießen 12 FU3
top: at the top	oben 4 FW2	(to) wave	winken 9 F1
tourist	Tourist/in 6 F1	wax figure	Wachsfigur 11 F5
tourist information center	Fremdenverkehrsamt/-büro/ -zentrale 6 F1	way	Weg 6 F
			Art und Weise, Methode 9 FU4
town	Stadt 1 F2	ask the way	nach dem Weg fragen 6 F
train	Zug 3 SF1	we	wir 2 F3
by train	mit dem Zug 5 F2	(to) wear	tragen 2 SF
(to) train	eine Ausbildung machen; trainieren 9 SF	weather	Wetter 10 SF
		wedding	Hochzeit 7 F5
transport: public transport	öffentliche Verkehrsmittel 5 FU1	wedding anniversary	Hochzeitstag 7 SF3
travel agency	Reisebüro 5 SF	Wednesday	Mittwoch 3 SF
(to) travel	reisen 5 FW1	week	Woche 1 F5
tree	Baum 6 SF1	weekday	Wochentag 4 SF1
trip	Reise 5 F5	weekend	Wochenende 3 SF
trousers	Hose, Hosen 11 FW1	at the weekend	am Wochenende 3 SF
true	richtig; wahr 3 F1	welcome: you're welcome	bitte schön; bitte sehr 1 FU7
(to) try	probieren; versuchen 8 F1	well	nun 1 F1
try on	anprobieren 11 F1		gut 5 FU1
T-shirt	T-shirt 5 SF1	went	Vergangenheit von *go* 9 FW1
Tuesday	Dienstag 3 SF	were	Vergangenheit von *are* 10 F1
(to) turn: turn right/left	nach rechts/links abbiegen 6 F1	west	(nach) Westen 6 F1
TV	TV 2 FU5	what	was; wie 1 FU7
watch TV	fernsehen 5 FW1		welche(r/s)? 9 F4
typical	typisch 4 F6	What a day!	Was für ein Tag! 9 FW2
		what about ...?	und ...? und wie ist es mit ...? 3 FW2
U		what are friends for?	wofür sind Freunde da? 7 F5
		What's she like?	Wie ist sie? 2 T
under	unter 6 FW	What's the matter?	Was ist (los)? 11 F1
unfortunately	leider; unglücklicherweise 12 F1	What time is it?	Wie spät ist es? Wieviel Uhr ist es? 3 SF
united	vereinigt 3 FW2	What's your name?	Wie ist Ihr Name? 1 FU7
United Kingdom, the	das Vereinigte Königreich 3 FW2	when	wenn; als 2 F4
United States, the	die Vereinigten Staaten 3 FW2		wann? 12 F1
untidy	unordentlich 2 FW1	where	wo; wohin 1 F1
up	hinauf, herauf 6 F4	Where are you from?	Wo kommen Sie her? 1 F1

which?	welche(r/s)? 6 F1, was 9 F1	world: in the world	(auf) der Welt 11 F5
while	während 9 F1	It's a small world.	Die Welt ist doch klein. 3 F2
white	weiß 6 SF	worse	schlimmer 9 F1
who	wer 2 F4	would like (to)	möchte/möchten/möchte(s)t 8 F1
	der/die/das 3 F4	(to) write	schreiben 3 FU6
whole	ganze(r/s) 10 F1	write down	aufschreiben 5 FU1
whose?	wessen? 10 F2		
why	warum 5 F5	**Y**	
wife	(Ehe-)Frau 1 F3		
will	werden 8 F4	(to) yawn	gähnen 9 F1
(to) win	gewinnen; siegen 8 F6	year	Jahr 3 SF
window	Fenster 8 FU3	time of year	Jahreszeit 7 F5
windy	windig 10 SF	yellow	gelb 6 SF
wine	Wein 8 FW1	yes	ja 1 F1
winter	(der) Winter 10 SF3	yesterday	gestern 9 T
with	mit 1 FU7	yoghurt	Joghurt 4 SF
woman, women	Frau, Frauen 3 F1	you	Sie/du/ihr 1 F1
won't	= will not		dich/dir; euch; Sie/Ihnen 5 F5
word	Wort 1 FW	young, younger	jung, jünger 3 F4
work	Arbeit 1 FU7	your	dein(e)/ihr(e)/Ihr(e) 1 FU1
at work	in/bei der Arbeit 1 FU7	yours	deine(r/s); Ihre(r/s); eure(r/s) 8 F4
finish work	aufhören zu arbeiten 4 F5	yourself	(Sie) sich (selber) 11 FU3
start work	anfangen zu arbeiten 4 F5		
working day	Arbeitstag 4 F6	**Z**	
(to) work	arbeiten 4 F1		
workman	Handwerker 4 FW1	zoo	Zoo 3 SF3

Quellenverzeichnis

Wir danken den folgenden Personen, Institutionen, Unternehmen und Verlagen für die freundliche Genehmigung von Copyright-Material, soweit sie erreicht werden konnten. Sollten Rechteinhaber hier nicht aufgeführt sein, so sind wir für entsprechende Hinweise dankbar.

S. 8, 9, 32, 36, 41, 50, 51, 56, 57, 58, 62, 79, 80, 87, 89, 90:   Jack Carnell
S. 22, 24, 29, 31, 43, 73, 75, 89, 92:   Stephen Fox
S. 9:   oben: Bavaria Bildagentur, Gauting (Panoramic Image)
S. 12:   British Airways Deutschland, Frankfurt
S. 14:   Dieter Reichler, München (MHV-Archiv)
S. 15:   Franz Specht, München (MHV-Archiv)
S. 19:   (Punch) Werner Lüning, Lübeck
S. 21:   Lufthansa-Bildarchiv, Köln
S. 22:   Sandra Verena Sigl
S. 30:   Foto Sexauer, Ismaning (MHV-Archiv)
S. 38:   British Tourist Authority, Frankfurt
S. 42:   MTA/Metropolitan Transportation Authority, New York
S. 47:   Drawing by Frascino: © 1987 The New Yorker Magazine, Inc.
S. 48:   British Tourist Authority, Frankfurt; links: Christian Regenfus, München
S. 49:   Ikea Einrichtungs-GmbH. SÜD, Eching; rechts: Duravit AG, Horneberg
S. 55:   (Punch) Werner Lüning, Lübeck
S. 59:   Illinois Office of Tourism, Chicago
S. 60:   British Rail/BMP DDB Needham, London
S. 63:   Drawing by Levin: © 1991 The New Yorker Magazine, Inc.
S. 64:   links oben: Drawing by Stan Hunt; © 1987 The New Yorker Magazine, Inc.;
Mitte und rechts: Family Cincle, North Matton;
links unten: United Feature Syndicate, Inc. © 1980, Boston;
rechts: (Punch) Werner Lüning, Lübeck;
S. 69:   New York State Department of Economic Development, Albany/
Wells, Rich, Green, Inc., New York
S. 70:   William Fox, Plymouth Meeting
S. 71:   (Punch) Werner Lüning, Lübeck
S. 72:   Thomasville Furniture, Inc., NC; Conrans, London;
Ikea Einrichtungs-GmbH SÜD, Eching
S. 73:   Mitte: Christian Regenfus, München (MHV-Archiv)
S. 75:   oben: Franz Specht, München (MHV-Archiv)
S. 78:   The Post Office, Swindon
S. 81:   links: Guinness World of Records, London;
British Tourist Authority, Frankfurt
S. 84:   Horst Wackerbarth, Photograph, Düsseldorf
S. 87:   rechts: Magnum Management GmbH, München
S. 95:   Christopher Simon Sykes/The Sunday Times, London
S. 96:   Ore-Ida Foods, Inc., Boise